The Song of Roland

The Song of Roland

Translated by
John DuVal

Introduced by
David Staines

Hackett Publishing Company, Inc.
Indianapolis/Cambridge

For my best friend, critic, and love, Kay.

For further information, please address
   Hackett Publishing Company, Inc.
   P.O. Box 44937
   Indianapolis, Indiana 46244-0937

   www.hackettpublishing.com

Cover design by Deborah Wilkes
Interior design by Mary Vasquez
Map by Erin Greb Cartography
Composition by William Hartman
Printed at Data Reproductions Corporation

Library of Congress Cataloging-in-Publication Data

Chanson de Roland. English
   The song of Roland / translated by John DuVal ; introduced by David Staines.
      p. cm.
   Includes bibliographical references and index.
   ISBN 978-1-60384-850-3 (pbk.)—ISBN 978-1-60384-851-0 (cloth)
   1. Roland (Legendary character)—Romances. 2. Epic poetry, French—
Translations into English. 3. Knights and knighthood—Poetry. I. DuVal,
John, 1940-
   PQ1521.E5D88 2012
   841'.1—dc23
                                                      2012014018

CONTENTS

ACKNOWLEDGMENTS

I would like to thank Fulbright College of the University of Arkansas, including Dean Bill Schwab, for funding my year at Cambridge University to write this translation and I would like to thank Wolfson College, in its tradition of enlightened generosity, for hosting and making a very good year available to my wife and me. Among the many new friends who made our experience at Cambridge delightful, Wolfson librarian Anna Jones must be singled out for her patience in making sure I had the books and the library connections I needed for the translation, as well as Robert Amundsen, Edward Johnson, and Tony Lenten, all three of whose generous support and criticism were invaluable.

I would like to thank Peter Haidu, Sarah Kay, and William Kibler for their helpful comments on early drafts. Thank you, Kay DuVal, for your astute criticism and inspired suggestions through every draft of the translation. Also, much thanks goes to Martin Kauffman for an unforgettable afternoon at the Bodleian Library, Oxford, showing us the Roland manuscript and telling us all about it. Thank you, Hackett editor Deborah Wilkes; your encouragement and the wisdom with which you have overseen this project from beginning to end have been invaluable. Thank you, project editor Mary Vasquez, for taking care of all these last-minute, hurry-up details. Thank you, David Staines, for your detailed editing; you have saved me from embarrassing mistakes. Many good moves come at your suggestion and whatever infelicities remain in the translation are all mine. Finally, again, thanks to the DuVal-Smith-Quigley-Wong clan for making my life a joy.

John DuVal
Fayetteville, 2012

INTRODUCTION

For the aristocratic audience of early twelfth-century France, *The Song of Roland* was a testament to their glorious past as a nation and an account of the present, a testament to the glorious days of Charlemagne three centuries earlier, and an account of the king and his knights, who were making their formidable presence increasingly felt in twelfth-century life. The poem thus unites two separate but related worlds, the eighth-century world of Charlemagne and the contemporary world of the rising knightly class.

Of the history of Charlemagne, Roland, and the tragedy in Roncevals, little is known. The most faithful account of the events of the year 778, the time of the actual occurrence of the massacre, comes from Einhard, Charlemagne's friend and biographer, who died in 840. In his *Life of Charlemagne,* the first biography of a secular figure of the medieval era, which he wrote around the third decade of the ninth century, he recounts the king's devastating attack on the country of Spain:

> Charles crossed the Pyrenees and received the surrender of all the towns and castles along the way; he returned with his army sustaining no losses. But recrossing the Pyrenees, he was made to experience Basque treachery. While his army was being forced by a narrow passage to proceed in a long column, some Basques were lying in wait to ambush his men from the top of the highest mountain, for the dense woods were well suited there for ambushes. They fell on the last part of the baggage train, driving the men from the protecting rearguard back into the valley, where they waged combat and slaughtered them to the last man. Then, having looted the baggage train, they dispersed quickly in every direction beneath the cloak of falling darkness. In this encounter, the Basques had the advantage of light armament and suitable terrain, whereas the French were disadvantaged by heavy armament and the ground's unevenness. Eggihard, the royal steward, Anselm, the count of the palace, Roland, the prefect of the Breton March, and many others were slaughtered in this engagement.

Einhard's *Life* focuses on Charlemagne; it is a short, personal biography of a great and beloved leader, written by one who knew him very well. And it survives in a vast number of manuscripts. Moreover, Roland is here only the prefect of the Breton March, the third of the three nobles named and therefore the least important of the three men who died in the battle; nothing else survives of Roland's identity, and his historical existence remains questionable.

In the nearly three centuries that intervene between Einhard's *Life* and *The Song of Roland,* the legendary stature of Charlemagne grows immensely from the realistic portrait of Einhard's king. He has become a mythic figure, the superhuman, almost supernatural French champion of the Church and of his country; he is, in essence, the defender of the true faith against the pagan infidels who are constantly striving to overcome and vanquish the Christian forces. And Roland himself, now safely enshrined as Charlemagne's nephew and his greatest warrior, is the epitome of loyalty to his king and to his God.

The late eleventh and early twelfth centuries were the era of the Great Crusades, which set Christian heroes against pagan warriors. A long series of religious wars that began toward the end of the eleventh century, the Crusades sought ultimately to restore Christian access to the holy places in and near Jerusalem, for the Crusades came about as a consequence of Muslim rulers forbidding access to all Christians to the sacred places. The Christians did recapture Jerusalem in 1099, a suitable date around which the composition of *The Song of Roland* might well have taken place.

As Einhard wrote, Charlemagne "loved foreign travelers and took great measures to take them under his protection." He had roads built for them, and he made it illegal to withhold accommodation from pilgrims in quest of distant shrines. When the Muslim lords denied all Christians entry to holy Jerusalem in the late eleventh century, people began naturally to turn their minds back to Charlemagne; he had always protected pilgrims. So strong was their belief in his power that during the crusade of 1101 rumors arose that Charlemagne had come back to life to guide and comfort his countrymen in this new time of crisis.

The Song of Roland unites the glorious past of the French nation with the contemporary crusades. Charlemagne opens and closes the poem—he is the avuncular center of the tragedy—and Roland is its true hero. The poem is a tribute to Roland's stature as the finest knight in the world, one doomed to his tragic end in his ceaseless battle for God and country.

Using the epic form now known as the chanson de geste (a song of a deed or action)—most chansons de geste focus on events that took place during the Carolingian period of the late eighth century and well into the ninth century, and their heroes are Charlemagne's knights or barons, who frequently fight pagan forces—the poet of *The Song of Roland* tells a tragic story, though it takes place amid the glory that was Charlemagne's world. This poem is certainly the oldest existing epic poem—and the best—in French literature.

This particular epic song was, indeed, a song, and the narrative poem was probably sung or partly sung by a minstrel, who may be the Turolde mentioned in the last line of the poem. Turolde may also be the copyist who entered the poem in his manuscript; indeed, Turolde may even be the composer of this epic story. Although Einhard's *Life of Charlemagne* may serve as a source for this poem, it is not the only source. Accessible now in written form, the poem was probably diffused and circulated orally for a long time before its final composition in this surviving form in the twelfth century.

There are references in the mid-eleventh century to the story of Roland and his companions, and additional frequent references to the story appear in the twelfth century. Even William of Malmesbury, the preeminent English historian of the twelfth century, noted that at the Battle of Hastings in 1066, a minstrel sang *The Song of Roland* to encourage the Normans.

Like most chansons de geste, *The Song of Roland* treats noble feats of the past. British literature has its *Beowulf*, though it was of much earlier origin; French literature has its *Song of Roland*. And the form of this French epic consists of *laisses*, or stanzas of irregular length, with the meter being decasyllabic, for the decasyllable was seen as the proper epic meter.

As the medieval audience listened to the singer, they heard an exciting story. Charlemagne, the great emperor of France, is returning home after seven long years conquering his southern neighbor, Spain. One problem remains: the city of Saragossa is governed by King Marsille, a pagan ruler. The opening *laisse*, therefore, establishes the opposition between Charlemagne, the good king serving the true God, and King Marsille, the pagan monarch who does not love and serve God. The war between them operates throughout the poem. King Marsille convenes his pagan council, which tells him to pretend to offer fealty and friendship to Charlemagne to prove his loyalty; in addition, the pagan king will pretend to convert to Christianity and become Charlemagne's vassal. Despite his promises, the king has no intention of doing any such thing. Charlemagne stands without defense from King Marsille's traitorous tricks.

In Cordoba, a city Charlemagne has just seized, Charlemagne greets the pagan embassy and listens to their promises. At his own council the next day, Count Roland, Charlemagne's nephew, recommends the rejection of the offer, preferring to send French forces to capture Saragossa and thereby avenge the recent beheading of their two ambassadors. To this call to arms, only Ganelon, brother-in-law of Charlemagne and stepfather of Roland, immediately answers, urging the acceptance of the treaty and pointedly rebuking Roland: "Advice that comes from pride should be reproved. / Let's cling to wisdom; leave foolishness to fools" (226–27). Charlemagne agrees with Ganelon, sending him, not Roland nor any other of the Twelve Peers, his trusted warriors, to King Marsille to arrange peace.

There is a bitter enmity between Roland and his stepfather, which is explained much later in the poem; Roland had, according to Ganelon's testimony, "cheated me in gold and gain, / So I had Roland killed, by my arrangements" (3678–79). But these words are the expression of an evil character who is himself motivated by greed (greed had supplanted pride in the eleventh century as the deadliest of the seven deadly sins). Under greed's control, and extremely jealous of Roland—of Roland's innate power over his companions and his obvious sway over Charlemagne—Ganelon is blind to Roland's sterling qualities, which make Roland both beloved and feared. As Charlemagne says of Ganelon, "You are the Devil! Mad and rabid blood / Has entered to your heart" (735–36). Ganelon's end will be a fitting conclusion to an evil life.

In the great walled city of Saragossa, Ganelon appears before King Marsille with Charlemagne's offer, informing him that if he refuses the terms, he will be put to death—a fictional addition by Ganelon. He promises Marsille that only half of Spain will remain to him—the other half going to Roland—his second fiction. He urges King Marsille to pretend to accept the offer, then ambush Roland and the rearguard in the narrow pass after Charlemagne has already traversed the mountains: Roland will be slaughtered, and Spain will be invaded no more. King Marsille accepts this treacherous plan, and Ganelon returns to the French troops.

To lead the French rearguard under the tight bluffs, Ganelon nominates Roland, who will take only twenty thousand Frenchmen for his forces. Although beset by dreams and fearful for his nephew and the troops under his surveillance, Charlemagne accedes, "Knowing that Ganelon will be the wreck / Of lovely France" (822–23). That Charlemagne followed Ganelon's advice, though fearing Ganelon would "be the wreck" of France, reveals Charlemagne's careful deliberation of the advice of all his advisors, even when he doubted their wisdom.

As the pagan forces march on Roland and the rearguard, Oliver, Roland's companion-in-arms, suspects Ganelon of betrayal, but Roland will embrace no such suspicion about his stepfather. Although Oliver begs Roland to sound his horn, Oliphant, to bring Charlemagne back from the north, Roland steadfastly refuses, "I'd be a fool to throw / Honor away" (1043–44). As the poet says, "Roland is valiant. Oliver is wise. / Both are marvelously noble knights" (1082–83). Archbishop Turpin blesses the French, "Confess your sins out loud and ask God's mercy. / I now absolve you into life eternal" (1121–22). As the French and the pagans engage in a long and protracted encounter—one hundred thousand pagans dead and only two thousand still alive!—the French lose many of their troops, with only sixty still alive. When Roland seeks to sound his horn and summon Charlemagne, Oliver sarcastically reproaches him: "Think of the shame your relatives would bear, / Knowing you blew your horn, yes, lifelong shame" (1676–77), and threatens to end Roland's engagement to his own sister. After the archbishop intervenes in their quarrel to urge the sounding of the horn, Roland gives a blast, and this sound summons Charlemagne, who has Ganelon placed under arrest before heading back to the pass.

In the subsequent fray, Roland sees his close companion, Oliver, killed, then the few remaining Frenchmen facing imminent slaughter. Amid a sea of dead bodies, Roland laments his own end, making a prayer for his salvation:

> The countries that he conquered and subjected,
> The men of France from whom he is descended,
> And Charlemagne, who cherished him and fed him.
> He cannot help but weep as he remembers.
> But now he must recall himself, confessing
> His sins to God and begging for His mercy:
> "Eternal God the Father, faithful ever,
> Who rescued Lazarus from death and rescued
> Daniel from the lions' den, defend me
> From my life's sins, which put my soul in peril."
> He holds his right glove, offers it, and stretches
> It up toward God. The Angel Gabriel
> Receives it from his hand. Then Roland rests
> His head upon his arm, clasps hands together,
> And goes on further to his end.
> God sends His cherubim with Gabriel
> And Michael Help-of-Sailors. They descend
> And carry Roland's soul to Him in Heaven.   (2335–52)

Roland dies a Christian hero's death. Now his soul ascends to Heaven.

Charlemagne arrives on the field of battle, but too late to prevent the terrible tragedy that has taken place. When he prays for a longer day, his prayer is answered: in their flight from the returning French troops, the pagans lose their lives in the Ebro River. Meanwhile, Baligant, the Grand Emir of Babylon and a noble warrior, comes to King Marsille, who promises to hand over to him the governance of Spain if he can defeat Charlemagne and his forces. Brimming with confidence, Baligant now prepares for a final encounter with the French forces.

At Roncevals, Charlemagne seeks out the body of Roland. On finding it, he laments his most grievous loss and, gathering up the bodies of Roland, Oliver, and Turpin, he has their hearts wrapped in soft silk and placed in a small white marble crypt. Then he prepares himself for battle against Baligant with an expressive prayer that recalls Roland's dying prayer:

> "True Father, today stand by me and defend me,
> You Who rescued Jonah from the depths,
> Pulling him forth from the great whale's belly,
> Who spared the repentant King of Nineveh,
> Who rescued Daniel when the lions pressed
> About him in the Babylonian den,
> And the Three Children in the furnace—You saved them!—
> Be with me Lord today, in love be present,
> And in Your mercy grant that I avenge
> The death of Roland, Roland, my dear nephew!"   (3029–38)

In the ensuing fray, Charlemagne harangues his men to victory; Baligant, who slays four French knights, prays to the three pagan gods. The French forces suffer the loss of seven thousand troops. The final encounter lasts all day long, with Charlemagne and Baligant meeting in single combat. Baligant proposes a pact, which the French king rejects. When Charlemagne receives a near-fatal blow, the Angel Gabriel rushes to his side: "Hearing the angel's urgings near at hand, / Charles's fears and hesitations vanish" (3529–30). He strikes the emir "with the sword of France" (3532) and Baligant falls dead.

Some pagans flee, though very few. In Saragossa, King Marsille "gives up his body, burdened / With sins, to earth; his soul, to evil spirits" (3563–64). Charlemagne captures the city, ending all vestiges of paganism within its walls, and more than one hundred thousand pagans receive baptism. He retains as prisoner Queen Bramimunde, the widow of King Marsille, and conducts her back to Aix. En route home, Charlemagne buries his three preeminent warriors—his nephew Roland; Roland's trusted companion, Oliver; and the wise Archbishop Turpin—in a white tomb at Blaye. When he is back at his palace in Aix, he encounters Alda, Oliver's sister, who comes to hear news of her betrothed, Roland. Stricken to the heart by his death, she herself falls dead at Charlemagne's feet.

Ganelon is then brought out for trial. A crowded court includes thirty of his supporting relatives. Ganelon is handsome; indeed, "If he were loyal, you would think, 'What valor!'" (3684). The barons cannot reach a verdict and report to Charlemagne their unwelcome news. Thierry of Anjou offers single combat on behalf of Roland, and Pinabel, Ganelon's relative, takes up the challenge. Thierry's success in combat leads to the hanging of all of Ganelon's relatives, and Ganelon himself is dragged to his death.

In a final moment of conversion, Queen Bramimunde, having listened to many sermons, lessons, and prayers, desires baptism, taking the new name of Juliana: "Christian she is, in knowledge and in faith" (3905). Alone in his vaulted chamber, Charlemagne receives a visit from the Angel Gabriel, who tells him that pagans have besieged yet another city. "How tired I am. How weary my life is" (3918), he laments, and the poem ends.

When the audience heard this story, they were duly impressed with their own recognition of France's past and one of its most glorious and tragic moments. All the men and women acknowledged the beauty of the story and the complexity of the narrative. They knew about Roncevals and the tragedy that had occurred there three centuries earlier. It had become the stuff of legend, and they relished the vibrant retelling of the story.

In this audience were both men and women, the latter a significant addition since there had been no women in earlier medieval audiences for the male-oriented stories of the heroic past. And their presence accounts, in part, for the significance of two women in the story, the stalwart Queen of Spain and Roland's beautiful betrothed, Alda.

Bramimunde's repeated references to Charlemagne connect her to the French king. After surviving the pagans' serious defeats, she adopts Christianity out of love and becomes a fitting and final proof of the power of faith. Meanwhile, Alda, who apparently fainted (though, in reality, she had fallen dead) at the news of Roland's death as Charlemagne himself fainted at the sight of Roland's dead body, subtly connects this epic poem to the nascent body of literature that would come to be called the "courtly love" romances. Alda, who cannot endure the news of Roland's death, is a heroine of the body of poetry that brings romantic love to the fore of the heroic life. Although this dimension of love is not possible in a truly heroic poem such as *Beowulf*, it is present here as the heroic age gives way to a more complete depiction of men and women. From this perspective will come the romances of the Arthurian cycle that will dominate French culture in the later part of the twelfth century.

The men populating *The Song of Roland* are knightly heroes who have a significant role to play in the governance of their countries. From both sides, the Christian and the pagan, come good knights who respect the vision of their class. Baligant, who worships the pagan deities, is, first and foremost, a fine warrior who could be a great man were he aware of the inadequacies of his pagan faith: "What valor he has shown through countless struggles! / O God, were he a Christian knight, how wonderful!" (3088–89). Even Ganelon, Charlemagne's respected knight and brother-in-law, espouses solid knightly virtues, though these are severely undercut by his monstrous sin of greed.

All the knights belong to a feudal society, bound to one another by fealty and bound to their ruler in a hierarchical world. Charlemagne rules over the Frenchmen, who are his vassals. He binds them to himself in homage and in love, and they endure all encumbrances and sufferings out of allegiance to him. In exchange for their loyalty, the king must be their protector and, if need be, their avenger.

Although Charlemagne is the poem's center, he has a reduced role. In Einhard's account of 778, he was a youthful and impressive monarch of only thirty-six years of age. In *The Song of Roland* he is a much older man, always pulling at his white beard and uttering loud lamentations. A brave and wise man, he is victorious in his single combat with Baligant, though he does receive supernatural assistance. He does not assume a minor position in the action—all the knights loudly support him—but his great role is now reduced. In another fifty years or so, the French Arthurian romances will remove Arthur to the remote background, and the knights of his Round Table will be the center of his romances.

The heroes of *The Song of Roland* are Roland, Oliver, Turpin, and the glorious knights who go down to defeat at Roncevals. The ideal knight, Roland has the innate ability to impart wise advice in council and the strength to be a powerful presence in battle. Most important in his character is his loyalty to his king—he is the proper vassal of his lord!—and his loyalty to God, who is represented on Earth by his king. With these qualities, Roland represents the virtues that are the essence of the perfect warrior. Oliver, Roland's companion-in-arms, is another Roland, loyal to his king and his God, and loyal, too, to his fellow knights on the battlefield. He watches over Roland, making sure that he is safe. Though perhaps more prudent and cautious than Roland, he is ever the servant to his lord. And the presence of Archbishop Turpin, the most important ecclesiastic figure taking part in the conquest of Spain, brings religion to this warring world, elevating the battle into a major religious struggle between the French—the men of God—and the pagan forces who strive to vanquish them.

A grouping of people from non-Christian lands, the Saracens—the pagan forces who worship Apollo, Mohammed, and Tervagant—are a curious mixture of folk beliefs and superstitious understandings. Although the terms "Muslim" and "Islam" do not occur in the poem, these followers of Mohammed are universally seen as negative agents in a world that strives to be perfect in a Christian frame of reference. Meanwhile, the contact the French had at this time with the Muslim world was severely limited, and they had little sympathy or understanding for what they did not know. The Saracens, therefore, come to represent the concrete embodiment of the oppositional forces to Charlemagne and his people.

The Song of Roland is the great tale of the unending war between the forces of good and the forces of evil, between those aligned here with the Christian God and those opposed to this allegiance. As Roland maintains,

> To serve his lord, a knight
> Should suffer hardships, deserts, winter ice
> And sacrifice his limbs, his hide, his life.
> —Frenchmen, prepare yourselves to strike and strike!
> No wit will mock our strokes with comic rhymes!
> Pagans are wrong. Christians are right!   (1000–1005)

And the epic form is the ideal vehicle for the poetic illumination of military exploits undertaken for religious purposes and the consequent tragedy of this particular enterprise.

Reading this new translation of *The Song of Roland,* the twenty-first-century audience sees again the alarms of battle, the sufferings of loss, and the ceaseless fighting for God and country. They witness the treachery and the machination of the infidels as they inflict countless horrors on the French; they watch the incredible heroism of Charlemagne, Roland, and many others; and they finish with singular appreciation for this magnificent twelfth-century epic and its superb translation.

Selected Bibliography

Editions of *La Chanson de Roland*

Bédier, Joseph, ed. *La Chanson de Roland*. Paris: l'Edition d'Art, 1927. Dual language edition and prose translation into modern French.

Brault, Gerard J., ed. The Song of Roland: *An Analytical Edition*. Vol. 2. University Park: Pennsylvania State Press, 1978. Edited text with facing translation.

Calin, William, ed. *La Chanson de Roland*. New York: Appleton-Century Crofts, 1968.

Jenkins, T. A. ed. *La Chanson de Roland*. Boston: D. C. Heath, 1924. The Anglo-Norman spellings are edited out and replaced by "standard" Old French spellings.

Jonin, Pierre, ed. *La Chanson de Roland*. Paris: Gallimard, Collection Folio, 1979. Includes a French translation.

de Laborde, Alexandre, ed. *La Chanson de Roland: Reproduction phototypique du Manuscrit Digby 23 de la Bodleian Library d'Oxford*. Paris: Société des Anciens Textes Français, 1933. Facsimile of the Oxford manuscript.

Mortier, Raoul, ed. *Les Textes de la Chanson de Roland*. 10 vols. Paris: Editions de la Geste Francor, 1940–44.

MS. Digby 23, Part 2. Early Manuscripts at Oxford University: Digital Facsimiles of Complete Manuscripts, Scanned Directly from the Originals. Oxford Digital Library. Available at http://image.ox.ac.uk. Retrieved on May 11, 2011.

Short, Ian, ed. *La Chanson de Roland*. 2nd ed. Paris: Le Livre de Poche, 1994.

Whitehead, Frederick, ed. *La Chanson de Roland*. Bristol, Eng.: Bristol Classical Press, 1993. Reissued with notes and introduction by T. D. Hemming.

Selected Manuscripts

Assonantal

Oxford manuscript Digby of the Bodleian Library, 4002 lines (O, primary source).

Manuscript IV, Library of St. Mark at Venice 6012 lines (V^4)

Rhymed

Manuscript VII of the Library of St. Mark's at Venice (V⁷)

Some Critical Studies

Brualt, Gerard J. The Song of Roland: *An Analytical Edition.* Vol. 1: Introduction and Commentary. University Park: Pennsylvania University Press, 1978.

Cook, Robert Francis. *The Sense of* The Song of Roland. Ithaca, NY: Cornell University Press, 1987.

Duggan, Joseph J. *A Concordance of the* Chanson de Roland. Columbus: Ohio State University Press, 1969.

———. The Song of Roland: *Formulaic Style and Poetic Craft.* Berkeley: University of California Press, 1973.

Haidu, Peter. *The Subject of Violence:* The Song of Roland *and the Birth of the State.* Bloomington: Indiana University Press, 1993.

Jones, George F. *The Ethos of* The Song of Roland. Baltimore, MD: The Johns Hopkins University Press, 1963.

Kibler, William W. and Leslie Zarker Morgan, eds. *Approaches to Teaching* The Song of Roland. New York: Modern Languages Association of America, 2006.

Kinoshita, Sharon. *Medieval Boundaries: Rethinking Difference in Old French Literature.* Philadelphia: University of Pennsylvania Press, 2006.

Pensom, Roger. *Literary Technique in the* Chanson de Roland. Genevé: Droz, 1982.

Uitti, Karl D. *Story, Myth, and Celebration in Old French Narrative Poetry.* Princeton, NJ: Princeton University Press, 1973.

Vance, Eugene. *Reading* The Song of Roland. Englewood Cliffs, NJ: Prentice-Hall, 1970.

TRANSLATOR'S INTRODUCTION

La Chanson de Roland is one of the first great poems of Modern Europe, yet people reading it sometimes ask, "Where is the poetry?" The language does not leap from one metaphor to the next as in *Beowulf.* There are no extended similes such as those that delight readers of Homer, Virgil, or Milton; or of Dante, for instance, at the beginning the *Inferno* when he describes the struggle to get back onto the right path:

> And as a man who, gasping for breath,
> has escaped the sea and wades to shore,
> then turns back and stares at the perilous waves,
> So too . . . .[1]

The few metaphors and similes that do occur are pretty conventional. There are some enchanting dream sequences and one lovely pictorial scene—the arrival of Charlemagne's enemy, Baligant, on the shores of Spain; otherwise, the colorful description is mostly confined to battle gear and battle wounds. The syntax, too, is unadorned and straightforward, with few modifying clauses and phrases. Nothing like the grammatical complexity of the first sentence of Chaucer's *Canterbury Tales* occurs in *La Chanson de Roland.* The lines are composed of grammatical units and almost always pause at the end. But poetry there is, in the magic of the storytelling. Instead of poetic adornments, we have poetic compression. The author wastes no time with explanations, but leaves those to the characters, who themselves are not talkative. The story rushes *bif, bam, bang,* from one line to the next and from one verse-paragraph (or *laisse*) to the next, sometimes with horrifying violence.

Perhaps the most poetic consequence of this compression is the sense of immediacy. Readers (or listeners) are intimately *with* the protagonists of each new verse-paragraph. As I was translating, I felt this intimacy so powerfully that whatever verse-paragraph I was working on impressed me as the most important to get right. The

---

1. Dante, *Inferno,* trans. Stanley Lombardo (Indianapolis/Cambridge: Hackett Publishing Company, Inc., 2009), 5.

sense of immediacy occurs even with minor characters. In *laisse* 193, two Syrian messengers from Emir Baligant ride to the court of King Marsille. These are "pagans," enemies of Charlemagne and his Christian heroes. We have no reason to care for them. Yet the compressed verse puts us into such intimate contact with them that we participate with them in their brief journey:

> "Ride fast," says Baligant, "don't linger."
> Both messengers reply, "Yes, Sire, we will!"
> One brother holds the glove, and one the stick.
> They ride full speed to Saragossa. Quickly
> They pass ten gates and gallop across four bridges
> And through the streets where merchants make their livings.
> Uphill they gallop through the pagan city,
> Approach the palace and can hear within it
> The noise of many pagans. . . .   (2631–39)

The poem is composed of *laisses,* that is, paragraphs of decasyllabic verse ranging in length from five to thirty-four lines. The lines within each *laisse* should end with the same assonance, and the assonance of each consecutive *laisse* should differ from the one before it. Almost every *laisse* is its own episodic unity, and time expands and contracts with miraculous elasticity from *laisse* to *laisse* and even contradicts itself in *laisses* 164 and 165, where Turpin dies, and then Roland sees him alive again, still praying for his soul's forgiveness; and in *laisses* 59 and 60, where Roland's manner of speaking reveals two contradictory natures.

For the translator into English, the problem with assonance is that vowel sounds in English are not consistent. From the town north of Philadelphia where I grew up, all I had to do was cross the Delaware River into Trenton to hear a different ă sound in *crab* and *castle.* Translating *Roland* last year in Cambridge, England, a city populated by speakers of English from several countries and continents, I was all the more aware of English-language vowel inconsistency. Although I have striven for assonance among the last stressed syllables of lines in each *laisse,* given the diversity of pronunciations in our language, not every assonance will ring perfectly true to every reader. I take consolation in the fact that they don't all ring true in the original, either, as transcribed in the twelfth-century Digby manuscript at Oxford. Some editors ascribe the occasional faulty assonance to scribal error, but if differences in Old French vowel pronunciation were as common as spelling differences, the author could not count on a widespread readership hearing all the assonances as he heard them. He could, however, count on his readers hearing most of them as his story gathered energy and propelled itself forward from *laisse* to *laisse,* sometimes martial in its rhythm, sometimes angry, sometimes elegiac, always poetic. I hope that in this translation into modern English, readers who do not hear the vowel sounds exactly as I do will hear enough that they will sense the poetry not only through the incidents of the story, but also through the sound.

The scribe of the Oxford Digby manuscript (O) marks the beginning of each new *laisse* with a single large, sometimes elegantly drawn red capital letter and ends a little more than half of them with the three capital letters *AOI.* AOIs also end the opening lines of eight *laisses.* And there are seven divided *laisses,* where the AOI marks a meaningful place for the *laisse* to end, but the assonance continues. The poem was recited or read aloud for an audience. No one knows whether the oral performer actually shouted those diphthonged AOIs, or whether they are the scribe's notations of some other aspect of the oral performance: the strumming of an instrument, the banging of wine cups on tables, prayerful amens, or dramatic pauses in the recitation. Perhaps they are simply the scribe's creative additions to the poem on the page. No editor or translator that I know of has left them out. The strange and magical inexplicability of those three uppercase vowels is, or has become, part of the poetry, poetry that, in its own way, pervades the epic.

For this translation, I consulted the editions listed below. Although Jenkins sometimes seems too liberal in "correcting" the O manuscript with variant readings from other sources, he conscientiously explains his decisions, some of which I adopted. His English-language glossary was very useful for this translation into English, as was the Whitehead/Hemming edition. Joseph Bédier's edition was useful to consult for its accompanying, somewhat free, prose translation into modern French. William Calin's explanatory footnotes in French were very helpful.

Bédier, Joseph. *La Chanson de Roland.* Paris: l'Edition d'Art, 1927. Dual language edition and prose translation into modern French.

Calin, William, ed. *La Chanson de Roland.* New York: Appleton-Century Crofts, 1968.

Jenkins, T. A., ed. *La Chanson de Roland.* Boston: D. C. Heath, 1924. The Anglo-Norman spellings are edited out and replaced by "standard" Old French spellings.

Whitehead, Frederick. *La Chanson de Roland.* Revised with notes and introduction by D. T. Hemming. London: Gerard Duckworth (Bristol Classical Press), 1993.

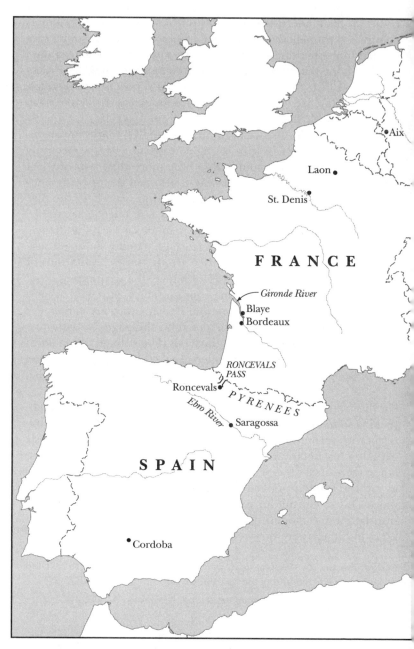

Roncevals Battlefield and Other Important Sites in *The Song of Roland*. Map shows country borders as they are today. Charlemagne's empire was considerably larger than modern France (though not so large as it was in the imagination of the author of *The Song of Roland*).

The Song of Roland

1[1]

King Charlemagne, our emperor, has stayed
Seven long years, waging war in Spain
And conquered all that land as far away
As to the sea. No castle blocks his way,
No city wall unbroken. All that remains   5
Is mountain Saragossa, under sway
Of King Marsille, who loves not God the Great,
But serves Mohammed and to Apollo prays[2]
And cannot stave off ruin, not even there.   AOI   [9]

2

Marsille the King still reigns in Saragossa.   10
He has gone for shade within a piney grove
And lies upon a yellow marble boulder.
At his command stand twenty thousand soldiers.
He calls his counts and counselors before him:
"Hear, lords of Saragossa, our misfortune!   15
King Charles of lovely France invades our homeland,
Plunders our country, hastens to destroy us.
I lack sufficient powers to oppose him.
I have no army to confound his forces.
Give me advice; wise counselors, inform me.   20
Save me from death and shame!" Of all his nobles,
Not one man answers him a word, but only
Blándandrin of Castle de Valfonde.   [23]

---

1. Bracketed numbers at the end of each laisse indicate where the equivalent
line can be found in the original French. Also, within the notes, bracketed
numbers indicate line numbers in the original French. For longer discussions
of editorial or translation decisions, see the Notes following the poem.

2. The slander that Muslims were pagans and that they worshiped anyone other
than the one God continued in Christendom throughout the period of the
Crusades.

3

Bláncandrin has been wise in strategies,
Well versed in vassalage and chivalry,   25
Mighty and valiant, eager to serve his liege.
He tells the king, "No need for you to grieve.
Send fierce and haughty Charles your fealty.
Send friendship, lions, bears, dogs of good breed;
And send a thousand molted hawks with these,   30
And seven hundred camels, too, and teams
Of mules to draw four hundred carts, all heaped
With silver and gold and other finery.
He'll have enough to pay his soldier-fees.[3]
Too long has he been fighting in our fiefs;   35
He will ride back across the Pyrenees
To Aix in France. You'll follow him and meet him
There as appointed, for St. Michael's Feast,
And you'll submit to Christianity
And be his man in honor, goods, and deeds.   40
If he wants hostages, we will release
Whatever he demands: ten at least—
Twenty—of our wives' own sons as guarantees.
Though he should die, send my own son with these.
Better the young men lose their heads than we   45
Forfeit our honor and authority
And be reduced, O King, to beggary.   AOI   [46]

4

"By my right hand, these fingers and these knuckles,"
Says Bláncandrin, "by this white beard, which flutters
Against my chest: soon to their own country   50
The Frenchmen will return. They will break muster
And each man hurry home to hearth and comfort.
King Charles will sit at Aix, his Chapel, trusting
And holding celebrations for your coming.
St. Michael's Day will come, then go, and nothing,   55
Not even a word, will he have had from us.
This king is proud. His heart is fierce and stubborn.
When you don't come, he will behead our sons.

---

3. Bláncandrin is expressing a certain contempt for Charlemagne, implying that some of his forces were mercenaries, which, according to the feudal arrangements of Charlemagne's empire, they were not.

Better they lose their heads than that we suffer
The loss of Spain the beautiful and sunny   60
And suffer countless other troubles."
"This strategy could work," the pagans judge.   [61]

5

Marsille the King adjourns his pagan meeting.
He summons Clarin of Balágatee
and Estamars and Eurropin the Peer   65
And Priamun and Garlan of the Beard,
Matthew and his nephew Machinee,
Jouner and Evilgood from Oversea,
And Bláncandrin, their leader, who will speak—
The ten most wicked men of Marsille's legions.   70
Marsille commands them, "Go to Cordoba and meet
King Charles where he holds court. Give him my greeting
And give him olive branches, which are sweet
Tokens of humility and peace.
And if you wisely do this task for me,   75
I'll give you silver and gold. And you will reap
Farmlands and vast estates and fiefs."
They answer him, "We have enough of these."[4]   AOI   [77]

6

Marsille adjourns his council and commands
The chosen ten: "My lords, an olive branch   80
Each one of you will carry in your hand
To Cordoba and plead with Charles the Grand
That for the sake of his own God he grant
Mercy on me. Before the month has passed,
I'll follow with a thousand men and clasp   85
The law of Christian men and be his man
In fealty and love. If he exacts
Hostages, hostages he'll have."
Bláncandrin says, "We'll get a useful pact."   AOI   [88]

7

Marsille has ten white mules brought out to him,   90
Gifts given by the King of Swátili.

---

4. See Notes on Editorial and Translation Decisions following the translation.

The saddles are silver, gold the reins and bits.
The messengers mount their mules, and all ten grip
The olive branches tightly in their fists.
They come to Charles. Though all of France's king,   95
He lacks protection from a traitor's tricks.   AOI   [95]

8

Charlemagne sits rejoicing in the fall
Of Cordoba. His knights have breached the walls
And broken down the towers with catapults
And bravely taken for themselves large hauls   100
Of silver, gold, and armor of great cost.
There's not one pagan left not killed or crossed
To Christianity[5] in Cordoba.
In a large orchard sits the emperor,
Roland and Oliver joining him in talk.   105
Nearby: Duke Samson; Anseïs the Strong;
Geoffrey of Anjou, the king's guide-on;
Gerin and Gerer, inseparable in war;
And many other noble barons also.
From lovely France some fifteen thousand warriors   110
Are sitting all about on white silk cloths.
The older barons settle down to talk
And play board games like chess and silver-toss.
The light-hearted young are fencing on the lawn.
Beneath a pine a gold throne is installed   115
Near to an eglantine. From there, King Charles
Of lovely France presides, white as the frost
His beard and flowing hair. He is straight and tall.
No man would ask, "Where is the king?" who saw him.
The messengers arrive, dismount, and walk   120
To greet the emperor with love and awe.   [121]

9

Bláncandrin speaks first: "May God Who reigns
And dwells in glory, to Whom we all must pray,

5. Jenkins, in a footnote, reports that "wholesale conversion by the sword is not historically true of Charlemagne" (p. 13). Later, however, it was common for Crusaders to carry out such wholesale conversion or simply wholesale slaughter of the populations of the towns they took. See Amin Maalouf, *Les Croisades vues par las Arabes* (Paris: Latès, 1983).

Save and protect you, mighty Charlemagne.
I bring these greetings from Marsille the brave.   125
He asks: 'How can salvation be attained?'[6]
My worthy king proposes that he share
His wealth with you: bears, lions, leashed greyhounds,
Seven hundred camels, a thousand hawks well trained
For seizing birds, four hundred mules all weighed   130
With gold and silver in a wagon train
Of fifty carts, with coins enough to pay
All of your soldiers. Too many years you've stayed
Inside this country. Now you should leave Spain
For Aix in France. My master will not break   135
His vow, but follow you and there keep faith."
Lifting his hands to Heaven, Charlemagne
Bows his head and begins to meditate.   AOI   [138]

10

The emperor's head is low. His face is hidden.
He doesn't rush to say what he is thinking.   140
His speech was always careful and deliberate.
Now he lifts his head. How fierce his visage!
He answers them: "Your words are good. Your king is
My enemy. If you have some provision
That will authenticate your words, what is it?"   145
The Saracen replies, "We will deliver
Hostages, ten of our young men, or fifteen,
Twenty, even—my son, though you could kill him.
Inside your royal halls you will have living
The noblest of our youths, in my opinion.   150
On the feast of Michael Rescuer-of-Pilgrims,
My king will follow you to Aix in tribute,
And there in waters sprung from God he wishes
To cleanse his spirit and become a Christian."
"His soul may yet be saved," Charles answers him.   AOI   155 [156]

11

The sun stays bright while afternoon still lasts.
Ten mules are stabled at the king's command.
He has a tent pitched on the orchard grass.
A dozen servants lead ten pagan Spaniards

---

6. See Notes on Editorial and Translation Decisions.

Into this tent to eat, sleep, and relax   160
All through the night until the dark has passed.
The king arises early to hear matins.
Before daybreak he listens to the mass,
Then goes beneath a pine and summons back
His barons to the council. He always asks   165
Advice from those he trusts: the men of France.   AOI   [167]

12

Beneath the pine the emperor has called
His barons back to council. It is dawn.
Duke Ogier and Archbishop Turpin come;
Old Richard and his nephew Henry also;   170
Count Acelin of Gascony; Theobald
Of Reims and his young cousin, Count Milon;
Gerin and Gerer; noble, wise, and strong
Count Oliver; Count Roland—all in all,
Of Frenchmen out of France: one thousand strong;   175
And he who did the treason, Ganelon.
And now the council starts that ended wrong.   AOI   [179]

13

The emperor addresses them: "Lord barons,
King Marsille has sent me emissaries.
He wants to give me of his wealth and chattels,   180
Lions and bears, greyhounds leashed for tracking,
A thousand molted hawks, seven hundred camels,
Four hundred mules with Arab gold to carry,
Pulling behind them more than fifty wagons.
But first he stipulates that I must travel   185
Back to lovely France; he'll follow after
And come from Spain to me at Aix, my Chapel,
Submit to Christian law, and as my vassal
Keep his dominions, mountains, farms, and pastures—
He says, but I can't tell you where his heart is."   190
"We must be wary now," reply the barons.   AOI   [192]

14

At the last word spoken by the emperor,
Roland, outraged, angry at these terms,
Leaps to his feet to argue they must spurn
Utterly the pagan offer: "Believe no word,   195

O King, that comes from King Marsille the cursed!
Seven whole years in Spain! My sword has earned you
Nople on this campaign, and Commilbury,
Pineland, and Bálasged, Tuéle, Valterne,
Seville—Seville, where King Marsille confirmed   200
Himself a traitor, sending messengers,
Fifteen pagans with the same fine words,
And olive branches, too. We all conferred,
And the French counseled lightly. You concurred,
Sent Básil and Basán, ambassadors,   205
From us to King Marsille, who seized them first,
Then cut off their heads on the Halt Hill. No, sir!
Wage the war you started though it burn
On longer than your life lasts. Lead us with courage.
Battle the Saracens. Besiege and burst   210
The walls of Saragossa. Let Spain be purged,
Avenge our friends, slaughter those murderers."   AOI   [213]

15

The emperor, when his nephew's speech is through,
Bows, strokes his beard, rubs his mustache smooth,
Answers neither approval nor reproof.   215
No Frenchman speaks but Ganelon, who moves
Scornfully forward to address his ruler:
"Do not," he says, "take counsel from a fool—
Not mine nor anyone's, if it's not useful.
Marsille sends promises to meet you soon   220
And join his hands in fealty to you.
Spain he will give you as a present, too,
And take upon himself our Christian rule.
He who advises you to spurn this truce
Cares nothing what kinds of deaths we must endure.   225
Advice that comes from pride should be reproved.
Let's cling to wisdom; leave foolishness to fools."   AOI   [229]

16

Duke Neïme rises from that noble crowd.
A better courtier cannot be found.
He speaks to Charlemagne: "You heard the count,   230
Lord Ganelon. His reasoning is sound,
If it be understood. You've put to rout
The armies of Marsille, and you've thrown down

With catapults his castles, walls, and towers.
You've conquered his people. You've burned down his towns.   235
It would be sinful, King, not to allow
The mercy that he asks for now.
The hostages will be sufficient grounds
For trusting. No more must this great war stretch out."
"The duke has spoken well," the Frenchmen shout.   AOI   240 [243]

17

"My lords, in Saragossa who shall be
The messenger we send to King Marsille?"
"I beg the gift to go," says Duke Neïme;
"Give me the glove and staff, and I will leave."
"You are a man of great sagacity,"   245
Replies the king. "By my mustache and beard,
You will not go that far from me.
Sit down when no one orders you to speak.   [251]

18

"Lord barons, whom shall we delegate to ride
Among the Saracens? To whom confide   250
This mission?" Roland stands and answers, "I
Will go to Saragossa." Oliver cries,
"Not you! You'd be the worst! You're fierce and wild.
Right off you'd get yourself into a fight.
Send me. I'll go if that's what Charles decides."   255
The emperor answers, "Both of you, keep quiet!
Not *you* nor *you* are going. Woe betide
If any of my Twelve gets this assignment—
I swear by my white beard!" Not one French knight
At this command has anything to reply.   260 [263]

19

Turpin of Reims, archbishop, now stands up.
"Let your Peers stay," he tells the emperor.
"For seven years campaigning in this rough
And rugged land our people have stayed stuck
Through hardship and war. Give me the staff and glove!   265
I'll go to the Saracen in Spain. I'd love
To get a look at him in his own country."
The emperor speaks testily: "Enough!

Sit back down, Turpin, on your white silk rug.
Be still unless I tell you to speak up.   AOI   270 [273]

                    20

"My noble knights," the Emperor Charles says,
"Choose me a border captain I can send
To King Marsille. Who will take my message?"
"My stepfather, Ganelon!" Count Roland says.
The barons answer, "Few could do it better!   275
Send him! There's not a diplomat more clever."
Aggrieved, Count Ganelon turns angry red.
He throws his marten furs from off his neck
And stands in his silk tunic, tall and splendid.
His eyes are green; his face is dark with menace,   280
His body noble—broad shoulders and thick chest—
And beautiful. All look on him with pleasure.
He says to Roland, "Fool, are you demented?
Though everybody knows that you're my stepson,
You judge me for the trip to Marsille's den.   285
If mighty God bestows on me the blessing
To make it home, I swear, I'll take such measures—
All of your life, by God, you will regret this."
"What?" Roland answers, "Pride and foolishness?
These people know I never minded threats.   290
We need to send a skillful emissary.
If the king wants, I'll go for you instead."   [295]

                    21

"No! You won't go for me!" Ganelon answers.[7]   AOI
I'm not your liege lord. You are not my man.
I serve King Charles and will, at his command,   295
Put his message into Marsille's hands.
Yet while I'm here, I swear I'll do some rash

---

7. This is the first of the AOIs that do not occur in the usual position at the end of a *laisse*, and it begins a temporary shift from that pattern; only one of the four AOIs that follow occurs in the expected end-*laisse* position. The sudden "misplacement" of four out of five AOIs may result from scribal carelessness, but it does stress a new element: the necessity of disaster, beginning with this part of the council "that ended wrong" (177). From the moment when Roland laughs (punctuated by that one end-of-the-*laisse* AOI, line 299), necessity will govern the action: Ganelon must go to Saragossa, and Roland and his companions must die.

And reckless deed. I must appease my wrath!"
When Roland hears these words, he laughs.   AOI   [302]

22

When the Count Ganelon hears Roland's laughter,   300
He almost bursts from sorrow, and his anger
Almost drives him crazy. He answers,
"You, I do not love. You have me branded
With a false judgment.[8] True Emperor, I stand here
Ready to go wherever you command me.   305 [309]

23

"To Saragossa I will have to go.   AOI
People, when they go there, don't come home.
I leave my wife (your sister), one son alone,
Most beautiful son a man could ever hope,
My Baldwin. He'll be a valiant knight when grown.   310
To him I leave my feudal lands and groves.
Take care of him. My eyes will not behold—"
"You're too soft-hearted," the king tells Ganelon.
"I gave the order, so you have to go."   [318]

24

The emperor says, "Ganelon, step up!   AOI   315
Come take from me your envoy's staff and glove.
You heard the judgment that the French knights judged."
"My lord," says Ganelon, "It's just that one—
Roland!—who judged me. Him I will never love!
Nor Oliver, his war-mate, no, and none   320
Of the Twelve Peers, who dote on him so much.
You witness, Sire: I'll see these people punished."
The king replies, "You shouldn't hold a grudge.
You will go there because I say you must."
"I'll go, and go without a safeguard—nothing   AOI   325
But what Sir Básil had, and Basán, his brother."   [330]

25

The king takes off his right glove, holds it out.
Ganelon, wishing he were elsewhere, lets down

---

8. See Notes on Editorial and Translation Decisions.

His hand and the glove slips to the ground.
"What's this?" the Frenchmen ask. "What loss is bound   330
Soon to befall because the glove fell down?"
"Lords, you will hear from me," declares the count.   [336]

26

"Sire, give me your leave," says Ganelon. "Dismiss me.
When people have to go, they shouldn't linger."
The king says, "Jesus' blessings and mine go with you."   335
He marks a cross on him with two right fingers,
And now the letter and the staff he gives him.   [341]

27

Ganelon the count walks to his tent.
There, with his finest silks and furs, he dresses
And puts on costly arms and armaments   340
And his gold spurs. He fastens to his belt
His sword Murgleis. His uncle, Guinemer,
Holds fast the stirrup for his foot's instep.
He mounts his steed Brownspot. You should have heard
His knights and many noble friends lamenting: 345
"Ah, Ganelon, your valor will be your end!"
"For years you've been at court among the French,
Who know and celebrate your nobleness."
"Not Charlemagne is able to protect
Whatever fool condemned you to this quest."   350
"Count Roland should have watched what he said:
Our Ganelon has family ties and friends!"
"Let us go, too!" some cry. Ganelon says,
"God forbid! Better one knight meet death
Than all you brave knights. Go to France instead.   355
Greet my wife for me; and Pinabel,
My peer and friend; and my son, Baldwin. Help
And pay him loyal service." Ganelon bends
His horse eastward and rides away from them.   AOI   [365]

28

Ganelon rides to meet the Saracens   360
Beneath an olive tree, where Bláncandrin
Sits in his saddle, on the watch for him.
They ride together, exchanging words with skill.
Bláncandrin says, "Your Charles is a great king.

He made Apulia and Calabria his.   365
He crossed the seas to England and inflicted
The tax called Peter's Pence upon the Britons.
Our Spanish wasteland—what does he want with it?"
Ganelon answers, "Charles's heart is big.
No one has proved his match, and no one will." AOI   370 [376]

                              29
"These men are great," says Bláncandrin, "these French.
Your master's dukes' and counts' advice has meant
Hardship for him and everybody else."
Ganelon says, "No bad advice except
Roland's—his pride will have its recompense!   375
Yesterday, in the shade where King Charles rested,
His nephew came, his chain mail still on, fresh
From pillaging near Carcassonne. He stretched
His hand out with an apple in it, red.
'Take, good Majesty! Take this,' he said.   380
'I give you crowns of all the kings of men.'
His pride should lead him to a sorry end.
Every day he gives himself to death.
Whoever kills him—we will have peace then." AOI   [391]

                              30
Bláncandrin says, "Roland is cruel and fierce.   385
He wants to bully men from their beliefs
And plant his banner over every region.
Whom does he count on to make his plans succeed?"
"The French," says Ganelon, "love him so dearly
They never fail him. He wins their full allegiance   390
With silver and gold, horses, battle gear.
He holds the emperor in his hand and means
To conquer every country in the East." AOI   [401]

                              31
Bláncandrin and Ganelon. They go
So far together that they swear an oath   395
To have Count Roland killed; so many roads
And mountain paths, then down to Saragossa.
And there, beneath a pine, they hitch their horses.
There sits in a pine tree's shade on his camp throne,
In Alexandrine silk, the king who holds   400

The realm of Spain, surrounded by a host
Of twenty thousand Saracens, mouths closed
To hear whatever's spoken. And behold,
Here come Lords Bláncandrin and Ganelon.   [413]

32

Bláncandrin steps up before the king   405
With Ganelon. He holds him by the fist.
"Mohammed save you. Apollo give you bliss,
Whose order we uphold. King, I delivered
Your words to Charles. All he did was lift
His hands to his God in praise and send you this   410
Preeminent ambassador of his.
He is a lord of France, noble and rich.
Will it be war or peace? You'll hear from him."
Marsille replies, "Let the man speak. We'll listen."   AOI   [424]

33

But the Count Ganelon is very thoughtful   415
Before the king. He stands, alert and cautious,
Then starts to speak, as one adept at talking:
"Hail, King Marsille. May God, the Most Exalted—
Whom we must worship—guide and save you always.
Hear what King Charlemagne the Mighty calls for: 420
He says you must submit to Christian law
And give him half of Spain in fiefdom. Also,
He says if you repudiate his offer,
His power will bind and shackle you and haul you
Off to his throne in Aix, where you'll be taunted,   425
Judged, humiliated, sentenced, slaughtered,
And die like a miserable vile dog."
Marsille is frightened. Violently he wants
To seize his javelin, a great spear wrought
With finely feathered gold, but his men halt him.   AOI   430 [440]

34

Marsille leaps to his feet. His face burns white.
He grabs his javelin. It shakes. The sight
Makes Ganelon grip his sword's gold hilt, which rises
Until two inches of the sword's blade shine
Above the sheath. "How beautiful and bright!"   435
He says to it. "I bore you a long time

In a king's court. King Charles won't say I died
Alone in a strange country. Their best knights
Will buy my life's blood at a high price."
The pagans say, "We must break up this fight."   440 [450]

35

The best of the pagans hurry to surround
Marsille and plead for him to sit back down.
The caliph tells him, "You hurt this cause of ours,
Flaunting your spear at the Frenchman. You should allow
Him speech, and listen!"—"Sir, I will endure his frowns,"   445
Ganelon replies. "I won't fail now.
Not all the money in the Spanish South,
Not all the gold God made could stop my mouth
From what King Charles, in his imperial power,
Commissions me and bids me to announce   450
To him, his mortal enemy." Then down
He flings his silken sable Alexandrine gown
(Which Bláncandrin retrieves from off the ground),
But never do his fingers, wrapped about
His sword hilt, loosen their tight grip. Out loud   455
The pagans say, "This is a noble count!"   AOI   [467]

36

Ganelon steps closer to the king:
"I'm not the one you should be angry with.
Charles, King of France, sent me to tell you this:
Receive the Christian law. To you he'll give,   460
In fief, one half of Spain. Spain will be split.
Half goes to Charles's nephew, Roland. Him
You'll find a proud co-sharer. If you resist,
He will lay siege to Saragossa City[9]
With all his forces. As soon as they break in,   465
You will be tied and manacled and ridden,
Not on a steed or stallion in fine trim,
Palfrey or mare or mule: his men will fling you
Onto a packhorse; to Aix you will be driven,

---

9. Ganelon does not make it clear who the "he" is: whether Roland or Charlemagne himself will lay siege to Saragossa.

Judged, and beheaded like a common criminal.[10]   470
My emperor commands me give you this."
He puts the letter in the king's right fist.   [484]

37

King Marsille is schooled to write and read.
He takes the letter and he breaks the seal
And throws the wax away. He looks and reads   475
What's written on it; then he looks up and speaks:
"Charles, King of France, reminds me of his grief
And anger over how my army seized
Basán and Básil and on Halt Hill's peak
Beheaded them. He says that if I seek   480
To save my body's life, I must release
My uncle, the Great Caliph, to his keeping.
Otherwise, I lose his love, says he."
At this, his son speaks up to King Marsille:
"This Ganelon's a lunatic. His speech   485
Is off the mark. No more impunity!
Don't listen to his folly. Give him to me.
I'll execute our justice." Ganelon hears.
He yanks his sword out from its sheath.
Then slowly he backs against a large pine tree.   490 [500]

38

The king moves to a deeper orchard area
And bids his best men follow. They obey him.
With him comes the crown prince, Jurfalé;
And white-haired Bláncandrin; and then the caliph,
The king's uncle, close to him and faithful.   495
Bláncandrin begins discourse by saying,
"Summon the Frenchman. He swore to me he'd aid us."
"Then fetch him!" He goes to Ganelon and takes him
By the fingers of his right hand and conveys him
Straight through the trees to start negotiating   500
The wrongful, lawless, and unjust betrayal.   AOI   [511]

---

10. With these embellishments (lines 466–70), Ganelon predicts some of his
own fall into disgrace. See 1795–98.

39

"Worthy Sir Ganelon," Marsille says, "I
Was somewhat hasty when I made to strike
You down in anger. Now it is only right
You have these sable furs. You couldn't buy   505
The gold fringes for four hundred pounds or five.
I'll have them for you by tomorrow night."
"Your Majesty, I won't refuse such kindness.
May God reward you," Ganelon replies.   AOI   [519]

40

"I wish, Count Ganelon," says King Marsille,   510
"To love you very much. I'd like to hear
About your Charlemagne. Old, isn't he?
By now he's used his time up, I believe.
He must have lived at least two hundred years,
Dragging his flesh from east to west to east,   515
And suffered so many blows upon his shield,
And brought so many kings to beggary—
When will he long to sit at home in peace?"
Ganelon says, "He won't. You can't conceive
The kind of man Charles is. Whoever sees   520
And gets to know our monarch knows a hero.
I can't begin to catalogue his feats
Of honor, his deeds of generosity.
I think that he would rather die than be
Bereft of the brave men who call him liege."   525 [536]

41

The pagan says, "This Charlemagne, I wonder—
This king is white-haired, old—over two hundred.
He's ridden his body through so many countries,
Countered so many blows from lances and bludgeons,
So many rich kings brought to beggardom,   530
Tell me, when will he give up the struggle?"
"He won't," says Ganelon, "not till Death summons
His nephew. No such hero ever was
Under the cloak of heaven. And such another
Is Oliver his friend. Greatly belovèd   535
By Charlemagne, the Twelve Peers cover,
With twenty thousand troops, all his frontiers,
And Charles stays safe and is afraid of nothing."   AOI   [549]

42

The Saracen remarks, "I am amazed
By Charlemagne. He's old, white-headed, pale;   540
He's lived two hundred years at least I'd say,
Conquered so many lands, parried the blades,
Bludgeons, and spears of so many knights, enslaved
Or slaughtered so many kings on darkening plains—
When will warfaring weary Charlemagne?"   545
"It won't while Roland lives," the Frenchman claims.
"From here to the East there's not a knight so brave,
And likewise Oliver, his brave war-mate.
With them the Twelve Peers, Charles's favorites,
Lead twenty thousand French, who keep him safe   550
From every foe. And Charles is not afraid."   AOI   [562]

43

"My dear Count Ganelon," Marsille remarks,
"My word can muster wonderful men at arms,
Four hundred thousand knights to swell my armies
To fight against the Frenchmen led by Charles."   555
Ganelon answers, "You're whistling in the dark.
Your losses would be much too great by far.
Leave foolishness to fools. Time to be smart:
Send money to King Charles, quantities large
Enough to strike amazement in French hearts,   560
And twenty hostages. He will depart
For lovely France, leading his larger army,
Leaving behind in Spain his small rearguard.
His nephew Roland will be there in charge
With courteous Oliver. There you will martyr   565
Both noble counts. Without his proud right arm,
Charlemagne will no longer have the heart
To wage his war against you any farther."   AOI   [579]

44

"My dear Count Ganelon, will you tell me this:
How may I manage to have Roland killed?"   570
"Yes," Ganelon replies, "I will.
Charles will have reached the great Ciz Gates while still
His rearguard winds behind him through the cliffs,
His nephew in command, Roland the Rich,
With Oliver, whom he puts such trust in,   575

And twenty thousand Frenchmen. You must fling
A hundred thousand pagans down on him.
He will be wounded and diminished—
Not that your own will not be sadly trimmed.
Let the French fight these hundred thousand first.   580
Then charge with a second army, just as big.
Roland can't slip through both the traps you spring.
You will accomplish knightly work and win
Peace for your land as long as you shall live.   AOI   [595]

45

"Whoever sees to Roland's death will carve   585
Out of the emperor's body his strong right arm.
Once having lost his wonder-legions, Charles
Never again will muster such an army.
Peace will settle on the world at large."
Marsille hears Ganelon, kisses his neck, and starts   590
Unloading heaps of treasure from a cart.   AOI   [602]

46

Marsille the King declares, "What use more talk?
What is decided shouldn't be put off.
Swear to betray Roland." Ganelon
Answers him, "Yes, Sire, if you think I ought."   595
On relics of his sword Murgleis[11] he falsely
Swears treason, puts his soul outside the law.[12]   AOI   [608]

47

From his ivory throne, Marsille the King of Spaniards
Commands a book be brought. On Tervagant
And Mohammed he vows that if he catches   600
The French rearguard with Roland, he'll attack
With all the regiments at his command
And Roland will have lived his last.
Count Ganelon replies, "Amen to that!"   AOI   [616]

---

11. For extra efficacy, the hilts of valuable swords were sometimes inlaid with
religious relics. See lines 2303–7 and 2452–55 for the relics in Roland's and
Charlemagne's swords.

12. The shortness of *laisse* 46 stresses the seriousness of the judgment that the
author expresses in this line.

48

Now comes the pagan Valdabron. He speaks,   605
Cheerful and radiant, before Marsille,
To Ganelon. "Here is my sword. Take, keep.
It's yours. There's not a better blade. Look here:
The gem-starred hilt alone is worth at least
One thousand minted Saracen gold pieces.   610
This is my friendship gift. May you reveal
Count Roland to us, Charlemagne's brave peer,
Leading the rearguard." Ganelon agrees.
"It will be done," he says. Each kisses each
Affectionately upon the chin and cheeks.   615 [626]

49

The pagan Climborin steps forward now,
Smiling of face, radiant of brow:
"Here, keep my helmet (no better can be found)
And give us helpful counsel to bring down
Roland's rearguard and Roland the proud count."   620
"It will be done," Ganelon announces.
They kiss each other on the cheeks and mouth.   AOI   [633]

50

Marsille's Queen Bramimunde speaks to him too:
"I love you, sir, because my lord approves
And prizes you," she says, "as all men do.   625
Favor your wife for me with these gold brooches,
Inlaid with jasper, amethysts, and jewels
Worth more than all the wealth of Rome, in truth,
More costly than your emperor's heirlooms."
Ganelon takes them and sticks them in his boot.   AOI   630 [641]

51

Now the king summons Maldebty, his treasurer,
And says, "You have King Charles's tribute ready?"
Maldebty answers, "All of it, Sire, yes.
Seven hundred camels, with gold weighed heavy,
And our best young men as hostages, all twenty."   AOI   635 [646]

52

Marsille grips Ganelon and pats his shoulder.
He tells him, "You are very wise and bold.
By the Salvation that you hold most holy,
Don't let your heart swerve from the path you've shown us.
Out of my wealth I give you twelve mules loaded   640
Heavily with pure Arabian gold—
That much each year! And take these keys to open
For you the great walled city, Saragossa.
King Charles will receive the larger gift of gold.
Make sure the rearguard captain will be Roland.   645
I swear: if I catch him on the valley road,
I'll kill him and the rearguard will be broken."
"It's late," says Ganclon. "I must be going."
He mounts his stallion, and he turns it homeward.   AOI   [660]

53

Meanwhile the emperor is getting ready   650
For his arrival in the town of Gelne,
Which Roland seized and razed. It will lie empty
A hundred years and still not be resettled.
The emperor waits for news of the immense
Spanish tribute that he should be getting.   655
Morning has risen and the bright stars are setting.
Count Ganelon rides up to the French tents.   AOI   [668]

54

Early awake, the Emperor of France
Listens to matins, celebrates the mass,
And stands before his tent on dewy grass.   660
Wise Oliver and Roland are at hand
And Duke Neïme and many other barons.
False and forsworn, Ganelon is back,
With his words artfully rehearsed. He stands.
"I bring you, King," he says, "from Spain's vast land   665
The keys to mighty Saragossa—and
Tribute, money, and treasure by the wagons,
And hostages—twenty noble Arab lads.
Although the caliph, whom you did demand,
Is absent, don't reproach the king for that.   670
With my own eyes I watched a host decamp:
Four hundred thousand fighting men, all clad

In mail and helmets, some with their visors clamped.
Swords cinched, the pommels' gold enameled black,
They tramped with their caliph down to the sea strand,   675
Fleeing Marsille, unwilling to compact
With Christian law. Their ships steered from the banks.
Just four miles out from land, thunderbolts flashed,
A whirlwind storm blew up, ships rose and sank,
And every pagan drowned. You've seen the last   680
Of them. If he had lived, I would have dragged
The caliph here. Before this month has passed,
I promise good Marsille will follow fast
Behind you into France and there contract
To serve your law and, with his two hands clasped,   685
Vow to hold Spain for you and be your man."
King Charlemagne replies, "May God be thanked!
Well done! I'll recompense you." Now great blasts
Of a thousand trumpets sound. The Frenchmen pack,
Break camp, lay luggage on their donkeys' backs,   690
And set out on the road to lovely France.   AOI   [702]

55

Charlemagne has laid waste to Spain and ripped
The towers down, ravaged the halls and cities.
Now he proclaims the long war is finished.
Toward lovely France they ride, and in the midst   695
Of every camp they pitch, Count Roland fixes
The guide-on flag up high upon a hill,
And the French lie all about in sight of it.
    Pagans ride north too. Clad to their chins
In chain-mail armor, helmets strapped, swords cinched,   700
Shields slung across their backs, lance handles gripped,
And visors closed and clamped, they ride and cling
To low valleys, and they camp in woods on ridges,
Four hundred thousand strong, till the night lifts.
God! What grief that the French don't know of this!   AOI   705 [716]

56

The dark has fallen at the end of day.
The mighty emperor, King Charlemagne,
Sleeps, dreaming that he stood at the Ciz Gates,
Holding a stout ash lance. Ganelon came,
Wrenched it out of his hands and wildly waved   710

And broke the lance. The splinters sailed
High in the sky above the darkened air.
Charlemagne sleeps on and does not waken.   [724]

57

That vision gone, another rocks his rest.
As he stood on his Chapel steps at Aix,   715
A cruel bear bit him on his right arm. Then
A leopard charged him from the dark Ardennes.
It pounced and bit and clawed and mauled his flesh.
Down from his hall a greyhound raced to rescue
King Charles within his troubled dream. It leapt,   720
Attacked, and tore the bear's right ear to shreds,
Then wheeled around to wrestle with the leopard.
"This is a fierce war," the Frenchmen said,
Not knowing which of them would come out best.
Charles sleeps on. He does not waken yet.   AOI   725 [736]

58

Dawn light advances as the darkness runs.
Horse bells begin to jingle. Morning's begun.
King Charles rides hard now by the rising sun.
Soon he cries out: "Lord knights of France, look up.
There stand the Gates of Ciz. Now you must judge: 730
Who guides my rearguard under the tight bluffs?"
Ganelon answers quickly, "My stepson.
For might and valor, Roland is the one."
The king glares hard at Ganelon and utters,
"You are the Devil! Mad and rabid blood   735
Has entered to your heart. Whom can we trust
To lead the vanguard then?" Says Ganelon,
"Ogier the Duke of Denmark. There is none
More valiant than the Dane. He'll guard our front."   [750]

59

Count Roland, when he hears himself decreed,   AOI   740
Answers by the laws of chivalry:
"My lord stepfather, you must hold me dear,
To judge the rearguard leadership on me.
King Charlemagne of France has not a steed,
No stallion, palfrey, mule—he-mule or she—   745
Pack horse, dray horse, nag that I won't keep

Secure for him while I still live and wield
A sword on his behalf."—"Yes, I believe
You speak the truth," Ganelon agrees.   AOI   [760]

60

When Roland hears the judgment laid on him,   750
He flares back up at Ganelon: "You stinking
Vile stepfather, low-class son of a bitch,
You think I'll let the glove fall from my fist
Like the staff Charles handed you, which you let slip?"[13]   AOI   [765]

61

"True Emperor," brave Roland says, "confide   755
To me the bow your fist still holds so tight.[14]
I think no one will want to criticize
The way I grasp the bow—not like the time
Ganelon's right hand let the staff slide."
The emperor lowers his head. He twists his white   760
Moustache and strokes his beard. He cannot hide,
For all his efforts, that his eyes aren't dry.   [773]

62

The Duke Neïme steps up. You couldn't name
A truer vassal. "Mighty Charlemagne,"
He says, "You hear how they debate.   765
Count Roland is hot tempered. No one can shake
The rearguard judgment from him now it's made.
Give him the bow you hold, and designate
The best support you have for his brigade."
The king holds out the bow, which Roland takes.   770 [782]

63

"Sir Roland, nephew," promises King Charles,
"Listen: I will give you half my army.
Take them to keep; and you won't come to harm."
Count Roland answers, "No. God strike my heart

---

13. For the problems surrounding the strange and wonderful contradictions of *laisses* 59 and 60, see Notes on Editorial and Translation Decisions.

14. See Notes on Editorial and Translation Decisions.

If I refuse the honor of this charge.   775
I'll take no more or less for my rearguard
Than twenty thousand valiant French at arms.
You, Sire, without one worry, will ride far
Through the Ports of Spain to France with your whole army."   [791]

64

Roland is mounted. He rides his great war steed.   AOI   780
His war-mate Oliver rides near.
Gerin and Gerer—the brave companion Peers—
And Otis come, and Bérenger with these,
And Astor and the ferocious Anseïs.
And here's Gerart of Russillon the Fierce,   785
And rich Duke Gaifiers. The archbishop speaks:
"I'm riding with Count Roland, by my beard!"
"I'm riding with you, too," Count Walter pleads;
"I'm Roland's man, and I will not retreat."[15]
More keep coming. Soon Count Roland leads   790
Twenty thousand valiant volunteers.   AOI   [802]

65

Roland calls up Count Walter de la Humme:
"Enlist a thousand knights of our French country.
Ride the ridges and occupy the summits.
Don't let one wagon of the king's be plundered."   795
"For you, I'll guard them!" Walter says, then musters
One thousand valiant knights of that dear country
And occupies the heights. No news of bloodshed
Will bring them back till, reduced to seven hundred,
Fighting King Almaris of Belferna   800
On that worst day, swords lifted, down they plunge.[16]   [813]

---

15. The twelve leaders in *laisse* 64 do not precisely coincide with the Twelve Peers listed in *laisse* 176. Of the four leaders who are not among the Twelve Peers, Archbishop Turpin was probably too prominent to go unlisted, and Walter de la Humme, even though he is not one of the Twelve, is dramatically important to this *laisse* for his eagerness to stand by Roland on the dangerous mission.

16. It is not clear in the manuscript whether Walter and his men fight King Almaris before or after they come down from the heights. The poet does not include this scene in his account of the battle when it comes.

66

The valleys are dark, and high up loom the cliffs.
The rocks are shadowed, the narrow passes grim.
The king's knights ride all day, and their good mood slips.
From fifteen miles you can hear their chain mail clink.   805
Filing out of Spain, the men begin
Descent to Gascony, their king's dominion.
Now they remember the homesteads where they lived,
The noble wives they had, the pretty girls.
There's not a one who doesn't weep for pity,   810
And the worst pity suffered is the king's,
Who left his nephew at the Gates of Ciz
And now, for all he tries, can't keep tears in.   AOI   [825]

67

Charlemagne's Twelve Peers are riding yet
Through rugged Spain with twenty thousand French,   815
Not one of them afraid. Not one fears death.
Charles rides in France, hooding his bowed head.
The Duke Neïme, who rides beside him, says,
"Why, Charles, do your spirits seem so leaden?"
And he: "How can you ask me such a question?   820
The grief I suffer—how could I not have wept,
Knowing that Ganelon will be the wreck
Of lovely France? Last night I dreamed he wrenched
My lance out of my grip and scattered the shreds.
The rearguard judgment came from him: I left,   825
Stranded in a foreign pass, my nephew.
Roland! I'll never have his like again."   AOI   [840]

68

The king cannot hold tears back from his eyes.
For pity a hundred thousand Frenchmen cry
And fear for Roland. Pagans have supplied   830
Ganelon the traitor with some prime
Returns for treason: gold and silver finery,
Laces, silks, and satins, horses to ride,
Camels, and lions.—King Marsille, meanwhile,
Calls Spanish barons to rally to his cry: 835
Counts, viscounts, dukes, emirs, and knights.
Four hundred thousand barons mobilize
For King Marsille in three days' time.

Drumbeats sound and resound from every height
Of Saragossa's walls. On a high spire   840
They raise Mohammed's statue, to which rise
Prayers and petitions for their enterprise.
The pagan army, in long hard stages riding
Valleys and hills and paths they know,[17] soon sight
French guide-ons and ensigns, flapping in the sky.   845
The Twelve Peers and the rearguard won't deny
Battle and bloodshed if the pagans want a fight.   [859]

69

Marsille's nephew thwacks his mule and drubs
It forward past the mid-ranks to the front.
Laughing and persuasive, he tells his uncle,   850
"Your Majesty, I served you long and suffered
Troubles and hardships for you; I have won
Battles for you on fields flowing with blood.
I beg a favor: let me have first thrust
At Roland. With my keen-edged steel I'll cut   855
Him down, then with Mohammed's help expunge
The French from Spain and win your land's freedom
From the Ports of Spain to far-off Durestunt.
Charles will be stricken. His armies will give up.
Never again will wars despoil your country."   860
King Marsille holds out to him the glove.   AOI   [873]

70

The nephew grasps the glove. Haughty and fierce,
He takes it from his uncle's hand and speaks:
"Dear uncle, great is the gift you've given me!
Elect twelve knights for me; with these elite   865
I will do battle with the Twelve French Peers."
Falsarun, brother of the king, receives
The first commission. "Nephew," he volunteers,
"I'm with you. To victory! Here are our spears.
With these we'll strike down Charlemagne's Twelve Peers.   870

---

17. Bédier, Jenkins, and Calin assume that "tere certaine" [856] is a proper
noun and a place name, but they are uncertain where it is. The poet, however,
is probably referring to the advantages of speed and secrecy that the land gives
to the Spanish Saracens. Much of the ground they are traveling is *certaine*, or
known to them.

Roland's rearguard will meet its destiny
Of death by us upon the battlefield." AOI   [884]

71

King Corsablix comes forward from the army.
Berber practitioner of evil arts,
He promises Marsille a liegeman's heart.   875
Not all the gold beneath God's shining stars
Could hold him from a fight with the rearguard.
Then spurring hard comes Málprimis Brigant.
This knight is faster on foot than horses are.
He speaks out to Marsille: "My lord, I'll charge   880
Headlong with lowered spear to Roncevals.[18]
If I find Roland, he will be my martyr."   [893]

72

Next Bálaguez comes forward, an emir.
Bright honest face, handsome in heart and limb,
But armed and in the saddle, lance atilt   885
Against his enemies, he's murderous and grim.
Honored for loyalty and heroism,
If Bálaguez were only Christian,
God, what a noble knight he would have been!
He pledges his allegiance to the king: 890
"In Roncevals I'll stake my life that if
I come upon Count Roland I will kill him
And Oliver, and the Twelve French Peers, all killed!
The French will die dishonored in the dirt.
Charlemagne grows weak, and his mind slips.   895
Stunned by his nephew's death, heartsick, war-sick,
He'll leave our Spain untroubled." King Marsille
Thanks him for the promises he gives.   AOI   [908]

73

There is an Almansour from Moriann.
No crueler rascal lives in Spanish lands.   900
He comes before Marsille and makes his brag:
"My twenty thousand men with shields and lances

---

18. Málprimis Brigant has the honor of being first to mention the fatal battle-field. It will be mentioned once per *laisse* through the next seven *laisses*.

Will ride with me at Roncevals and will attack.
If I find Roland, he will die. No day will pass
That Charles won't weep for him while his old age lasts." AOI   905 [915]

74

Then there is Turgis of Turteluse, the count,
Commanding and ruling Turteluse the town.
He yearns to see the Christian forces routed.
He lines up with the other six and shouts,
"There's nothing, King, for you to fret about.   910
Roman St. Peter isn't worth a mouse
To him we serve: Mohammed! By his power
We'll conquer. The honor of the field is ours.
At Roncevals I mean to overpower
And kill Roland. No one can save him now.   915
Look at my sword. It's keen and long, and bound
To cross with Durendal. Word will go round
How my sword bent down his. And once so proud,
The French will die who dare to hold their ground.
Charles will be shamed. Weeping, he will lie down,   920
And never, in any land, put on a crown."   [930]

75

Now there emerges from a regiment
Count Escremiz of Valterna. He presses
Up to Marsille among the pagans present:
"In Roncevals I mean to put an end   925
To Roland's pride and there cut off his head,
And Oliver's. Roland's Twelve Peers, death-destined,
Will perish there with all the other Frenchmen.
The French will die. Their land will be swept empty.
Chivalry will be lost, Charles left defenseless."   AOI   930 [939]

76

More pagans come to join them: Esturganz
And Astramarz, his mate and war companion,
Both of them traitors, lying and underhanded.
Marsille gives orders: "Ride, my noble vassals,
To Roncevals, where the long valley narrows,   935
And lead my pagan armies into battle."
They answer, "Yes, Your Highness! You command us.
Roland and Oliver—we will attack them

And the Twelve Peers. For them there's no safe passage
From certain death. Our swords are sharp and slashing.   940
With warm French blood we'll rinse them to the handles.
The French will die. King Charles will mourn them sadly.
We'll give you Greater Europe for the having.
Come with us, King, and look upon the vanquished.
We'll give the emperor into your hands."   945 [954]

77

Lord Márgariz runs up to volunteer.
He governs from Seville to Cazmarine.
He is so handsome, every woman dreams
To be his love. If they can only see him,
They faint from bliss or laugh with blushing cheeks.   950
No pagan like him for pure chivalry!
Above the other voices, loud and clear,
"O King," he shouts, "don't be afraid. I'll meet
Roland at Roncevals and there defeat
And slay him. Oliver and the Twelve Peers   955
Cannot escape the death that I decree.
Look at my gold-hilt sword, given to me
By the Emir of Primes. How it will bleed
With red French blood! The French will die, France grieve
With shame, and Charles the Old of the White Beard   960
Not live one day not prostrate from his grief.
Within a year our armies will have seized
All France and will bed down in St. Denis."
The pagan king nods thanks to Márgariz.   AOI   [974]

78

Chernuble, who is Múnigre's cruel ruler,   965
Comes forward next. His hair hangs to his boots.
He can bear greater weight for his amusement
Than four well-fed, hardworking large pack mules.
Sun never brightened Múnigre. The moon
Stays always dark, where no grain ever grew.   970
Rain never fell, and never falls the dew.
All of the rocks are black. People presume
Devils dwell in the country of Chernuble.
"My sword is cinched," he cries, "ready to sluice
Red blood in Roncevals. If Roland moves   975
Across my path and I don't charge that fool,

Call me a liar! My sword will subdue
His Durendal. The valley will be strewn
With French. France will lie empty as a tomb."
These Twelve take their commission and assume   980
Command over a hundred thousand troops.
Ambitious for the war to be renewed,
They don their armor in a pine wood's gloom.   [993]

79

The pagans dress in chain mail to the thighs,
Some hauberks double-, most of them triple-ply,   985
And Saragossa helmets with steel visors,
And Viennese steel swords. Their shields are wide,
The lances that they carry are the pride
Of Spain's Valencia. Their ensigns rise
And flutter scarlet, blue, and white.   990
They've left their palfreys, donkeys, mules behind.
They mount war steeds and ride in a close file.
The day is beautiful. The sun is bright.
Every rider's armor glints and shines.
A thousand trumpets sound, and their music flies   995
Across the ridges to the rearguard lines.
   "I think," says Oliver, "we'll get to fight
With Saracens, my friend." Roland replies,
"God grant we do! Our business is to bide
Here for our king. To serve his lord, a knight   1000
Should suffer hardships, deserts, winter ice
And sacrifice his limbs, his hide, his life.
—Frenchmen, prepare yourselves to strike and strike!
No wit will mock our strokes with comic rhymes!
Pagans are wrong. Christians are right!   1005
Never will *my* deeds argue otherwise!"   AOI   [1016]

80

Oliver rides and looks from a hill's crest
At a green valley. Pagan regiments,
Off to his right, ride in his direction.
He calls to Roland, his battle-mate and friend: 1010
"I'm looking back toward Spain and can detect
The glare of hauberks and the gleam of helmets.
This will mean countless sorrows for our French.
Ganelon—the traitor!—knew this when

He judged us for the army's rear defense."   1015
"Oliver, keep quiet," Roland says.
"He's my stepfather. Not a word against him."   [1027]

81

Oliver observes from a high mound
And sees the land of Spain stretch to the south
And Spaniards swarming toward where he looks out,   1020
Their spears and ensigns set. The helmets crowned
With gold and jewels, the saffron chain-mail gowns,
And the shields shine in his eyes. The crowd
Of regiments is more than he can count
Or measure. His vision is confounded   1025
By such vast motion, and his mind astounded.
To give the French an accurate account
Of all that he has seen, he hurries down.   [1038]

82

Oliver says, "The pagans I have seen!
Never has anyone seen more than these.   1030
Their vanguard shows a hundred thousand shields;
Their helms are strapped and their chain mail gleams.
The pagans grip the handles of their burnished spears.
Now for a battle, vicious beyond belief.
—Frenchmen! Take strength from God and victory   1035
Is in our hands! Do not give up the field!"
The Frenchmen say, "God curse whoever flees.
Even from death, not one of us retreats!"   AOI   [1048]

83

Oliver says, "The pagan power is more
By many thousands than our little force.   1040
Friend Roland, lift up and wind your horn.
Charles will hear it and ride back from the north."
Roland replies, "I'd be a fool to throw
Honor away and lose in France my glory.
With Durendal I mean to strike strong blows   1045
Till the blade runs blood. The heathen hosts
Will curse the wind that blew them to this port.
Death sentences hang over all our foes."   AOI   [1058]

84

"Roland, dear friend, sound Olifant. Its din
Will summon far-off Charles. He will not linger,   1050
But hurry back with all his barons with him
To rescue us." Roland says, "God forbid
A deed of mine bring shame upon my kin
And lovely France be shamed for what I did.
With Durendal I mean to strike until   1055
Its long steel blade is bloody to the hilt
Before I sheath it. It was an evil wind
For our vile foes that blew them to these hills.
I swear to God: their dying now begins."   AOI   [1069]

85

"Wind your horn Olifant, Roland dear friend!   1060
King Charles will hear us where the mountains end
And ride to our rescue with the valiant French."
Roland says, "God forbid that it be said
By any man alive that infidels
Drove me to horn blowing! Not one breath   1065
Of blame will reach my kindred. In the press
Of battle I will strike and strike again
With Durendal, a thousand strokes and then
Seven hundred as the blade runs red.
The French fight well and *will* fight. Nothing protects   1070
Those soldiers out of Spain from certain death."   [1081]

86

Oliver says, "I don't see any blame!
All I see is Saracens from Spain
Flooding across the mountains and the plains,
The meadows, hills, and valleys. Look how great   1075
The enemy army is. Look and compare
Our little company." Roland exclaims,
"But my desire is great! God and his angels
Save me from causing France to be dispraised!
I'd rather die. Better be dead than shamed!   1080
The harder we hit, the greater love from Charlemagne."   [1092]

87

Roland is valiant. Oliver is wise.
Both are marvelously noble knights.

Now they're on horseback, ready for the fight.
They won't back down from battle. They'd rather die.   1085
Both are good barons, their words high and defiant.
Now the vile pagans come furiously riding.
"Look," says Oliver, "at their front lines.
They're close, and Charles is farther all the time.
You didn't blow your Olifant, for pride.   1090
If Charles were here, our men would come out right.
Look upward through our rearguard files
And see the consternation in their eyes.
When these are gone, never will be their like."
Roland: "Don't waste your breath on bad advice.   1095
To hell with any heart that quivers and shies.
We're staying where we are. Let *them* take flight.
We'll win the melees and the single fights."   AOI   [1109]

88

When Roland sees the battle is impending,
He grows more dangerous than lion or leopard.   1100
"Oliver!" he calls. "Hear me, you Frenchmen!
Friends and dear companions, no talk of surrender!
The Emperor of France, when he selected
Us for his twenty thousand—he expected
No cowardice from any that he left here.   1105
To serve his lord, a worthy knight shall welcome
Brute hardships, freezes, thirst, and scorching deserts,
And willingly sacrifice his blood and flesh.
Thrust with your spears! With Durendal, my present
From Charlemagne, I'll strike their regiments,   1110
And if I die, who owns my good sword next
Will know that once a worthy knight possessed it!"   [1123]

89

And now comes forward Lord Archbishop Turpin.
He wheels his horse around and spurs it
Up on a little hill to preach his sermon: 1115
"My lords, the king assigned us here. Our purpose:
To fight and give our lives in the king's service
So all of Christianity may flourish.
The battle is upon you. Your role is certain.
See Saracens riding near, intent on murder.   1120
Confess your sins out loud and ask God's mercy.

I now absolve you into life eternal.
Die, and as holy martyrs you inherit
Heavenly thrones and sit in azure circles."
The French dismount and kneel down on the earth   1125
To have their sins absolved. Archbishop Turpin:
"And for your penance, strike your adversaries!"   [1138]

90

Charlemagne's barons rise and stand up straight,
Absolved, and all their sins are washed away.
Archbishop Turpin blesses them and makes   1130
The sign of the cross over the French brigades.
Now they are on warhorses and arrayed
In knightly armor and glistening chain mail.
"Oliver, you were right," Roland declares.
"Ganelon betrayed us all. He traded   1135
Us for the gold and silver Marsille gave.
This deed will be avenged by Charlemagne.
A bad deal for Marsille: for the gold he paid,
All the return he gets is our steel blades."   AOI   [1151]

91

Count Roland, leading twenty thousand French   1140
On Veillantif, his swift warhorse, has led
The rearguard through the Spanish passages.
He is armed and in armor, handsome, confident.
With a firm grip, he points his lance to heaven.
The white ensign flaps down the lance's length,   1145
And the fringes flutter on his fists. His strength
Is great, his body straight and elegant,
Face bright with glad and laughing eyes. His friend,
Count Oliver, stays close behind. The French
Call Roland *Safeguard*. Roland looks again,   1150
Proudly and fiercely toward the Saracens,
Then mildly and humbly back at his own men
And with noble courtesy addresses them:
"My lords, move forward slowly. Steady, steady.
These Saracens come looking for their deaths.   1155
What plunder we will have at the day's end!
No king of France ever won more." That said,
With lowered lances, the Frenchmen move ahead.   AOI   [1169]

92

"I'm done with talk," says Oliver at last.
"You didn't care to blow your Olifant,   1160
Or care for Charles himself, that great, good man.
He's not to blame. He thinks we're through the pass.
Those up ahead can't help it that we're trapped.
Ride now, and fight as fiercely as you can.
—Lord barons! Hold the field of battle!   1165
For God's sake, concentrate on swift attacks,
Striking and taking blows that they give back.
We must not fail to raise our battle-rally
In honor of our emperor's red standard!"
A loud cheer rises from the rearguard ranks.   1170
(Whoever heard that cheer, "Mountjoy!"[19] would laugh
And joyfully remember great deeds passed.)
Each spurs his warhorse forward in a dash
To strike the first foe with his lance.
They mean to fight. What else but to attack?[20]   1175
Nor do the pagans fear the men from France.
Frenchmen and pagans meet with a loud clash.   [1187]

93

The nephew of Marsille, Aelroth by name,
Gallops ahead of all the men of Spain,
Screaming his oaths and slanders all the way   1180
Against our French: "Vile French, we joust today.
The one who should defend you has betrayed you.
Crazy King Charles abandoned you in Spain!
Lovely France will lose its former fame,
And Charles, the right arm from his shoulder blade."   1185
When Roland hears these insults, God, what rage!
He spurs his Veillantif, lets go the reins,
And with his long spear thrusts with deadly aim,
Shatters the shield, bursts open the chain mail,
And pierces the chest. The ribs and backbone break,   1190

---

19. See Glossary and Index for *Mountjoy.*

20. The French is, "Si vunt ferir, que fereient il el?" [1185], literally, "They are going to strike. What else would they do?" a line nicely balanced in sound by the *f* and *r* consonance and in meaning by the two possible interpretations: the men are brave, and there's nothing else they will do; the men are trapped, and there's nothing else they can do.

And the lance thrusts the soul from the rib cage.
He digs the spear deeper, shakes Aelroth in the air,
And flings him onto the ground, where his neck breaks
In two. Roland speaks to him anyway:
"Mongrel son of a bitch, Charles isn't crazy.   1195
Our king is loyal and abhors betrayal.
The king did right to leave us back in Spain,
And France won't lose its fame.—Frenchmen! We claim
First blood. Strike, Frenchmen, strike for Charlemagne!
We're in the right. These bastards have the blame.   AOI   1200 [1212]

94

There is a duke. His name is Falsarun,
Uncle to Aelroth and Marsille's brother,
He's Lord of Datliún and of Balbiún.
A meaner reprobate there never was.
His two big ugly eyes, which bulge in front,   1205
Measure between them at least half a foot.
Seeing his nephew killed grieves him so much
He hates the French and breaks forth at a run,
Singing the battle cry of pagandom.
"Frenchmen," he threatens them, "the day is come   1210
When lovely France's glory will be smudged."
Count Oliver, outraged by the insult,
Digs in his golden spurs, attacks, and thrusts
His long lance through the pagan's shield and cuts
The chain-mail hauberk open; the lance shoves   1215
Ensign streamers deep into the lungs.
He flings the body headlong in the dust.
Now he looks down and says, "You useless lump,
All of your claims and threats mean less than nothing.
—Hit them, you French! This battle will be won!   1220
Mountjoy!" he cries, and lifts his ensign up.   AOI   [1234]

95

The Berber Corsablix, who wears the crown
Of a strange and barbarous kingdom in the south,
Arouses the other Saracens and shouts,
"Barons of Spain, the victory is ours!   1225
Look at them. This wretched little rout
Of Frenchmen will be easy to confound.
The hour destined for their death comes round,

And where is Charles? He's nowhere to be found."
Archbishop Turpin hears. Without a doubt   1230
He hates him from the center of his bowels.
With golden spurs he urges his swift mount,
Lowers his lance, charges, aims, and jousts
With knightly skill and concentrated power,
Bursts shield, bursts hauberk, jabs the body out   1235
And up from the saddle, shakes it like a trout,
And roughly casts it down.
Looking back he sees him dead, but shouts,
"You lie, you lousy loud-mouthed pagan lout.
My lord King Charles protects us even now.   1240
We French don't flee. We're here to stay and clout
Your pagan friends. Let your dead skull announce:
They'll all lie dead before the night comes down.
—Strike, Frenchmen, strike! Remember your renown.
Thanks be to God, the first blow struck is ours.   1245
Mountjoy! Mountjoy! Maintain the battleground!"   [1260]

96

Sir Gerin jousts Lord Málprimis and hits
The costly shield, which is not worth a pin,
Dead center in the crystal eye. The shield splits,
And the right half spatters on the ground in splinters.   1250
The spear drives through the mail and through the skin
And flesh, entrails, and spine. Sir Gerin flings
The pagan's body down into the dirt
As Satan carries off the pagan's spirit.   AOI   [1268]

97

Gerer, his friend, strikes Emir Bálaguez,   1255
Shatters his shield, tears his mail to shreds.
The stout lance penetrates the pagan's belly
And pokes out through the other side. Then Gerer
Tosses the body and leaves it where it fell.
Oliver says, "Our battle's going well."   1260 [1274]

98

Duke Samson hits the Almansour and shivers
The shield of ornamental gold and lilies.
The costly hauberk offers no resistance.

The spearhead bursts the heart and lungs and liver.
He throws him dead, whether one wills or wishes.   1265
The archbishop says, "That stroke was well delivered."   [1280]

99

Count Anseïs at breakneck gallop rides
At Turgis of Turteluse, and his spear rives
The shield above the golden center eye
And rips the chain mail where it's double plied.   1270
The steel point penetrates the flesh and knifes
So far it sticks out through the other side.
He throws him headlong on the grass to die.
Count Roland tells him, "Struck, like a noble knight!"   [1288]

100

Then Éngeler, the Gascon of Bordeaux,   1275
Spurs, drops the bridle, lets his swift horse go,
Strikes Escremiz Valterna such a blow
It shreds the shield the pagan tries to hold,
Breaks the collar of the hauberk open
And nails the body through the collarbone.   1280
He throws him from the saddle to the road.
"Losing," he tells him, "was all that you could hope."   AOI   [1296]

101

Otis jousts the pagan Esturganz.
He hits the upper edge of his shield and smashes
White and vermillion gules. The lance advances   1285
Straight through the bursting chain-mail hauberk straps
Into Estruganz's heart and rams
The pagan's body lifeless from the saddle.
"You won't heal soon," he says as he looks back.   [1303]

102

Bérenger strikes Astramarz's shield   1290
And shatters it. Sharp steel fragments pierce
Deep in the pagan's flesh. Down he careens
To join a thousand pagan dead. Of the Elite
Twelve Saracens: ten dead; two living peers:
Chernuble and Count Márgariz.   1295 [1310]

103

A gallant, valiant knight, Sir Márgariz
Is beautiful and agile, strong and quick.
He spurs his steed toward Oliver and hits
The shield's gold center, and the steel point rips
Tangentially the shirt along the ribs.　　　　　　　　　　　1300
God has saved Oliver! He isn't hit.
The lance hilt cracks. Oliver stays fixed
Firmly in stirrups and gallops off uninjured,
Rallying the rearguard with his bugle ringing.[21]　　　　[1319]

104

The battle is fierce. It rages everywhere.　　　　　　　　1305
Roland is always where he isn't safe.
While his lance lasts, he jousts with deadly aim,
But after fifteen hits, he throws the stub away.
He unsheathes Durendal, gleaming and naked,
Spurs straight at Chernuble and swings his blade,　　　1310
Breaks through the helmet's carbuncle and jade,
Slices down through the hair and scalp and brain,
Dissects between the eyes the pagan's face,
Unstitches all the closely-linked chain mail,
Splits downward to the juncture of the legs　　　　　　　1315
And the gold-braided saddle, and it stays
Not there, but cleaves the horse's spine and lays
Man and horse lifeless on the grassy plain.
He says, "Son of a low-born bitching slave,
Today Mohammed's giving you no aid.　　　　　　　　　1320
Not by the likes of you are battles gained."　　　　　　　[1337]

105

Roland rides wherever the battle's roughest,
With Durandal, attacking, slashing, thrusting,
Distributing death, trampling enemies under.
What jousts! He heaps one body on another　　　　　　　1325
Into the spongy grass where warm blood slushes.
Both his arms and his chain-mail shirt are bloody.
His horse is bloody from the mane to rump.
Oliver at slashing is no sluggard,

---

21. See Notes on Editorial and Translation Decisions.

And the Twelve Peers perform chivalric wonders.   1330
All the French knights slash and cut and bludgeon
The Saracens, who swoon and die and suffer.
The archbishop says, "May God reward our valor.
Mountjoy!" he cries. "Remember Charles's colors."   AOI   [1350]

106

Oliver gallops back and forth and fights.   1335
His lance is broken to a fourth its size.
With it he batters Malun, a pagan knight,
Right through the shield all flowered gold and white,
Crushes helmet, crushes skull. Out burst eyes.
Brains spatter underfoot, where there now lie   1340
Seven hundred dead. He turns and smites
Turgis and Esturgoz, who fall like flies.
Wood splinters on the hand that holds it tight.
"Oliver, what are you doing?" Roland cries.
"Why fight with wood? What about steel and iron?   1345
Your sword Hautcler? What's wrong with it? Just right,
With its gold hilt and the glass-sharp edge, for striking!"
"Too many targets, Roland! There's no time
To draw my sword," Oliver replies.   AOI   [1366]

107

Count Oliver has drawn his faithful sword   1350
At last, just as his battle-mate implored.
He swings it down with all chivalric force
On Justin, Count de Val Ferrée. The sword
Cleaves helmet, head, neck, spinal cord,
The saffron mail, the flesh to where it forks,   1355
The costly saddle, all with jewels adorned,
And carves the backbone of the pagan's horse.
Down to the ground he shoves the double corpse.
Roland remarks, "I knew that stroke was yours.
Such strokes earn favor of our emperor."   1360
"Mountjoy!" the Frenchmen shout of one accord.   AOI   [1378]

108

Gerin rides Sorrel. Gerer rides parallel
On Stagcatcher. These two close battle-friends
Let loose their bridles, spur their steeds ahead,
And double-spear the pagan Tímozel,   1365

One through the shield, the other the chain hauberk.
Both spears enter and break inside his breast,
Knocking him into a fallow-field death bed.
(Which of them dealt the death blow I can't tell.)
The Gascon Peer Sir Éngeler now fells   1370
Espérveris, the son of Count Borel.[22]
Archbishop Turpin slays the sorcerer
And pagan necromancer Sízlorel,
Whose dark equations once forced Jupiter
To guide him through the labyrinths of Hell.   1375
"It's time," he tells the corpse, "you paid your debt."
"You ground that bastard down," Count Roland says.
"These are good strokes, aren't they, Oliver, friend?"   [1395]

109

Meanwhile, what a cruel and stubborn battle!
Pagans and French take blows and give them back,   1380
Attack, defend, attack, and counterattack.
How many fight with shattered, bloodied lances!
How many standards and colorful guide-ons cracked,
And Frenchmen dead before their youth can pass!
Mothers and wives will not see them in France,   1385
Nor will the French, who look back for their banners. AOI [1403]
  Charlemagne weeps. Worry near drives him mad.
What good does it do? No rescue is at hand.
In Saragossa, Ganelon served him badly
And sold his people in a pagan land,   1390
For which he will forfeit his life, legs, hands,
And thirty valiant members of his family,
Who at the hearing will be judged to hang[23]
And never did expect to die like that.   AOI   [1411]

110

What a marvelous and bitter fight!   1395
Roland, Oliver! They strike with skill and might.
More than a thousand blows the archbishop strikes,
And neither do the Twelve Peers lag behind.
And every Frenchman thrusts and strikes and smites.
Pagans by the hundreds—thousands!—die.   1400

---

22. See Notes on Editorial and Translation Decisions.
23. This judgment at the "hearing" will take place in *laisse* 288.

Their only guarantee from death is flight.
Will they or nil they, here they lose their lives.
  France is losing its bravest guardian knights.
Fathers and mothers never will have sight
Of them riding home—nor Charles, who rides and bides   1405
Beyond the pass. All France is horrified
To hear loud winds and thunder. Storms of ice
Destroy the fields and forests. Bolts of lightning
Flash intermittently. Quakes open wide
Cracks in the earth from Sans to Mount St. Michael's,   1410
From Besanson to the high Atlantic tides,
And crumble stronghold walls. The noon sun shines
No brighter than the moon in murky night.
When the sky crackles open—that's the only light.
People can't see and cry out in their fright: 1415
"This is the end!" "End of the world!" "End times!"
Not realizing, when they contemplate these signs,
The death of Roland is what they signify.   [1437]

                              111
The French warfare is valiant and effective.
The pagan dead lie heaped throughout the meadow;   1420
Out of a hundred thousand, not two left.
"Ours are good vassals," Turpin says, "none better.
You couldn't find more valiant under heaven.
Let it be told in the *Chronicles of the French:*
"King Charlemagne had valiant fighting men."   1425
They comb the field for wounded friends, lamenting
Their fallen, pitying the family members
For what they soon will have to suffer.—Then,
Marsille's main army crashes down on them.   AOI   [1448]

                              112
Straight through the valley King Marsille is coming   1430
With the huge host of fighting men he summoned:
Twenty divisions of knights with helmets buckled,
All bright with jewels and sapphire-tinted bucklers
And chain-mail tunics. Seven thousand trumpets
Proclaim their coming. Hoofbeats and horns and drumbeats   1435
Resound throughout the country.
"Oliver," says Roland, "war-mate, brother,
False Ganelon has sworn to our destruction.

His treachery will out. He will be punished.
Our emperor will wreak revenge upon him.   1440
The war we wage today will be so bloody
People will say no worse there ever was.
I'll strike with Durendal. Oliver, brother,
You strike with sharp Hautcler. Think of the countries
We bore our swords to, fought with them and won   1445
Together with them! Our deeds will not be subjects
Of the satiric little songs of jugglers."   AOI   [1466]

113

Marsille beholds his barons where they died.
He sounds his horns and trumpets, and he rides
Forward with his army. In the front lines   1450
Rides evil Duke Abisme. You could not find
A crueler Saracen, more steeped in crime.
God, the Son of Mary, he denies.
He's black as field peas cooked for a long time.
All of the gold God made he does not prize   1455
So much as treachery, back-stabbing, lies,
And murder. No one ever saw him smile.
He's brave, relentless, reckless, which is why
He's Marsille's darling. His soldiers keep their eyes
On his dragon guide-on and rally to his side.   1460
Archbishop Turpin can't help but despise
This pagan. How eagerly he yearns to strike him.
"This Saracen," he tells himself, "looks vile.
A heretic, I think." He makes up his mind:
"I'd better kill him. Cowards I do not like,   1465
And cowardliness I never could abide."   AOI   [1486]

114

Archbishop Turpin mounts the first attack,
Riding the steed he seized from King Grossall
In Denmark when he killed him. This great stallion
Has strength and spirit, hollow hoofs, silver shanks,   1470
White tail and yellow mane, short thighs, broad back,
Long flanks, high head, and little ears. He's fast
And lets no other horses block his path.
Turpin spurs bravely, lets the reins fall slack.
No chance for Duke Abisme to wield his lance.   1475
The lord archbishop charges him, and *slash,*

Strikes Abisme's shield, which gleams and flashes
With gemstones—amethyst, turquoise, topaz,
And carbuncles of fire. (In Val Metás,
A devil gave it to Emir Galaff,   1480
Who sold it to Abisme.) The archbishop slashes,
And the shield's not worth a bead of broken glass.
He cuts Abisme from front ribs to the back
And dumps him dead upon a stretch of grass.
"Valiantly struck!" exclaim the men of France.   1485
"The cross is safe in the archbishop's hands."   [1509]

115

The Frenchmen see so many knights from Spain
Swarming and covering the battle plain
They call to Roland and Oliver. They beg
All Charlemagne's Twelve Peers to keep them safe.   1490
Archbishop Turpin speaks to them: "Be brave,
Lord barons. No bad thoughts, and for God's sake,
Hold your ground lest men compose refrains
Making fun of those who ran away.
Better die fighting. The end is near. That's plain.   1495
We know we will not live beyond today.
Nevertheless, I guarantee your safety:
Among the Holy Innocents[24] who gave
Their lives to save the Savior, you will reign
In Paradise." The French take heart and raise   1500
Their voices: "Mountjoy, Mountjoy for Charlemagne!"   AOI   [1525]

116

There is a wealthy Saracen, who owns
One half the property of Saragossa,
Named Climborin. Is he a good man? No.
He and Ganelon swore a friendship oath,   1505
Kissing on the mouth, a pact he closed
With a gift helmet, encrusted with gemstones.[25]
He swore to lay all Greater Europe low,
Uncrown the emperor and smash his throne.
Barbamouche Beardfly is his horse, which goes   1510

---

24. The Holy Innocents were the babies slaughtered by Herod in his attempt to kill the baby Jesus. See Matthew 2:16–18.

25. See Notes on Editorial and Translation Decisions.

Faster than falcon or swallow. Now he approaches
Count Éngeler, the Gascon of Bordeaux,
Spurs his swift Barbamouche, lets the reins go,
Aims his lance, and strikes him such a blow
The shield shatters. The chain mail does not hold.   1515
The steel point penetrates the flesh and bone.
He shoves it through up to the hilt, then throws
Éngeler's body backward onto the stones.
"These Christians are a joy to beat," he boasts;
"Strike, men! Divide them! Break their closed ranks open!"   1520
The Frenchmen say, "God, what a woeful stroke."   AOI   [1544]

117

Roland calls to his battle-mate and says,
"Friend Oliver, Count Éngeler is dead.
There wasn't a better knight among our men."
Oliver answers, "God give me quick revenge!"   1525
Racing with golden spurs, he grips Hautcler—
The blade all bloody—aims it straight ahead,
Strikes, and twists the blade inside the flesh.
Down the pagan falls. A crowd of devils
Takes his soul. Then Oliver kills Alphaien,   1530
Beheads Count Escababi, unhorses seven
More Arab warriors. Not one of them
Will get much glory in a fight again.
"Looks like my friend is angry," Roland says.
"Next to my score, he's doing very well.   1535
Fighting like that earns Charlemagne's respect.
Strike, Frenchmen! Strike, you valiant French!"   AOI   [1561]

118

A pagan champion named Valdabraun,
Marsille's godfather, emerges from the throng.
This rogue commands four hundred ships of war.   1540
There's not a pirate who is not his pawn.
He occupied Jerusalem by fraud,
Defiled the Temple of King Solomon,
Throttled the Patriarch in baptismal waters.
He swore his troth to Ganelon the false,   1545
Gave him his sword and money. Gramimond,
His horse, is faster than a sparrow hawk.
Valdabraun eyes Duke Samson, brave and strong,

Kicks his sharp spurs, rides, thrusts, breaks shield and hauberk,
And the lance point penetrates the body, drawing   1550
Straight through the wound the colorful ensign cloths.
He shakes his lance, and Samson's body falls.
"Strike, pagans, strike! We're going to crush them all."
"God," the French say, "his death is a great loss."   AOI   [1579]

119

Roland has seen the slaying of Duke Samson.   1555
The grief he feels for the duke—you can imagine!
He spurs towards Valdabraun. Faster and faster
He rides. He wields his priceless Durandal
Above his head, then swings it down in anger
And cleaves the helmet, spattering the sapphires,   1560
Slicing through skull and tunic, body, saddle
(All jeweled and trimmed in gold), cutting the stallion
Deeply through the spine. Praise or disparage,
Roland has killed them both. The pagans clamor,
"That was a woeful blow against our baron!"   1565
"I cannot love you pagans," Roland answers.
"You people are wrong, and still you're arrogant."   AOI   [1592]

120

Grimthought, a Moor from Africa, appears,
Son of King Grimtail, in hammered-gold armor gleaming
Brighter in sunlight than his pagan peers.   1570
He rides his sturdy stallion, Crazyleap.
No other horse can equal it in speed.
He strikes Lord Anseïs with his long spear,
Breaks the blue and scarlet buckler, pierces
The chain-mail hauberk, breaks the links to pieces;   1575
And the spear's wood shaft thrusts the point of steel
Deep into his flesh. The days of Anseïs
Are finished in this moment. The French knights weep
And cry out, "Anseïs, what a sad deed!"   [1604]

121

Lord Turpin ranges the field. You never knew   1580
A chaplain chanting mass to comfort troops
Who swung a sword with greater fortitude.
He shouts to Grimthought, "Evil come to you!
You slew a hero that I love and rue."

He spurs his horse and, with a stroke straight through   1585
The colorful gold Toledo shield, uproots
The pagan from the stirrups. Onto the dew
He flings the corpse beneath his horse's hoofs.   [1612]

122

Grandonies, the son of King Capél
Of Cappadocia, leads his regiment   1590
Upon the horse he calls Marmoriés.
Quicker than bird in evening ever sped,
He spurs, drops reins, hits Gerin. The spearhead
Shatters the scarlet shield hung from the neck,
Breaks the chain-mail tunic open, enters   1595
The flesh, pulling in ensign cloths of yellow.
He dashes Gerin's body on a rock, where head
And neck both break. Then he kills Gerin's friend
And war-mate, Gerer. Likewise, Bérenger,
And Guyun of St. Anthony as well,   1600
And Astor, Duke of Valerie-Valere
High on the Rhone—the pagan kills all of them.
Great is the joy of all the Saracens.
The Frenchmen say, "Many of ours are dead."   [1628]

123

Count Roland grips his bloody-handled sword.   1605
He hears his brave French barons lament and mourn,
And at the sound he feels his own heart torn.
"Pagan!" he cries, "may every ill be yours!
The men you killed—I'll see that you pay sorely
For every one of them." He spurs his horse.   1610
The two are close. Which one will come out worse?   [1635]

124

Grandonies was a noble, valiant pagan,[26]
Hard fighting for his lord, strong, tough, and brave.
Seeing Roland charging straight his way,
He knows him by his bearing and his strength,   1615
His power, his fierce and concentrated gaze.

---

26. The author's sudden use of the past tense to describe Grandonies indicates
that the answer to the question posed at the end of the previous *laisse* is obvious.

Suddenly Grandonies is too afraid
To move. He wants to run away. Too late.
Roland is on him. Down Roland swings the blade,
Down through the helmet's noseguard, through the face,   1620
The mouth, the teeth, the Algerian chain mail,
The golden saddle, and the swift steed's mane
And back and belly. Man and beast fall slain.
Loud lamentations from the men of Spain!
"Our Safeguard strikes good blows," the Frenchmen say.   1625 [1652]
Horrible and great the battle rages.
The Frenchmen strike with spears and gleaming blades.
What a spectacle of men and beasts in pain!
Thousands of wounded, bleeding, dead, and maimed
Heap up pell-mell about the battle plain   1630
Face down, face up. The Saracens fight bravely.
The suffering is more than they can bear.
Like it or not, they yield ground and are chased
Out of the field by the knights of Charlemagne.[27]   AOI   [1660]

125

The battle rages, marvelous and deadly.   1635
The French knights fight furiously and well,
Slicing fists, rib cages, backbones, necks,
Through outer garments into living flesh.
Loud is the outcry of the Saracens:
"Mohammed curse you, Northern Continent!   1640
No other land has peopled such aggressors.
Great King Marsille," they cry, "we are hard pressed.
Ride, King Marsille, ride to our rescue!"   [1670]

126

Roland calls to his war-mate, Oliver.
"My friend," he says to him, "you must admit   1645
How splendid a knight the lord archbishop is.
No knight beneath the firmament exists
For striking with a lance or spear like him."
Oliver answers, "Let's give him some assistance."
Again they plunge in where the fighting's thick.   1650
Horrible are the thrusts, grievous the hits.
The Christians suffer unbearable afflictions.

---

27. See Notes on Editorial and Translation Decisions.

Roland and Oliver—what deeds they did!
The archbishop spears and thrusts. (One can confirm
His deeds in letters, documents, and writs.   1655
Chronicles of the French sums up his kills:
More than four thousand.) The French withstand the first,
Second, third, and fourth onslaughts. The fifth
Breaks up their ranks, and all are killed but sixty,
Who will exact revenge before *they're* killed.   AOI   1660 [1690]

127

Roland sees his loyal barons down.
He looks around to Oliver and shouts,
"Brother! What do you think, dear noble count?
Look at them all fallen, these men of ours.
Poor lovely France, to have to do without   1665
So many valiant knights! Dear King, great Power,
Charlemagne, why aren't you with us now?
Oliver, brother, how can we hold out?
How can we let him know we've been pinned down?"
Oliver answers, "Roland, I don't know how.   1670
Better to die than people call us cowards."   AOI   [1701]

128

"I'll wind my Olifant," Roland declares.
"Charles will hear it beyond the pass through Spain.
The French will come riding back and flood this plain."
Oliver answers, "Then you would be disgraced.   1675
Think of the shame your relatives would bear,
Knowing you blew your horn, yes, lifelong shame.
You wouldn't when I asked. Now if you change,
Never say you blew it for my sake.
If you blow your horn, you won't be brave.   1680
Your arms are dripping blood." Roland explains,
"I've struck some mighty blows today."   AOI   [1712]

129

Roland says, "This battle's getting hard.
I'll wind my horn and send news up to Charles."
Oliver says, "That wouldn't show much valor.   1685
You wouldn't blow your horn when all this started,
Although I asked. If Charles were here, no harm

Would come to us. It's not their fault they're far
And riding ever farther. By my heart,
If I could see my noble sister Alda,   1690
She'd never lie with Roland in her arms."   AOI   [1721]

130

Roland asks, "Why are you mad at me?"
Oliver says, "Your valor is the reason!
Wisdom serves more than thoughtless bravery.
Better good sense than unbridled chivalry.   1695
Frenchmen are dead because you didn't heed.
Now Charles will never profit from our deeds.
He would be here if you had heeded me,
The battle won for us, and King Marsille
Killed or imprisoned. Would God we'd never seen   1700
Your valor, Roland! Charles will not receive
More aid from us. No greater man will be
Again till trumpets sound eternity.
France will be brought to shame, and you die here.
This is the breakup of the Twelve French Peers.   1705
There will be nothing left of us by evening."   AOI   [1736]

131

Hearing the two friends quarrel, Archbishop Turpin
Kicks forward with his mother-of-pearl spurs
And rides between the two of them to urge,
"Sir Roland, please! And you, Sir Oliver!   1710
Don't turn against each other now. It's certain
Winding your Olifant will not defer
Our dying, but it will, when it is heard,
Avenge our deaths. Blow for the king's return!
No mirth this evening for our murderers!   1715
Our French will get down from their steeds and search,
Looking for us about the trodden earth.
They'll find us, dead and tattered, and confer
Our bodies back to France on beasts of burden
And weep for us all the way. We will be buried   1720
In holy ground within the walls of churches
And not feed dogs, wild pigs, scavenger birds."
Roland replies, "You give good counsel, sir."   AOI   [1752]

132

Roland lifts up his Olifant and winds
That ivory clarion with all his might.   1725
The road to the North is long. The hills are high.
The horn blast echoes and re-echoes thirty miles.
Charlemagne hears it. So do all his knights.
"Our men back there," he shouts, "they're in a fight!"
"If anyone else," Ganelon replies,   1730
"Suggested that, I'd call it a huge lie."   AOI   [1760]

133

Despite the pain, Count Roland eagerly grasps
And winds his horn with all the strength he has.
Blood surges from his mouth. The pressure cracks
His temples open and the blood spurts. The horn blast   1735
Rings out for miles across the craggy lands.
Charlemagne hears it from beyond the pass.
Neïme hears it. So do the knights of France.
The king exclaims, "That's Roland's Olifant!
He never winds it but he's hot in battle!"   1740
"There is no battle. White-bearded King, old man,
You talk like a child," Ganelon reprimands
The emperor. "It's Roland's pride—so vast,
Why God puts up with it I cannot grasp.
He captured Nople against your own command.   1745
The Saracens sallied. Then Roland, that good vassal,
Killed them and from a spring of water splashed
The tell-tale blood from all the meadow grass.
He'll blow his horn to chase some little rabbit.
He's riding with his Peers, joking and prattling.   1750
Nobody on earth would dare attack him.
Ride on! Why are you wasting time? The path
Still stretches northward to the heart of France."   AOI   [1784]

134

Count Roland winds his horn. Mouth bleeds. Blood trickles
Out of his temples, and the pressure cinches   1755
His head with pain. The mountain crags are ringing.
Charles hears the sound. The Frenchmen stop to listen.
Charles says, "That horn was blown from a long distance."
"A battle's being fought, in my opinion,"
The Duke Neïme hastens to answer him;   1760

"And you're betrayed by him who says it isn't.
Arm yourself! Let your Mountjoy be lifted.
Ride to the rescue of your noble kindred.
You've heard! You know the trouble Roland's in."   [1795]

135

Charlemagne has his trumpeters wind their horns.   1765
The French dismount and dress themselves for war:
Hauberks and helmets, gold-inlaid steel swords,
Tough spears, tough shields artfully adorned.
Gold, red, white pennants mark each battle corps.
Now they remount. The barons spur their horses   1770
Into the pass and southward through the Ports
And gallop the narrow road that threads the gorge.
Not one lord speaks to his companion lord.
Each thinks, "Roland, if you still live, we will support
You to a man and add our strokes to yours."   1775
But what's the use? Too long in lovely France they've loitered.   [1806]

136

The sun is brilliant as it lingers westward.
Their armor flames and glistens in reflection;
So do the chain-mail hauberks, helmets,
The shields with flowers painted in the metal,   1780
The spears and flashing ensign flags and pennants.
The emperor rides hard and bitter-tempered,
While sorrowful and angry ride the Frenchmen,
Worried for Roland. Every one of them
Weeps to think of what may lie ahead.   1785
The emperor has Ganelon arrested
And handed to the cooks to be sequestered.
He gives Besgun, his chief cook, these directions:
"Guard him for what he is, a common felon.
The man betrayed my knights and my dependents."   1790
Besgun consigns him to his hundred best
And meanest scullions, mess boys, kitchen men.
They pluck his beard and mustache, pound his flesh,
Four punches each, and beat him with boards and trenchers.
They forge and seal a collar round his neck   1795
And bait him like a bear. To even better
Abuse, humiliate, and disrespect him,

They throw him on a packhorse. At their pleasure
He'll lie there till the king comes back to get him.   [1829]

137

The Spanish hills are dark, immense, and high;   AOI   1800
The valleys, low. Torrents rush deep inside.
Up front and back, loud bugles sound replies
To Olifant. Angry, the emperor rides.
His French are angry, too. They ride and sigh,
While not a knight among them stays dry-eyed.   1805
"God, guard Roland!" inwardly they cry,
"Until we reach the field. Then side by side,
Fighting for him, what mighty blows we'll strike!"
What use all this to him? They will arrive,
Having left late, late. They can't get there in time.   AOI   1810 [1841]

138

Angrily Charlemagne rides, his white beard fixed
Over his tunic. His brave French ride with him,
Every one of them in anguish, wishing
Their force could reach the field where Roland still
Defends himself as Saracens close in.   1815
"If Roland's wounded, how can he still live?"
The riders question one another grimly.
God, never will a captain or a king
Lead such good men as Roland's last still-standing sixty!   AOI   [1850]

139

Roland surveys the field and sees his men   1820
On slopes and plains, so many lying dead.
Knightly and generous, he weeps for them:
"May your souls rise to God, you noble French.
God grant you Paradise, and lay your heads
Down softly on celestial flower beds.   1825
I never knew more loyal, valiant men.
You served me long, continually, and well.
For Charlemagne we won great lands together.
The emperor fed you long, for this cruel end.
Sweet land of lovely France! You are bereft   1830
In one day's debacle of all your best.
Barons of France, because of me you're dead.

I cannot save you now, cannot defend you.
May God, who never lies, be your protection.
Oliver! I must not fail you, friend.   1835
If wounds won't kill me, grief will be my death.
Let's strike into the thick of it again!"   [1868]

140

Back into the battle Roland comes.
With Durendal he hews and hacks and thrusts.
He slices through the Saracen Faldrún   1840
De Pui; then three more foes; then twenty-one
Of their best fighters. Never did warrior hunt
Hotter for vengeance. Pagan barons run
From him like deer before the hounds. "Well struck!"
The archbishop cries, "The way a good knight must   1845
Who rides a steed and bears a lance and buckler!
If he's in battle and he isn't tough,
He's not worth dirt, might as well be a monk
In one of those cloisters, muttering prayers for us
For all our sins. Mountjoy! Raise standards up!"   1850
Roland cries, "Strike, you Frenchmen, strike! Spare none!"
On hearing this, the Christian barons plunge
Into the fray, with more losses to suffer.   [1885]

141

Soldiers aware no quarter will be given
Fight back more savagely while they still live.   1855
The French fight back like lions. On a hill
King Marsille on his warhorse, Gaignun, sits.
He's ripe for battle. He spurs, aims, spears, hits
Lord Bevon of Dijon. The French shield splits.
The spear breaks through the hauberk. Bevon slips   1860
Dead from the saddle. Marsille rides on full tilt,
Strikes Baron Gerart of Russillon, kills him,
Then kills Sir Ivon and Sir Yvoris.
Roland sees all and cries to the pagan king:
"May God in Heaven cast you into the pit!   1865
You killed my battle-mates, and for that sin
You'll learn my sword's name when you feel its sting."
Valiant in battle, Roland spurs and swings
And lops the king's right hand off at the wrist,
Then wheels his horse and with another swing   1870

Beheads young Jurfalé the Blond, the prince,
Marsille's one son. "Help us, Mohammed, rid us,"
The pagans cry, "deliver us, and give us
Vengeance against this Charlemagne, who filled
Our sunny Spain with felons such as this.   1875
We'll hold the field though all of us be killed."
They tell each other, "It's useless to resist!"
A hundred thousand pagans turn and quit.
They leave the field, and no commander's bidding
Will bring them back, and nothing ever will.   AOI   1880 [1912]

142

Who's left to care? Although Marsille heads home,
His caliph uncle, Marganice, won't go.
He holds Alfrera, Carthage, Gumalio,
And all the cursed land of Ethiopia.
Black people fight in Marganice's hosts,   1885
Each with two big ears and a big nose.
Fifty thousand of them ride and patrol
The field of battle. Angry and ferocious,
They cry their standard up and scream their boasts.
Count Roland shouts, "Our martyrdom approaches.   1890
We don't have long to live. That I now know.
Make them pay with their lives! If they pay low,
The shame is yours. Strike with your swords! Strong blows!
Defend your lives and deaths with every stroke.
Let no disgrace of lovely France be spoken.   1895
Our Charlemagne will come. When he beholds
The Saracens scattered dead, some fifteen foes
For every one of us, he will bestow
The blessings of a king upon our souls."   AOI   [1931]

143

When Roland sees this host of enemies   1900
Blacker than ink, riding with Marganice,
With no white showing but their teeth,
He says, "I realize now and I believe
We die today on this red battlefield.
Strike back to the battle, barons! Follow my lead."   1905
"Shame on the slowest!" shouts Oliver, his peer.
Once more the French assault the pagan shields.   [1939]

144

The pagans see the Christian ranks are down.
Then they take heart and tell each other proudly,
"The emperor is wrong. The right is ours."   1910
Marganice sits firmly on his mount.
He kicks with golden spurs and wheels around,
Strikes Oliver from behind, and the spear pounds
Through the chain-mail hauberk, and the point gouges
Through his rib cage. "You're badly hit!" he shouts.   1915
"Charles, riding north, should not have let you down.
He wronged our people. Killing you now counts
As vengeance for the sacking of our towns."   [1951]

145

Oliver feels the death blow has been dealt.
He grips Hautcler with its burnished cutting edge,   1920
Slices through the caliph's golden helmet,
Shattering crystals, flowery trim, and gems,
Splitting the face back to the baby teeth, then sheds
The dead man from his blade. "Damn you," he says,
"I don't say Charles won't suffer from our deaths.   1925
But you will not be bragging of my death
To any lady in the land you left.
No wife or maid will hear you boast you shed
One drop of my blood, or of any men."
Then he cries out for Roland: "Roland, come help!"   AOI   1930 [1964]

146

Oliver feels his wound and knows he's dying.
His will for vengeance isn't satisfied.
In the crush of battle, he strikes and thrusts and strikes.
He hacks off lances, shields, and bucklers; slices
Feet and fists, saddles, ribs, and sides.   1935
Whoever saw him dismembering pagan knights
And flinging their bodies into ghastly piles
About the battlefield would call to mind
All past chivalric deeds. "Mountjoy!" he cries
And loudly calls up Charlemagne's ensign.   1940
"Roland!" he calls his friend and peer, "come ride,
Friend and companion! Ride with me in this fight.
We suffer worse not fighting side by side."   AOI   [1977]

147

Roland looks hard at Oliver. The hues
Of his friend's face are turning ashen blue   1945
As blood runs down between his armor's grooves.
Blood clots drip down under his horse's hoofs.
"God," Roland says, "I don't know what to do.
Dear friend, your valor is the death of you.
Greater than yours, no baron ever knew.   1950
Poor lovely France, to lose and be denuded
Of her best knights. Great loss, great sorrow, too,
Sad day that Charlemagne must rue."
Roland slumps forward on his horse and swoons.   AOI   [1988]

148

There slumps Roland, fallen on his horse,   1955
And there is Oliver, whose wound is mortal.
So much more blood from his back wound pours,
He can't see far or near to know the form
Or face of any man that comes before him,
Not even Roland, his friend through countless wars.   1960
Blinded, he strikes out upward with his sword
At Roland's gemmed gold helmet. The blade stops short
In the steel noseguard, then cuts up past his forehead.
Roland looks, and in language sweet and courtly,
Asks, "Oliver, are you hitting me on purpose?   1965
It's Roland, who loves you! You didn't warn
Or challenge me." Oliver retorts,
"I hear you now. Friend Roland, know for sure
I couldn't see you. May God see and restore you—
I did hit you. Will you forgive me for it?"   1970
"You didn't hurt me. What's to forgive? Of course!
I do forgive you, here and before the Lord.
They bow to each other from their separate horses,
And thus their love and their parting are recorded.   [2009]

149

Oliver feels the creeping in of death,   1975
And his eyes turn inward in his head.
He cannot see, and he hears less and less.
He gets down from his horse, lies down to rest.
He calls to mind his sins, and he repents.
He joins his hands, lifts them up, and begs   1980

The Lord to let him have a place in Heaven.
He blesses Charles and lovely France, and he blesses
Especially, more than any, Roland his friend.
His heart fails him. His helmet weighs down his head.
His whole body sinks and presses to the earth.   1985
He cannot linger. Oliver is dead.
Roland, good baron, weeps, is overwhelmed
By sorrow worse than the sorrow of other men.   [2023]

150

Roland, when he sees his friend is fallen,
No longer living, face in the ground, still calls   1990
Again and again to him though he is gone:
"Your valor, Oliver, was your downfall.
We've been together years and days, and always
I never betrayed you; you never treated me wrong.
Your dying tortures me that I live on."   1995
He loses consciousness again and sprawls
Forward on Veillantif, senseless and tossing
This way and that because his boots stay caught
In his gold stirrups, and his body won't fall.   [2034]

151

By the time Roland's senses have recovered,   2000
The armies of the pagans will have cut
The French forces down to almost none.
Archbishop Turpin still has not succumbed—
None left but him and Walter de la Humme,
Who rode down fighting from the ridge above   2005
To fight the Spaniards. Spaniards have overcome
And slaughtered his intrepid seven hundred
For all his efforts. Now he rides through the crush
Seeking for Roland to help him in the struggle.
"Where are you, Count Roland? I never feared or stumbled   2010
When you were riding near. It's Walter, the one
Who slew the pagan general Maëgut,
The nephew of the old white-haired Droún.
I am your vassal, whose valor, sir, you loved.
My shield is broken, my lance is just a stub,   2015
My hauberk's torn. A steel spearhead is stuck
Deep in my flesh. I know my death has come,
But I'll pay pagans for what they've done to us."

Roland hears. He wakens, straightens up,
And spurs his horse toward where the voice comes
    from.   AOI   2020 [2055]

152

Roland is racked with pain and rage. He rides
Into the crush of battle, thrusts and strikes,
Kills twenty Spaniards. Riding at his side,
Walter kills six; and the archbishop, five.
"These three are monsters!" the pagan soldiers cry.   2025
"Fight, lords! Don't let them get away alive.
Whoever doesn't rush them is no knight,
He's coward who lets one of them survive."
They bang their shields and raise a hue and cry
And close in on the Frenchmen from all sides.   AOI   2030 [2065]

153

Count Roland is a noble fighting peer;
Walter is good at all chivalric feats;
Archbishop Turpin, valiant, bold, and fierce.
They strike and hack the pagans but still keep
Guard of each other against their enemies.   2035
A thousand foes dismount and on their feet
Accompany four thousand more who wheel
On horseback all around the three French heroes
But do not ride too close to them for fear
Of the French swords. They keep away and heave   2040
Large stones and lances, knives, spearheads, and spears,
Shoot darts and arrows. The first barrages stream
At Walter's head and heart. He falls dead on the field.
More break through Turpin's helmet, burst his shield.
His head is wounded, his chain-mail hauberk pierced.   2045
Into his flesh drive four iron-headed spears.
At last he falls when arrows kill his steed
And it topples sideways out from underneath.
When the great archbishop falls—O God, what grief!   AOI   [2082]

154

With four spearheads embedded in his flesh,   2050
Turpin of Reims feels stricken unto death
But leaps to his feet from the hard ground where he fell.
He looks at Roland, runs to him, and says,

"I have not lost! A brave knight, while there's breath,
Fights on." He draws his burnished sword, Almace,   2055
Charges, and rains down on the Saracens
A thousand blows. (Charles will find evidence
Of how he spared no enemies near the end:
Around him lie four hundred stricken men,
Some wounded, some gouged, some of them beheaded,   2060
All told in the *Chronicles*. Sir Giles was present,
For whom God works great signs; this saint attests
In Laon Abbey charters to these true events.
Who doubts these facts will never comprehend them.)   [2098]

155

Roland fights very well, as he knows how.   2065
His body sweats, he's hot, and his pulse pounds
Painfully in his brain from when he sounded
His Olifant. He knows he must find out
If Charlemagne is coming. He puts his mouth
To Olifant again. It weakly sounds.   2070
    The emperor stops short, listens, then shouts:
"My lords, it's Roland! Sad news! The count,
My nephew! I hear his horn announce
His dying hour. Gallop full speed to the south
If you would join him! Trumpeters: sound!   2075
Sound trumpets all the way to the battleground!"
You should have heard the horns: a hundred thousand
Resounding down the valleys from the mountains.
The pagans hear. They do not laugh. They shout,
"King Charlemagne will be attacking now!"   AOI   2080 [2114]

156

The pagans say, "The emperor is coming.
Those are the French! Listen to their trumpets.
If Charles arrives, all of us will suffer.
If Roland lives, he'll start the war all over.
Our homeland Spain never will be recovered."   2085
They pick among themselves four hundred
Armed knights, the best on the field that they can muster.
They circle Roland, raise a cry, and storm upon him.
Roland has much to do now—more than enough.   AOI   [2123]

157

Count Roland, when he sees them closing in,   2090
Gets ready for them. Tough, powerful, and grim,
He will not yield an inch, not while he lives.
Firm in his stirrups, with his gold spurs he kicks
Forward on his warhorse Veillantif
And crashes straight to where the battle's thickest.   2095
Unhorsed, Archbishop Turpin runs with him.
They shout to each other, "Strike, brother! Hit on hit!
You heard the emperor's brass trumpets ring.
They trumpet the arrival of our king."   [2133]

158

Count Roland never could abide a coward   2100
Or a self-serving baron, or a proud one,
Or vassal that his master couldn't count on.
He calls to Turpin, standing on the ground,
"I'm up on horseback, sir, and you're dismounted.
For love of you, whatever be the outcome,   2105
I will slow down for you and will allow
No one between us. What's good or ill is ours
To share together. Strike with combined power,
And the best strokes will come from Durendal!"[28]
"Curse us if we don't strike!" Lord Turpin shouts.   2110
"Charles will avenge us. I hear his trumpets now."   [2145]

159

The pagans say, "God, we were born to grief!
It's the worst day a soldier can conceive.
We have lost our leaders; we have lost our peers.[29]
Valiant King Charles is coming back. We hear him.   2115
French trumpets blare. We hear the Frenchmen cheer,
Their 'Mountjoy! Mountjoy!' growing ever nearer.
Roland is so abominably fierce

---

28. For this one line in the O manuscript, the V[4] manuscript has two lines, which could be translated, "In this assault, the pagans will find out / The names of Almace and Durendal," Almace being Turpin's sword. Jenkins, in his edition, substitutes the two lines from V[4] for the one line in O, thus portraying Roland as more generous than competitive near the end of his life.

29. Listen to the lovely chiasmus in the original line: "Perdut avum noz seignurs e noz pers" [2148].

No living knight can bring him to his knees.
Let's throw things at him, curse this place, and leave."   2120
The pagans throw lances, javelins, and spears;
Pikes, feathered darts, and knives burst Roland's shield
And tear his chain-mail hauberk into pieces
But do not wound him. But Veillantif, his steed,
Takes thirty wounds and stumbles from underneath   2125
His master, where he dies.[30] The pagans flee
And leave Count Roland standing on his feet.   AOI   [2163]

160

Anxious and angry, the Saracens take flight
Back toward Spain as fast as they can ride.
Count Roland does not follow where they fly.   2130
Veillantif, his good warhorse, has died.
Now he's afoot, whatever he wants or likes.
He walks to help Lord Turpin where he lies,
Unstraps his comrade's helmet, gently slides
The helmet from his head and then unbinds   2135
His hauberk and tears his tunic off in stripes
To stop and bind his wounds. He holds him tight
Against his chest; then on the green hillside
He lays him down. There he entreats him mildly,
"Archbishop, dear noble friend of mine,   2140
Give me your leave to leave you for a while.
All of our friends, their bodies where they died—
We cannot leave them lying through the night.
I'm going to look for them and, when I find them,
Bring them for you to see and recognize."   2145
"Go and come back," the wounded lord replies;
"This battlefield, thank God, is yours and mine."   [2183]

161

Roland, alone, goes through the field of battle.
He searches hills and level spots and valleys.
Here he finds Gerin and Gerer, dear companions.   2150
There he finds Anseïs and there Duke Samson,
And the old Duke of Russillun, Gerart.
One by one he carries back these barons

---

30. Note that Roland's commitment to stick by Archbishop Turpin prevents him from defending himself by attacking the throwers.

And ranges them below their lordly chaplain,
Who cannot help but weep. He lifts his hand up   2155
And blesses them, then says, "For you, such sadness.
May God in Glory bring you to His mansions
To rest in roses and lilies of the valley.
I feel my own death coming on me fast.
I will not see the Emperor of France."   2160 [2199]

162

Roland goes back and searches high and low,
And he finds Oliver, the friend he rode with.
He gathers him against his chest and holds him,
Lifts, carries him to where the Peers repose
At the archbishop's knees. There he lowers   2165
And lays him on a shield. Turpin leans close,
Makes signs of the cross above his body, intones
A prayer of absolution. Their sorrow grows.
They feel great pity. "Oliver," says Roland,
"You were the son of Duke Reinier the Bold,   2170
Who held the Runer Valley as your homeland.
For breaking spears and shields, for overthrowing
Insolent men and bringing proud men low,
For counseling decent people and upholding
Good men at arms, for conquering thieves and rogues,   2175
No better knight than you was ever known."   [2214]

163

Roland, when he surveys his Peers, all dead,
And Oliver, his own belovèd friend,
His eyes grow wet, and all the color empties
From face and head. For sorrow, seeing them,   2180
Like it or like it not, he can't stand steady
But falls forward in a faint upon the meadow.
"Your valor is your grief," the archbishop says.   [2221]

164

When Turpin sees Roland unconscious on the grass,
He feels grief worse than he felt for any man.   2185
He reaches out and grips the Olifant
To carry water in for his companion
From a fast-flowing stream in Roncevals.
He takes a little stumbling step and staggers

Forward, for now he is too weak to stand.   2190
With so much blood lost, all his strength is sapped.
He doesn't manage to struggle on much farther
Before his heart gives out and he collapses.
Death comes upon his body with great anguish.   [2232]

165

Count Roland's mind returns from dark to light.   2195
He stands, but his head bursts from the inside.
Roland looks up, then down along his line
Of barons on the green grass where they lie,
And past, and sees a noble knight lie dying.
It's the archbishop, ordained by God on high,   2200
Confessing his sins, with his hands clasped tight
And lifted in entreaty to the sky,
Pleading with God to grant him Paradise.
Turpin is dead now, Charles's valiant knight
And champion against the pagans all his life,   2205
Preaching eloquent sermons, fighting great fights.
Grant him Your holy blessings, God Almighty.   AOI   [2245]

166

Roland is looking down at the archbishop.
Beside the body, he sees the entrails spilling.
Brains bubble from the forehead, but, white as lilies   2210
And beautiful across his battered rib cage,
His two hands make a cross. For benediction,
Roland laments for him in his tradition:
"Ah, gentle knight, baron of noble lineage,
I offer you to God. Nobody living,   2215
Since the Apostles lived and the first Christians,
Strove so eagerly to do His bidding.
No one was so prophetic and so skillful.
To champion faith, no one was so winning.
Now may your spirit suffer no affliction.   2220
May Heaven open wide and let you in!"   [2258]

167

Count Roland senses his own death approach.
His ears feel the pressure, how his brains explode!
He prays, "God, take my dear companions' souls,"
Then prays for himself to Gabriel. He holds   2225

His Oliphant and Durendal, his sword,
So that for them he suffer no reproach.[31]
As far as an arrow shot from a crossbow,
He goes toward Spain, then up a grassy slope
To a high bluff where stand two lovely oaks.   2230
At last he reaches four large marble stones,
Then topples backward on the green grass. Roland
Has fainted. Now his death approaches.   [2270]

168

High are the hills. Two trees spread out above.
Four marble boulders glimmer in the sun.   2235
Unconscious on the green ground Roland slumps.
A Saracen is watching him, someone
Who played dead, lay down quietly among
The other bodies, and smeared himself with blood.
He rises and reaches Roland at a run.   2240
He once was handsome, valorous, and tough.
Pride makes him mortally delirious.
He pulls the armor from Roland's limbs and trunk
And says, "King Charles's nephew! Now he's not worth much.
I'll take this sword back to Arabia."   2245
Roland awakes; his sword is being tugged.   [2283]

169

The sword's removal wakes Roland from his swoon.
His eyes open. All he says is, "You?
You are not one of us, none of my troops."
He grips his Olifant and does not mean to lose it.   2250
With it he hits the thief's helmet, breaks its jewels,
Breaks steel and bone and skull. Out the blood spews.
From the disfigured face, the eyes obtrude.
The pagan falls dead, his head at Roland's boots.
"Saracen son of a bitch, you dared assume   2255
What's mine, for right or wrong, would fit your use?
No one who hears of this won't call you *fool*.
Now Olifant is broken almost in two,
The gold trim cracked, scattered are all its jewels."   [2296]

---

31. To abandon either his sword or his horn, even while dying, would be shameful.

170

Roland realizes he cannot see.   2260
As steady as he can, he gets to his feet.
He's lost the color from his brows and cheeks.
A red-brown boulder lies within his reach.
Hurting, he strikes ten times, and his blade shrieks
But does not break or lose one notch of steel.   2265
"Help me," he cries, "help me, Mary Queen!
Ah, Durendal, your strength was woe to me.
Once I am dead, I cannot be your keeper.
I won so many battles on the field
And conquered so many countries and regimes   2270
Now held by Charlemagne of the White Beard,
No knight must hold you who would flee from fear.
A knight who was good did hold you many years.
In holy France, no better will ever be."[32]   [2311]

171

Roland hammers the hard stone with his blade,   2275
Which does not even nick, though the steel wails,
And when at last he knows it will not break,
"Ah, Durendal, my valiant," he complains,
"You gleam and glimmer in the sun like flame.
When Charles was in the Valley of Moriane,   2280
God had His angel give you to him, saying,
'Give this to one of your knights.' To me he gave you.
With his two hands, he cinched you to my waist,
The noble king! With you I won the states
Of Anjou, Poitou, Brittany, and Maine,   2285
Provence and Lombardy and Aquitaine,
Low lands of Flanders and Normandy the Great,
Burgundy, Bavaria, Romagna, Romania,
Poland, and Constantinople, which I made pay
Homage to Charles, then Saxony, then Wales,   2290
Scotland, and far-off Ireland. I constrained
England to be his particular domain.
I suffer for you now, who overcame
Countries and provinces for Charlemagne.
I'd rather die than let this sword remain   2295

---

32. Like the translation, the original ("Jamais n'ert tel en France l'asolue")
[2311] does not make clear whether Roland is referring to his sword or himself.

In pagan hands. Great Father God, I pray,
Don't let it happen. Do not let France be shamed."   [2337]

172

Count Roland strikes the red-brown stone—the strokes
He hammers on it, more than can be told.
The sword blade shrieks, but the good hard steel stays whole   2300
And bounces toward the sun. At last he knows
It will not break. Softly to himself he moans,
"Ah, Durendal, so beautiful and holy,
With relics nestled in your hilt of gold:
A tooth of St. Peter, a vial of St. Basil's blood,   2305
A lock of St. Denis' hair, and with all those,
A precious patch from Holy Mary's robe.
It is not right that any pagan hold you,
Good Durendal. You must serve Christians only,
And never cowards! With you I've overthrown   2310
So many countries, so many earthly thrones
For Charlemagne of the White Beard to own,
Magnanimous and mighty emperor."   [2354]

173

Roland can feel his death as it comes pouring
Into his heart, into his head and forehead.   2315
He lies down on the grassy meadow floor
Beneath a pine, with Durendal, his sword,
Under his body, and Olifant, his horn.
He turns his head so that he faces forward
Against the fleeing pagans. Charles and his cohorts,   2320
Seeing him lying there will be assured:
"The noble count, he died a conqueror."
He beats his breast, repents his sins, implores
Forgiveness, glove held up and offered to the Lord.   AOI   [2365]

174

Roland feels his living moment finish.   2325
His face toward Spain, he lies on a hilltop.
With one hand he beats his breast and whispers,
"Mea culpa; God in Your grace, have pity
For all my sins, the great ones and the little,
From my birth date until this day that kills me."   2330

To give his right glove up to God, he lifts it.
Angels from Paradise descend to him.   AOI   [2374]

175

Beneath a pine tree, Roland lays his head,
Face still toward Spain. How much he recollects!
The countries that he conquered and subjected,   2335
The men of France from whom he is descended,
And Charlemagne, who cherished him and fed him.
He cannot help but weep as he remembers.
But now he must recall himself, confessing
His sins to God and begging for His mercy: 2340
"Eternal God the Father, faithful ever,
Who rescued Lazarus from death and rescued
Daniel from the lions' den, defend me
From my life's sins, which put my soul in peril."
He holds his right glove, offers it, and stretches   2345
It up toward God. The Angel Gabriel
Receives it from his hand. Then Roland rests
His head upon his arm, clasps hands together,
And goes on further to his end.
God sends His cherubim with Gabriel   2350
And Michael Help-of-Sailors. They descend
And carry Roland's soul to Him in Heaven.   [2396]

176

Roland is dead. God has his soul for keeping.
The emperor at Roncevals appears.
There is no track upon the ground, no field,   2355
Not three square feet—not one—he doesn't see
Littered with French or pagan knights. He screams,
"Roland, where are you? Where are you, nephew dear?
And the archbishop? And Oliver? Where is he?
Gerin and Gerer? Anseïs the Fierce?   2360
Gerart of Russillon, whom I held dear?
And where are Otis, Ivon, and Yvoris?
Bérenger? Éngeler of Gascony?
Where is Duke Samson? Where are the Twelve Peers
I left behind?" What use are his loud pleas?   2365
No one answers. "God," he says, "woe is me!
The battle started, and I wasn't here."
Like a wild man, he weeps and tears his beard.

The barons of his army also weep,
While twenty thousand faint upon the field   2370
And pity overwhelms the Duke Neïme.   [2417]

177

In Roncevals there's not a single knight
Who does not weep for pity at the sight
Of nephews, brothers, sons, who does not sigh
For friends and liege lords left on the field to die.   2375
Many barons faint at what they find.
Immediately Neïme considers wisely:
"Look up!" he tells the emperor. "A mile
Ahead of us on the great road, see dust rise.
There many pagans must be taking flight.   2380
Ride to avenge this sorrow. You must ride!"
"Alas! They're already far," King Charles replies.
"Advise me what I should do. What would be right?
They cut the flower of France. Look, here it lies.
—Milon, Oton, Gebuin!" the emperor cries,   2385
"And Teobald of Reims! You are assigned
To guard the field, the valleys, and the heights.
Defend the men who died. Let them still lie.
Let not one animal, let not one lion,
And no man near them, not one serf or squire.   2390
I do forbid that anyone come nigh
Until, God willing, we return from fighting."
"Sire, we will," they lovingly reply,
And with a thousand knights they stay behind.   AOI   [2442]

178

The king gives orders: "Let the trumpets sound!"   2395
Now he rides southward with his great power.
The Spaniards show their backs, while the French thousands
Unite their minds and strengths to catch and confound them.
The king looks westward. Sunlight begins to founder.
He gets down off his horse, and down he bows   2400
His forehead to the green and grassy ground
And prays to God, "Don't let the sun go down!
Hold back the dark, O Lord. Let light abound!"
The angel who often speaks to him comes now.
"Ride, Charles," he commands. "Daylight will be allowed.   2405
God is aware that France has lost its flower.

Ride and wreak vengeance on that criminal crowd."
Hearing these words, the emperor remounts.   AOI   [2457]

179

He wins a wonder from the King of Glory.
The sun in heaven shines and goes no lower.   2410
The pagans flee. The French keep getting closer
And reach them at the Valley Tenebrosa.
They hound them farther on toward Saragossa,
Spearing and slicing them with mortal strokes.
They cut them off at all the paths and roadways.   2415
For the retreating men, one way lies open:
The Ebro River, deep and rapid flowing,
And on it not a single barge or boat.
They pray to their god Tervagant and throw
Themselves into the flood. Their prayers are hopeless.   2420
The costly armor weighs too much for floating.
Some sink like stones. The current rolls them over
Along the river bottom. Those who float
Choke on the waves. All drown. None makes it home.
The Frenchmen cry, "Alas, alas for Roland."   AOI   2425 [2475]

180

When Charles looks out at all the pagans slaughtered,
Some by swords, most of them by water,
And all the booty that the battle brought them,
He bows his head, and with the grass for altar,
Bows down to God, thanking Him, exalting.   2430
When he gets up again, the sun is gone.
"It's time to pitch our camp," he tells his warriors.
"It's dark, and Roncevals is too far off
To reach tonight. Our horses are exhausted.
Unsaddle them and let them graze unhaltered   2435
About the meadows after they are watered."
The French reply, "We will. These are good orders."   AOI   [2487]

181

The emperor commands the camp be readied.
The French dismount. Around, the land is empty.
They take the saddles off their horses and divest them   2440
Of golden bits and bridles, to graze unfettered
About the meadows where the grass is freshest.

Tonight no other service is expected.
All are exhausted. All lie down on earth.
Throughout the weary night, no one stands sentry.   2445 [2495]

182

The emperor lies down upon the plain.
Beside his head he keeps his long lance safe.
He has not taken off his saffron mail
Or any armor. His gem-starred helmet stays.
He keeps Joyeuse still cinched, his matchless blade,   2450
Which changes colors thirty times a day.
We know about the Roman spear that made
The wound in crucified Lord Jesus' waist.
King Charles obtained the spearhead, God be praised.
Into the sword's gold hilt he had it placed.   2455
Therefore Joyeuse is Charlemagne's sword's name
To celebrate the honor that God gave.
Joyeuse! In gratitude, French knights should raise
Their standard with the cry, "Mountjoy!" That way,
No force that comes against them can prevail.   2460 [2511]

183

The night is crystal clear, and the moon gleams.
Charles has bedded down, but he lies grieving
For Roland and Oliver, whom he loved dearly,
And the Twelve Peers, for all the brave French heroes
He left at Roncevals, dying and bleeding.   2465
He cannot stop his sorrow, and he keeps weeping.
He prays to Heaven for their souls' redeeming.
The king is worn. For all the hurt he's feeling,
He finally sleeps, all his strength depleted.
Throughout the meadowland, French knights lie sleeping.   2470
Too tired to stand, their horses end up eating
While lying down, whatever grass is nearest.
Great learning comes to those well versed in grief.   [2524]

184

King Charles sleeps on like one exhaustion-stricken.
God sends the Angel Gabriel to visit.   2475
The angel comes and stands guard at his pillow
And there uncovers for the king a vision
Full of terrifying signs and signals

Of a great battle still to fight. The king lifts
His eyes up to the sky and sees grim whirlwinds,   2480
Ice storms, and thunderstorms. Lightnings cut zigzags
This way and that across the sky and kindle
Oceans of fire that rain on his divisions.
Tough spears of ash and apple can't resist them.
The flames burn shields down to the gold hand-grips.   2485
The helmets and the hauberks twist and crimp.
King Charles sees all the pain his knights are in.
Leopards and bears contend to eat his Christians.
Devils and imps and snakes and vipers sting them.
Dragons and more than thirty thousand griffons   2490
Hurtle themselves upon the French to kill them.
"Help us!" the French cry. "Help us, Charles, our king!"
The king can't hold back tears of grief and pity.
A lion, huge and proud in face and figure,
Bursts out from where the forest growth is thickest   2495
And charges Charles, but the intended victim
Wrestles with the lion limb to limb.
Who stands, who stumbles, cannot be distinguished.
The dream concludes. And the king's sleep continues.   [2554]

185

After this dream, another vision comes.   2500
He is in France at Aix and stands in front
Of a stone slab beside a chained bear cub.
From the Ardennes Mountains thirty more bears rush.
He hears them shout as if with human tongue,
"Unchain him, King! Give him back to us.   2505
You have no right to bind him to your judgment.
We have the right to liberate our cousin."
Down from the palace a swift greyhound comes running,
Cuts off the largest bear and leaps upon him
On the green lawn some distance from the others.   2510
The king can look upon the wondrous struggle
But cannot tell which animal has won.
Only so much the angel has uncovered.
The king sleeps on until the sun comes up.   [2569]

186

To Saragossa Marsille flees at last,   2515
Gets off his horse where olives cast their shadow,
Takes his sword and byrnie off, unclasps

His helmet, lies clumsily on the green grass.
He sees himself bleeding where his fist was hacked
And loses consciousness from loss of blood and anguish.   2520
Queen Bramimunde, his wife, is there. "Alas!"
She cries for him and weeps and wrings her hands.
About her twenty thousand soldiers stand,
Cursing Charlemagne and lovely France.
Enraged, they hurry to Apollo's chapel,   2525
Insult their god and blame him for what happened:
"What shame you laid on us when you abandoned
Our king, ungrateful god! Why did you leave him stranded?
Whoever serves you gets poor wages back."
They rip his crown and scepter off and hang him   2530
From a tall pillar by his hands, then drag him
Down to their feet, and with their clubs they batter
The statue till the wood and marble shatter.
They rip the carbuncle from Tervagant.
Into a ditch they haul Mohammed's statue,   2535
For dogs to gnaw upon and pigs to trample.   [2591]

187

At last Marsille recovers from his faint
And bids that he be carried to his stateroom
With all its ornamental scripts and paintings,
While Bramimunde, his lady, tears her hair,   2540
Laments and calls herself a wretch, and wails,
"O Saragossa, woe to you today,
Bereft of a great king who wisely reigned!
Our gods committed treason: they betrayed him
This morning in the battle when they failed him.   2545
The emir is a coward," she exclaims,
"If he won't come do battle with these brave
French knights who fight their wars without a care
For life or death so long as they obey
Their king, their flowing-bearded Charlemagne,   2550
So brave and heedless in the wars he wages
That from the battlefield he'll never run away.
Will no one come to kill this Charlemagne?"   [2608]

188

For seven years the emperor has been
In Spain and kept a mighty power with him,   2555

Capturing castles, cities, fortresses,
Pursuing King Marsille, who from the first
Wrote desperate letters to the Grand Emir
Of Babylon, named Baligant, that prince
Who'd reigned since Virgil wrote and Homer lived,   2560
Begging him to come and rescue him
In lofty Saragossa. Unless he did,
His gods would have to go. Into a ditch
His idols would be cast. The French would win
Whatever terms of peace from him they wished.   2565
He'd settle with Charles and then become a Christian.
The Grand Emir is far; at first he lingers,
Then calls up conscripts from his forty kingdoms,
Commands his royal galley be outfitted,
And has more barges, warships, galleys built   2570
In Alexandria, the seaport city.
When this armada is at last equipped,
His armies board. As summer is beginning,
Out onto the sea he thrusts his ships.   [2629]

189

His hosts make up a huge and alien crew.   2575
They row and sail and steer beneath the moon.
From masts and sterns and figureheads, carbuncle jewels
And lanterns dissipate the deep-sea gloom
And wash the oceanic night with beauty.
At last the shores of Spain come into view,   2580
While far inland the country is illumined.
A coast guard runs to bring Marsille the news.   AOI   [2638]

190

The pagan people: they never will let go.
These leave the sea for where fresh waters flow.
They sail up past Marbrise and past Marbrow.   2585
They sail far up the Ebro, and then row.
Their strings of carbuncles and lanterns glow
All through the night and light the way they go.
When morning breaks, they come to Saragossa.   AOI   [2645]

191

The sun is shining and the day is clear.   2590
The Grand Emir steps out onto the beach.

The men of Spain come down from land to meet him.
Seventeen kings attend the Grand Emir,
Too many counts and dukes to number here.
They spread a white silk cloth upon the green   2595
Underneath a shady laurel tree
And there install a throne of ivory.
There Baligant the Emir takes his seat.
The rest attend him, standing on their feet.
They pay attention while their master speaks: 2600
"Listen, you noble knights, to my decree:
The Emperor of France—he ought not eat
Or sleep unless permission comes from me.
Throughout all Spain, this man makes war on me.
I go to lovely France. Him I shall seek.   2605
I dedicate my life, and will not cease
Until he dies or spurns his Christianity."
The emir slaps his right glove on his knee.   [2664]

192

Once he has spoken, he is so inflamed
That all the gold on earth could not restrain him   2610
From riding straight to Aix, where Charles holds state.
His counselors counsel him and heap on praise.
He calls two knights to hear him and obey.
Clarifan and Claren are their names.
He says, "You are the sons of Malatrain,   2615
Who was my messenger. Now *you* convey
This message for me to Marsille of Spain.
Tell him I have come to give him aid
Against the French. We have a war to wage.
I'll fight against them if they don't escape me.   2620
Give King Marsille this gold-trimmed glove to wear
On his right fist. Also, do not fail
To hand him this baton, with gold inlay.
Then have him come to me with oaths to swear
Of loyalty to me. I shall invade   2625
And conquer France and capture Charlemagne.
Unless he falls down at my feet and prays
For mercy and repudiates his faith,
I'll snatch the crown myself from his white pate!"
"Your Majesty speaks well," the pagans say.   2630 [2685]

193

"Ride fast," says Baligant, "don't linger."
Both messengers reply, "Yes, Sire, we will!"
One brother holds the glove, and one the stick.
They ride full speed to Saragossa. Quickly
They pass ten gates and gallop across four bridges   2635
And through the streets where merchants make their livings.
Uphill they gallop through the pagan city,
Approach the palace and can hear within it
The noise of many pagans bearing witness
With tears and shrieks that the gods give no assistance.   2640
"Mohammed, Tervagant, Apollo are indifferent!
What will become of us?" they wail and whimper
One to another. "We're stricken and bewildered."
"We've lost our King Marsille." "The king is crippled.
Yesterday Roland cut off his right fist."   2645
"And Jurfalé, the blond young prince, is killed.
Today all Spain will be a French dominion."
The messengers dismount at a stone pillar.   [2704]

194

They leave their horses where an olive shades them.
Two Saracens take their horses by the reins.   2650
Each brother clasps the other brother's cape
As up and up they climb the palace stairway
And walk into the royal vaulted chamber.
Politely they make perverted salutation.
"May Lord Mohammed, who holds us all," they say,   2655
"Lord Tervagant, and Lord Apollo save
The king and guard the queen."—"You must be crazy,"
Says Bramimunde the Queen. "Our gods broke faith
At Roncevals. That's where their powers failed us.
They didn't keep our knights from being slain.   2660
My lord rode out to battle and they failed him.
Look at him now—Count Roland amputated
The king's right fist. Now Spain is Charlemagne's.
What will happen to me, most wretched lady?
Why not just kill me? Will some man do that favor?"   AOI   2665 [2723]

195

"Lady," says Claren to the queen, "don't prattle.
We're messengers from pagan Baligant,

Who bids us tell you he will save your master.
He sends his stick and glove. We came to land
From Ebro River with four thousand rafts,   2670
Also with barges, galleons, and galleys—
I couldn't count how many ships he has.
Our lord is rich and powerful. He plans
To seek out Charlemagne in far-off France,
Kill him or make him spurn his faith." "Small chance!"   2675
Says Bramimunde. "His trip will turn out bad.
Your lord can find the French nearer than France.
For seven years they've occupied our land.
Charlemagne is a noble, brave combatant.
He'd rather die than run away from battle.   2680
All other kings? To him they're callow lads.
He's not afraid of any living man."   [2740]

196

"No more of that!" suddenly shouts Marsille.
"Sir messengers," he tells them, "speak to *me*.
You see me maimed to death. No heir will I leave.   2685
I have no son or daughter left. Last evening
I lost my one son on the battlefield.
Go tell the Grand Emir to come and see me.
He has some claim on me as my emir.
If he wants Spain, I say she's his to keep.   2690
Let him defend her from the enemy.
I'll counsel him on how he will defeat
King Charlemagne and bring him to his knees
Within four weeks. Here! Take him the keys
To Saragossa. Tell him not to leave!"   2695
"Well said, my lord," the messengers agree.   AOI   [2754]

197

"This emperor," Marsille says with a scowl,
"Has killed my men and laid waste all around,
Trampled my farmlands, ruined and ravaged my towns.
Seven miles off, according to my count,   2700
Tonight beside the Ebro he beds down.
Tell the emir to come with all his power
Against King Charles to joust him and confound him.
He holds the keys to Saragossa now."
The messengers take the keys from him and bow.   2705
They walk back through the palace doors and out.   [2764]

198

The two messengers mount and ride in haste
Rapidly from the city, all the way
To the emir, to whom they now convey
The keys to Saragossa. The emir exclaims,   2710
"What happened? Where is the King of Spain?
I told you, 'Bring him here!'" "The king is maimed
And dying," Claren says. "King Charlemagne
Rode home to lovely France the other day
With his main army through the mountains of Spain.   2715
Roland, captaining the rearguard, trailed
In the Spanish Pass with Oliver, his mate,
Twelve Peers, and twenty thousand French invaders,
Armed and in armor. There brave Marsille waylaid them
And attacked Roland. They jousted face to face.   2720
Roland charged; with Durendal, his blade,
He swung and cut through King Marsille's chain mail
And lopped his right fist off. And Jurfalé,
Marsille's belovèd only son and heir—
Roland killed him! And many other brave   2725
Barons of Spain were killed. Marsille escaped.
He could not stay. But Charles is giving chase.
Marsille sends word and pleads with you to save him.
He says the land of Spain is yours to claim."
Baligant hears and nods and meditates   2730
And feels such sorrow that it almost drives him crazy.   AOI   [2789]

199

"Yesterday was a battle," Claren says,
"At Roncevals. There died King Charles's nephew.
Count Roland; so did Oliver, his friend,
And the Twelve Peers that Charlemagne loved best;   2735
And with them perished twenty thousand French.
Marsille's right fist was severed, and he fled,
Chased by the emperor. No Spanish knight is left
Not slain or sunk to Ebro's riverbed.
Beside its banks the French have pitched their tents   2740
Near us and too far forward to effect
An orderly retreat if you want vengeance."
Baligant scowls, but the thought that he can catch
The emperor makes him happy nevertheless.
He leaps up from his ivory throne and says,   2745

"Out of your ships! Onto your horses, men!
Ride and attack before the French suspect.
If they escape, Marsille will be unavenged!
For his right fist, I'll have King Charles's head."   [2809]

200

Down from their ships, knights from Arabia troop.   2750
They mount their horses and get onto their mules.
They ride. What more can these knights do?
The emir calls Grimálfin, whom he approves,
And says, "You take command of all my troops."
He mounts a swift bay steed and takes the route   2755
To Saragossa, riding with four dukes.
They soon arrive and stop at a stone stoop.
Four counts attend the emir's stirruped boot
As he dismounts. They reach the doors and enter through.
They climb the palace steps to Bramimunde.   2760
She runs to them. "Sire, I am destitute.
My lord is shamed. I am about to lose him."
She falls at his feet. He uplifts her, and the two
Walk together to Marsille's sickroom.   AOI   [2826]

201

As soon as King Marsille sees Baligant,   2765
He tells two Spanish Saracen bystanders,
"Grab hold of me by my arms; prop up my back."
One of his gloves he takes in his left hand.
"Sir, Saragossa and my Spanish lands,
With honors pertaining to them, I now grant   2770
To you, my lord emir. I've lost my grasp,
Myself, my people—all the men I had."
The emir says, "That only makes me sadder.
But I can't stay to talk. King Charles won't tarry
For me in Spain. And yet, despite all that,   2775
I take the glove." Weeping, he turns his back,   AOI
Goes out the room, down steps, and out the palace,
Mounts and spurs his horse, and gallops back
To his knights, straight on until he leads their ranks,
Shouting orders to them as he gallops,   2780
"Ride, pagans! Ride! They already fly toward France!"   AOI   [2844]

202

That morning, when the eastern sky breaks darkness,
King Charles awakens as his angel guardian,
Gabriel, marks a blessing on his forehead.
The king gets up, at last takes off his armor,   2785
As do the knights and barons of his army.[33]
Now they remount their horses and ride hard
And far along long roads both wide and narrow,
Back once again to view the harm and horrors
Left from the battle fought at Roncevals.   AOI   2790 [2854]

203

When Charlemagne enters Roncevals and sees
The many dead, he cannot help but weep.
He tells his Frenchmen, "Lords, wait for me here.
I'm walking farther for a while to seek
My nephew. Once at Aix, at a high feast,   2795
With barons boasting of their battle feats,
All Roland said was, if some foreign field
Were where he died, he would make sure to be
Farthest advanced of all his knights and Peers,
With his head turned to face the enemy,   2800
And so die conquering." With no more speech,
He walks a stone's throw farther than his people
Up a green slope and underneath two trees.   [2869]

204

The emperor, as soon as he arrives,
Looks for his nephew. On the fields he finds   2805
Vermillion flowers that his knights' blood dyed
And feels such pity, he cannot help but cry.
Charles walks beneath two trees, and there he spies
Grooves in three stones that Durendal has sliced,
Looks down, and on the green grass recognizes   2810
His nephew. Wild with rage—that's no surprise—
He leaps down, runs to where the body lies,
And lifts it in his arms. With a great sigh
Of anguish he faints beside his fallen knight.   [2880]

---

33. The armor will be carried behind the main army in wagons.

205

The emperor recovers from his swoon.   2815
Acelin the count, Neïme the duke,
The brothers Thierry and Geoffrey of Anjou
Guide him to shade, but his eyes don't move
From his nephew. "Roland," he says, "adieu.
God grant you mercy. Knighthood never knew   2820
A knight to face great battles, fight, and conclude them
With victory—none ever like to you!
My honor is slipping. It cannot endure!"
Charles swoons again. What else can he do?   AOI   [2891]

206

From his deep swoon, Charlemagne recovers.   2825
Four of his knights help to lift him up.
He looks down at his nephew, sees how comely
His body is. His flesh has lost its color.
His eyes turn inward, and the whites are muddied.
Charles loyally mourns aloud and kneels above him: 2830
"Friend Roland, God lead you to a saint's homecoming
To rest in gardens that are sweet and lush.
Your ride through Spain brought evil to your uncle.
No one is left to guard my honor's luster.
No day that comes will ever bring me comfort.   2835
My power fades and my bright reign is sullied.
No friend like you exists beneath the sun,
And none so valiant among my sons and cousins."
He weeps and tears his hair out in thick clumps.
A hundred thousand Frenchmen grieve. Among them,   2840
Not a one can keep his eyes from flooding.   AOI   [2908]

207

"I'm going back to France now, Roland, friend.
When I hold court in Laon, there will come men
From many foreign lands, and they will question,
'Where is the noble count, your mighty general?'   2845
I'll answer, 'In a Spanish valley, dead.'
With grief and trouble I will hold my realm together.
Never will come a day without regret.   [2915]

208

"Friend Roland, lovely youth, heroic captain,
People will come to me in Aix, my Chapel,   2850
Asking for news, and I will have to answer,
'Dead is my nephew, who won me lands and grandeur.'
At that my provinces will rebel: the Saxons,
Bulgarians, Romanians, and Magyars.
Apulians and Palermese will band   2855
With upstart rebels in Africa and Calif.
Troubles will start, bringing me grief and anguish.
Who will command my men against all factions
Now he is dead, who once was our commander?
Lovely France, today you lie abandoned.   2860
I do not want to live into such sadness."
He tears at his white beard and with both hands
Tears hair from his white head. He fails to stand.
A hundred thousand horrified French collapse.   [2932]

209

"God have mercy on you, dear friend Roland,   2865
And may God's Paradise receive your soul.
Whoever killed you left my kingdom homeless.
I feel such sorrow for my own dear nobles
Who died for me that death is all I hope for.
May Mary's Son grant that I not behold   2870
The Gates of Ciz before my soul has flown
And left my tired body to be lowered
Into the earth with my belovèd soldiers."
The emperor tears at his white beard and moans.
"Ah," says Duke Neïme, "he feels such woe!"   AOI   2875 [2944]

210

Geoffrey of Anjou says, "Charlemagne,
Great Emperor, this grief should be contained.
Order a search for all our people slain
By Marsille's regiments of Spain
And have them taken to a common grave."   2880
Charles answers, "Blow your bugle to proclaim it."   AOI   [2950]

211

A bugle blast from Geoffrey of Anjou!
The French dismount. The king commands his troops

To find and bring the French the Spaniards slew.
They lay them in a common grave to view them.   2885
Bishops and abbots give the dead their due.
Monks, tonsured priests, and canons sing the funeral,
Make signs of the cross, and extend absolution.
Incense and myrrh and aromatic fumes
Make sweet the spot where they will be entombed.   2890
With ceremony they bury the brave youths,
Then leave them there. What else can they do?   AOI   [2961]

212

The emperor holds Roland back, and with him,
Oliver, and Turpin the archbishop.
Surgeons open their ribs in front of him,   2895
Remove their hearts, and wrap them in soft silk,
Then place them in a small, white marble crypt.
They wash the three knights' heads and trunks and limbs
Lovingly with wine and spiced elixirs
And wrap them carefully in soft deerskins.   2900
The king tells Theobald and Gebuin,
Milon the count and Marquis Oton, "Bring
Three carts to carry these three heroes in."
Over the three, they lay Galatan silk.   AOI   [2973]

213

The emperor longs for France and means to start.   2905
Two messengers from Baligant's vanguard
Come riding in, proclaiming, "Proud King Charles,
It would be wrong of you to flee this war.
Baligant's army, riding at full charge,
Comes after you. Don't run. You won't get far.   2910
His host from Araby is very large.
Now we will see how valorous you are."   AOI   [2981]

214

The emperor tugs his beard as he thinks hard
About the carnage, Roland, and the rearguard.
He looks at his people with a fierce regard.   2915
Loud and clear he shouts out the alarm:
"Run to your horses, barons of France! To arms!"[34]   AOI   [2986]

---

34. See Notes on Editorial and Translation Decisions.

215

First to be armed is Emperor Charlemagne.
He puts his tunic on of bright chain mail.
His helmet is strapped. Joyeuse is at his waist.   2920
Even against the sun its gleam won't fade.
He hangs his Biterne shield from his neck and shakes
His lance by the handle, point high in the air,
Then mounts his Tencedor, the steed he gained
At the Marse Ford, the time he threw Malpalin   2925
Of Nerbone out of the stirrups to a wet grave.
He spurs, lets loose the reins,
And as a hundred thousand of his soldiers gaze,
Forward to his army's lead he races.   AOI
"God and St. Peter at Rome!" shouts Charlemagne.   2930 [2998]

216

All around the valley's fields and meadows,
One hundred thousand Frenchmen are assembled.
Of arms and gear they have a good selection,
Spirited steeds and finely crafted weapons.
Now they are mounted, eagerly expectant   2935
And looking for a battle if one threatens.
They hang their colorful pennants from their helmets.
Charles sees how beautiful they look and beckons
To Jozeran of Provence, Neïme, and Antelme
Of Maience, and he says, "Look at them, friends!   2940
These barons you can trust. It would be senseless
To be afraid as long as we have them.
Unless the Arabs turn, we'll have our vengeance
For Roncevals and the killing of my nephew."
"God grant we do!" the Duke Neïme says.   AOI   2945 [3013]

217

Charles calls Rabél and Guinemán. "My lords,"
He tells the two of them, "Here are my orders:
Rabél, take Roland's place; you, Oliver's.
You carry Olifant; you, Roland's sword.
With fifteen thousand French, you two ride forward.   2950
Gebuin and Count Loranz will lead one more[35]

---

35. See Notes on Editorial and Translation Decisions.

French division of the same size as yours."
Neïme and Jozeran count files, arrange, and sort them.
If they can find a way, they'll have great warfare.   AOI   [3025]

218

The foremost two divisions, then, are French.   2955
The third to form is the Bavarians,
Approximately twenty thousand men.
They will not let their battle line be bent.
Of all his knights at arms, Charles loves these best
Next to the French, who won him his possessions.   2960
These fighters are so fierce, they must be led
By no one less than Ogier, Duke of Denmark.   AOI   [3034]

219

After the emperor has called up three,
He names a fourth division, which Neïme
Establishes of valiant cavaliers,   2965
German barons out of Germany—
Twenty thousand, the witnesses agree—
Armed to the teeth in brilliant battle gear.
They'd rather die than yield a contested field.
The Duke of Trace, Lord Herman, is their leader.   2970
He'd die before he'd do a cowardly deed.   AOI   [3043]

220

Count Jozeran and Duke Neïme now form
A fifth division made up all of Normans—
Twenty thousand, according to French reports—
With lovely arms and swiftly running horses.   2975
They'd rather die than leave the field of war.
For a good fight, there is no fiercer force.
Richard the Old will lead these Norman lords
And strike with his sharp lance as he rides before them.   AOI   [3051]

221

Brittany supplies the Sixth Division.   2980
Thirty thousand Breton knights are in it,
All famous for their noble horsemanship.
With painted lances they hold their pennants lifted.
Oedun, the brave commander of the Sixth,

Calls Theobald of Reims to come to him,   2985
With Marquis Oton and Count Nevelin.
"Lead my men," he says; "that is the gift I give you."   AOI   [3059]

222

Charlemagne has six divisions ready.
The Duke Neïme establishes the Seventh:
Twenty thousand barons from Auvergne,   2990
And from Poitou there ride about as many.
They ride good horses and wield exquisite weapons.
Up on a little hill they move together.
With his right hand, King Charles gives them his blessing.
Their leaders: Jozeran and Godeselmes.   AOI   2995 [3067]

223

Neïme now designates the Eighth Division.
One half of it is Flemish; one half, Frisian;
In all, some forty thousand fighting Christians.
They will not fail at holding their position.
The king declares, "They will perform their mission."   3000
Rembalt and Hamon of Galicia
Will lead the Eighth Division with distinction.   AOI   [3074]

224

Duke Neïme and Jozeran assign
Fifty thousand knights to Division Nine,
Half from Lorraine, the other twenty-five   3005
From Burgundy. They're ready, and they ride
With helmets strapped, their chain-mail tunics tied,
And their short-handled, sturdy spears held high.
Should the Arabians decide to strike,
They will strike back and give them fight for fight.   3010
Duke Thierry of Argonne commands the Ninth.   AOI   [3083]

225

The Tenth Division is of men of France,
One hundred thousand of our greatest captains,
Bold, ferocious, vigorous, and handsome,
With hoary heads, white beards, and white moustaches.   3015
They wear their chain-mail armor double wrapped,
Swords fashioned by skilled French and Spanish craftsmen.

Each decorated shield tells who the man is.
They mount their horses and they call for battle.
"Mountjoy!" they call. Charlemagne commands them.   3020
Geoffrey of Anjou bears the Oriflamme,
Which was St. Peter's, *Romaine* its name in Latin,
But now the Frenchmen, for their battle rally,
Call out, "Mountjoy!" when they see this standard.   AOI   [3095]

226

Down from his steed the emperor descends   3025
And lies down prone upon the grassy meadow,
Looking east to where the sun ascends.
Deep from his heart he prays to God and says,
"True Father, today stand by me and defend me,
You Who rescued Jonah from the depths,   3030
Pulling him forth from the great whale's belly,
Who spared the repentant King of Nineveh,
Who rescued Daniel when the lions pressed
About him in the Babylonian den,
And the Three Children in the furnace—You saved them!—   3035
Be with me Lord today, in love be present,
And in Your mercy grant that I avenge
The death of Roland, Roland, my dear nephew!"
He finishes his prayer, stands up again,
Makes the sign of the cross for God's full blessing,   3040
And mounts. Neïme and Jozeran attend him
And hold his stirrup. He grasps his shield and settles
His sharp sword in its sheath. He sits erect,
Handsome, hardy, confident, majestic,
With a bright face, generous and pleasant.   3045
Well seated on his horse, he guides its steps.
The trumpets sound behind him and ahead,
But Olifant rings out above the rest.[36]
Their minds on Roland, the Frenchmen's eyes are wet.   [3120]

---

36. Jenkins questions whether the author "has forgotten that the Olifant was badly cracked at line 2259" (p. 218). But the three sentences of lines [3118–20] run so faultlessly together to complete the long *laisse* that they sound perfectly true, and Roland's spirit is so alive to his fellow combatants that they do indeed hear his horn as they ride to battle.

227

The emperor rides skillfully and nobly.   3050
Outside his tunic he lets his white beard flow.
For love of him, they too let their beards show,
One hundred thousand Frenchmen on the road.
They thread through hills and past tremendous boulders.
They edge high cliffs with fearsome depths below,   3055
Ride down the mountain paths to rolling slopes,
As deep into the realm of Spain they go.
On a wide meadow they take a brief repose.
   The scouts return to Baligant. "We've spoken,"
One Syrian says, "to Charles, the haughty foe.   3060
His men are fierce and will not fail their lord.
Arm yourself. The time for battle's close."
Baligant says, "It's time for deeds of glory.
Sound forth the trumpets! Let my pagans know!"   [3136]

228

Throughout the army throbs the beat of drums   3065
Accompanied by bugle blasts and trumpets.
Pagans dismount to don hauberks and doublets.
Nor does the emir linger here or slumber.
He dons chain mail with gold and saffron colors.
He cinches his sword to the left. Out of presumption,   3070
Because he learned Charles calls his sword *Joyeuse,*
He calls his sword *Precious,* and the name has come
To be his standard and the cry they thunder
Riding into battle. He holds his shield and buckler,
With its gold hand-grip and crystal border, strung   3075
Down from his collar by a strong silk muffler.
The Emir Baligant in his right fist clutches
The lance he calls *Maltéd,* which means *bad trouble.*
Its heavy handle is thicker than a bludgeon.
Another man would need a mule to lug it.   3080
He heaves himself onto his horse. Marculus
Of Sea's End holds his stirrup so it won't budge.
His loins are broadly arched, his thighs like trunks.
His torso is immense, slender his stomach,
His shoulders wide. His face is bright and rugged.   3085
His look is fierce. His curls are snowy clusters.
His flesh is fair as flowering fields in summer.
What valor he has shown through countless struggles!

O God, were he a Christian knight, how wonderful!
He spurs his horse's flanks so they run bloody.   3090
Straight to a gulch he rides, and the horse jumps
The fifty feet from one brink to the other.
The pagans shout, "He rescues all our countries!
Any knight of France who dares confront him,
Whether he wants or not, he will die suffering.   3095
Oh, what a fool King Charles was not to run!"   AOI   [3171]

229

One look at the emir inspires awe.
His beard is white as flower-flooded lawns.
He's wise and very learnèd in his law.
He's proud and fearless in a war's onslaught.   3100
His son Malprámis is chivalrous and strong.
Like his forefathers he is tough and tall.
"Gallop!" he shouts. "Father, we mustn't dawdle.
I'll be amazed if we see Charles at all."
"We will," says Baligant; "he's a great warrior.   3105
His valor is the theme of epic songs,
But with his nephew Roland gone,
Charles cannot hold out against us long.   AOI   [3183]

230

"My son, Count Roland was valiant and renowned,
And Oliver, a brave and valiant count.   3110
But they are killed, and the Twelve Peers struck down,
Whom King Charles doted on, who were so proud,
And twenty thousand more, French knighthood's flower.
What's left for Charles is knights of no account.
My messenger, the Syrian, announced   3115
That Charlemagne is riding toward us now
With ten divisions more. The knight who sounds
The Olifant must be a man of prowess.
His battle-mate's response is clear and loud.
They lead the First Division, fifteen thousand.   3120
The emperor has named his youthful scouts.
As for the rest, expect them to fight proudly."
"Father," Malprámis answers him, "allow me
To strike first blow against King Charles's rout."   AOI   [3200]

231

"Malprámis, my dear son," says Baligant,   3125
I gladly grant the favor that you ask.
Unceasingly assault the men of France
With Torlus the Persian king at your right hand
And Dappledeath the King of Leutzistan.
If you bring low the Frenchmen's arrogance,   3130
I will bestow on you a stretch of land
From Marchis Valley up to Cheriant."
Malprámis answers, "Sire, I give you thanks."
He gallops beside him to accept the grant
Of lands King Flurit governed in the past.   3135
(The lands turned out unlucky after that.
Malprámis never was invested as their master.)   [3213]

232

The emir rides and reviews his regiments.
Behind him rides Malprámis the Immense.
Persian King Torlus and King Dappledeath   3140
Establish the divisions: three times ten,
Comprising knights of wondrous skill and strength,
The least division, fifty thousand men.
The First Division: Butentrotiens.
Knights of Blos and Nuble form the Second.   3145
The Third are Micenies, who have big heads.
All up their backs and shoulder blades and necks
They grow thick piggy bristles to protect them.   AOI   [3223]
The Fourth is formed by Browns and Slavs. The next
Are Sorz and Sorbiennes. And after them   3150
The Sixth Division: Armenians and Deadmen.
People from Jericho make up the Seventh.
From Niger, the Eighth; from Gros, the Ninth assemble.
Fort Balida supplies Division Ten,
Made up of men who harbor bad intentions.   AOI   3155 [3231]
The emir swears oaths that he believes effective:
"By our Mohammed's power and his flesh,
King Charles is mad to ride in our direction.
There will be battle; unless his purpose bend,
He'll never wear his golden crown again.   3160 [3236]

233

They order ten additional divisions.
The First are ugly Canaanites, who issue
From Fuit Valley along their ugly rivers.
The Second are the Turks, the Third the Persians,
The Fourth the Pinceneis, noses out like pincers.   3165
The Sultras and Aversians form the Fifth.
The Sixth Division: Ormalies and Iggies.
The Seventh is the men from Samuel's lineage,
The Eighth from Bruise, the Ninth from Clavers City,
The Tenth from Occian, the dry and windy,   3170
Whose desert people do not do God's bidding,
The worst people you ever heard of living.
All of these Occians have iron-hard skins.
Helmets and hauberks were never made to fit them.
In battle they are treacherous and vicious.   AOI   3175 [3251]

234

Ten more divisions are ordered by the emir:
The First Division, Giants of Malprese;
The Second, Huns; the Third, from Hungary;
The Fourth Division from Along-Baldise;
The Fifth from far-off Valley-Wet-With-Tears;   3180
The Sixth from Maruse. The men of Leu will be
The Seventh with the Astrimoniyees.
The Eighth: Argoilles; the Ninth are Clarbonese;
The Tenth Division is the Slingshot-Beards,
Recruited from a God-forsaken people.   3185
Chronicles of the French lists ten times three
Divisions that made the mighty host complete.
The trumpets sound out loud and clear
As pagans ride to war like noble peers.   AOI   [3264]

235

A mighty man is Baligant the Great.   3190
In front of him his dragon staff parades.
Mohammed and Tervagant also lead the way,
And vile Apollo's image is displayed.
Beside him ride the warriors of Canaan.
With a loud voice, they promise and proclaim,   3195
"Anyone who wants our gods to save him
Must pray and suffer penitence and pain."

The pagans bow their chins and heads and lay
Their shining helmets on the ground and pray.
The French say, "Die, you bastard pagans!   3200
May foul confusion rain on you today!
God, protect our Emperor Charlemagne.
The battle will be won in our God's name."   AOI   [3278]

236

The Emir Baligant, who's very wise,
Summons his son and two kings to his side.   3205
"Ride out in front," he tells them. "Lead and guide
All of my divisions, except that I
Will reserve three, the ones I most rely on:
The Turks, the Ormalies, the Malprese Giants.
I'll lead the Occians of the hard hides   3210
To joust with Charlemagne and the French knights,
And if the emperor and I collide,
I'll cut his head off. Let him realize
His end will be unalterably decided."   AOI   [3290]

237

The armies are huge and the divisions wondrous.   3215
Between them lies no ridge or ditch, no clump
Of trees, no tree, no thicket to hide under.
On level land they look straight at each other.
Baligant cries, "Men of my pagan countries,
Ride to the battle! Throw yourselves to the struggle!"   3220
Ambors of Holiferne extends the ensign upward.
"Precious!" they cry, and clang their swords and bucklers.
The Frenchmen shout, "Down with you to destruction."
Again and again, "Mountjoy, Mountjoy!" they thunder.
The Emperor of France shouts, "Sound the trumpets!"   3225
The trumpets sound, and Olifant rings above them.
The pagans say, "King Charles's force looks good.
We'll have our fight—and with it grief and bloodshed." AOI   [3304]

238

The field they face each other on is wide.
The gems in their helmets gleam, and the gold shines.   3230
Their shields and saffron cuirasses are bright,
As are the pennants and their spears of iron.
Trumpets ring out. Their music floats the skies.

Olifant's flourishes lift even higher.
   The Emir brings his brother up beside him,   3235
Canábeus, a dreadful king and tyrant
Of Sevre Valley and the adjacent heights.
He points toward the divisions Charles aligned.
"Look," the emir says, "look there at the pride
Of famous France, how fiercely the emperor rides.   3240
He's back there riding with his bearded knights.
They loose their beards outside their armor, white
As snow that lies on surfaces of ice.
Their swords and spears are sharp, and they can smite.
Today we're in for a long and vicious fight   3245
As never has been known before our time."
Baligant gallops farther than a spear's flight
In front of all his troops. "Pagans," he cries,
"Follow me! I'll show you where to ride."
He grips his lance, lifts it, shakes it on high,   3250
Then down at Charles he points the tip of iron.   AOI   [3328]

239

When Charlemagne looks back at the emir,
He sees the dragon and the ensign, and he sees
Such a large swarm of knights from Araby,
It seems to occupy the battlefield   3255
Except the plot of ground with his ten legions.
The emperor cries for all his men to hear:
"Loyal French barons, you pride of chivalry!
Think of your many hard-fought victories.
There are the pagan armies, cowardly, mean.   3260
I wouldn't give a cent for their beliefs.
Their knights may be big. What's that to you or me?
Come ride with me, whoever wants to be
My knight!" He spurs his steed,
Tencedor, and puts him through four leaps.   3265
"Ours is a valiant king," the French agree.
"Ride, noble King! We will not fail you. Lead!"   [3344]

240

The air stays clear; the sunlight, gay and dazzling;
The armies beautiful, with grand combatants.
Nearer they ride; the advanced divisions clash.   3270
Up front, Rabél and the Count Guinemán

Let loose their bridles and let their steeds run fast
And spur them on. So do the men of France,
Aiming to hit their marks with their sharp lances.   AOI   [3351]

241

Leading the French, Rabél's a noble count.   3275
He rakes gold spurs and urges on his mount
And strikes Torlus, who wears the Persian crown.
The lance bursts through the shield and byrnie, gouges
Into the body, then thrusts the body out
Of the saddle onto the brambly ground.   3280
"God be our help and aid," the Frenchmen shout.
"Charles has the right. We will not let him down!"   AOI   [3359]

242

Count Guinemán spears Dappledeath. He splits
And shatters his shield with all its flowered trim
And bursts the byrnie. The lance and ensign ribbons   3285
Penetrate his chest. Into a ditch he flings
The body dead, laugh or weep as you will.[37]
The French applaud the deed and praise his skill.
"Strike without holding back, you barons. Quick!
Charles upholds right against the pagan lineage.   3290
We're here to do God's justice with our king."   AOI   [3368]

243

Malprámis sits upon a pure white stallion
And rides wherever the French are thickest packed,
Everywhere dealing great blows with his lance.
One after another he flings them from their saddles.   3295
Out in the front rides Emir Baligant.
"Barons," he shouts above the noise, "my barons!
I've housed and nurtured you as my own vassals.

---

37. As in the Battle of Roncevals, the particularities of the "pagan" deaths are
very like the deaths of the French, but the audience reactions were probably
different: sorrow and chagrin for a French knight lanced through and through
and thrust onto the ground; joy and triumph and even laughter for the same
death meted out to a "pagan." The "laugh or weep as you will" ("ki qu'en plurt
u kin riet," 3364) may be the narrator's comic (or half-comic) rebuke of the
predictable laughter of some in the audience.

Look at my son, riding in search of Charles.
He rides against the French to challenge and smash them.   3300
I ask no better vassal than Malprámis.
Ride to his help! Strike with your sturdy lances."
Hearing these words, the pagans ride and rally
And strike cruel blows. Carnage covers the landscape,
And on it lasts, the fierce and bloody battle,   3305
No battle fiercer, never before or after.   AOI   [3382]

244

The hosts are huge; the fighting vast and deadly.
All of the divisions have crashed together.
The pagans battle furiously and well.
God knows how many sturdy lances spent   3310
And their wood splintered, how many shields in shreds.
Lance ends and chain-mail links litter the meadow.
Grass, once delicately green, runs red.
The emir calls and encourages his men:
"Strike, barons. Strike the Christians dead!"   3315
Back and forth, the combatants get no letup.
Never were such deeds done, and never again.
They fight straight into night, and still no end.   AOI   [3395]

245

The emir calls and encourages his forces.
"Fight, pagans! That's what you've come here for.   3320
I'll give you girls and women who are gorgeous.
I'll give you fiefs and honors, lands, and rich rewards."
"Our duty—fight and win!" reply his lords.
They break so many lances, they are forced
At last to unsheathe a hundred thousand swords.   3325
And so the carnage continues to get worse.
Whoever is there knows what a thing is war.   AOI   [3404]

246

King Charles keeps calling to the French. "My brave
Lord barons! I trust and love you!" he exclaims.
"You've served me well—so many battles waged,   3330
So many kings cast down and kingdoms gained.
I know how well you've served me. I'll repay you:
Myself, my moneys, and my rich domains.
Avenge your sons, your brothers, and your heirs

Who died at Roncevals the other day!   3335
You have the right—you know it!—against the pagans."
"King Charles, you speak the truth!" the Frenchmen say.
With one voice twenty thousand knights proclaim
Their loyalty to Charles and pledge their faith.
Not for distress or death—they will not fail him.   3340
They shake their lances, draw their swords, and race
Once again into the bloody fray.
On and on this great and marvelous battle rages.   AOI   [3420]

247

Everywhere in the battle, Baligant's son,
Malprámis, gallops, meting out destruction   3345
On the hard-pressed French. Neïme sees all he's done.
He angrily spurs his horse, valiantly plunges
His spear through the shield's crest and the double
Chain-mail wrapping of the hauberk, thrusts
His yellow colors through the body, dumps   3350
Malprámis dead with seven thousand others.   [3428]

248

Baligant's brother, Canábeus of Sevre,
Has seen the Duke Neïme transfix his nephew.
He spurs his horse ahead, and his fist clenches
His crystal-handled sword. The sword descends   3355
On Duke Neïme and slices through his helmet
And five tough straps of metal-plated leather.
Half of the helmet peels away. The rest
Doesn't protect the duke worth half a cent.
The blade swings down and cuts along his head,   3360
Sheering onto the ground a chunk of flesh.
It was a hard blow, and the duke's knocked senseless
And would fall from his horse, without God's help; instead,
He grasps his horse and holds onto its neck,
But if the pagan turns and comes again,   3365
Neïme, the noble vassal, will be dead.
But Charlemagne is riding to the rescue.   AOI   [3443]

249

Neïme the duke is hurt and nearly slain.
Canábeus is riding back, with his sword raised.

Charles shouts, "You bastard, you've made a big mistake!"   3370
He aims his lance, bravely attacks the pagan,
And bursts the shield against the hauberk chains
And into his enemy's chest. The pagan sways
And dies. His horse runs riderless across the plain.   [3450]

250

King Charles looks back and is heart-sorrowed   3375
To see how Duke Neïme has fallen forward
Wounded onto his horse's neck, blood pouring
Bright red onto the grass. Now he implores:
"Neïme, come ride beside me through the warfare.
The dog who wounded you is dead. I gored   3380
Him with my spear." "That I believe, my lord,"
Says Duke Neïme, "and I can promise surely
That if I live, I'll do great service for you."
Loyally, lovingly, they ride their horses
Together, with twenty thousand Frenchmen more,   3385
All of them spearing and hacking with their swords.   AOI   [3462]

251

About the battlefield gallops Baligant.
With his long lance, he strikes Count Guinemán.
He hits the count's white shield, hammers it back
Against his heart, bursts the hauberk clasps,   3390
Scatters the links, and splits his chest in half.
Baligant knocks him dead out of the saddle.
Next he slaughters Gebuin and Loranz,
And Richard the Old, chief of the Norman ranks.
Pagans cry, "Precious! Ours is a noble standard!   3395
Strike, barons! Our victory is granted."   AOI   [3472]

252

You should have seen the knights of Araby,
The Occians, Argoilles, and Bascalese,
Slaughtering skillfully with swords and spears.
Nor do the French incline to leave the field.   3400
Back and forth the armies kill. By evening
The battle's just as fierce, the deaths increase.
Before nightfall, there will be more to grieve.   AOI   [3480]

253

They hit each other, Arabians and Christians.
Lance handles break from their grips and their spears shiver.   3405
Anyone who saw their shields so twisted
And heard white hauberks snap and burst their linkage
And sword blades ring on helmets—whoever witnessed
Knights falling from their saddles, flung from their stirrups,
Men moaning, men dying in the dirt,   3410
Would call to mind what battle suffering is,
Because this battleground is heaped with misery.
The emir keeps calling Apollo to assist him,
Mohammed, too, and Tervagant: "Gods, listen!
I've been your servant and have done your bidding   3415
And have erected you in golden images—"   AOI   [3493]
His dear Grimálfin rides up to deliver
Bad news: "My lord," he tells him, "everything
Is going against you: your son, Malprámis, killed;
Canábeus, your brother, slain with him.   3420
Two Frenchmen fought them well and to the finish.
One was Charlemagne in my opinion,
A powerful warrior, lordly and prodigious,
With a long beard as white as April lilies."
The emir bows his head; dark grows his visage,   3425
His grief so great he almost dies from it.
He summons Jangle Oversea, his wizard.   [3507]

254

"Jangle, come speak with me," the emir says.
"You always have been valiant and perceptive.
You've always counseled well, and I've attended.   3430
What now with the Arabians and Frenchmen?
Will we at last win victory over them?"
"Lord Baligant," says Jangle, "you're a dead man.
Your gods will guarantee you no protection.
King Charlemagne is valiant, strong, relentless.   3435
His barons are the fiercest fighters ever.
Call up your Arabs, Giants, Turks, and Enfruns.
Whatever happens, there's no time for rest."   [3519]

255

The emir yanks his hauberk, thrusts beard out,
Where it shines whiter than the hawthorn flower.   3440

Whatever the cost, he will not hide his countenance.
He puts his clarion trumpet to his mouth
And blows. The pagans hear his call resound,
Take heart and rally throughout the battleground.
Occians bray and whinny. Argoilles growl   3445
And snarl and bark and bare their teeth and howl.
They throw themselves madly where the Frenchmen crowd,
Break the French ranks, and cut the French knights down.
With one attack they slaughter seven thousand.   [3530]

256

Cowardliness is something Ogier hates.   3450
There is no better fighter than the Dane.
Seeing the French divisions fold and break,
He shouts to Thierry of Argonne, berates
Count Jozeran and Geoffrey, the guide-on bearer,
And even reprimands King Charlemagne: 3455
"You see how many of our men are slain!
May God rip from your head the crown you wear
If you don't strike back and avenge your shame!"
There's not a knight, who, hearing Ogier, fails
To spur his horse full speed, let loose his reins,   3460
And thrust and strike wherever he meets pagans.   [3542]

257

King Charles strikes bravely, and his forces rally.   AOI
Neïme and Ogier bravely thrust and slash,
And Geoffrey of Anjou, with Charles's banner.
Ogier the Duke of Denmark, very valiant,   3465
Lets loose the reins, at full speed spurs his stallion,
And hits Ambors, who bears the pagan dragon.
Down falls Ambors, dead upon the grass.
The dragon comes down too, and the emir's standard.
Baligant sees his guide-on fall, and the damage   3470
Done to the fallen emblem of Mohammed,
And at the sight almost begins to grasp
That Charles has right on his side, and he hasn't.
Hundreds of pagans scatter from the battle.
"Attack them, my Frenchmen!" cries the King of France.   3475
"For God's sake, ride to my aid, you barons!"
"Shame that you even have to ask!" they answer.
"Attack them! Shame on whoever lags!"   AOI   [3559]

258

The daylight darkens. They fight on into evening.
With swords the French and pagans slash and beat   3480
And cut each other. How valiantly their leaders
Lead the attacks! They don't forget to cheer
Their battle standards. "Precious!" shouts the emir.
"Mountjoy!" Charles shouts his standard. Each hears
And knows the other's voice, clear and unique   3485
Above the brawl. They charge. Midfield, they meet
And break their lances through each other's shields,
Bursting the hauberks, though the broken spears
Don't pierce the flesh. The saddle cinches ease,
The saddles slip, and the two kings career   3490
Onto the hard ground. Up they leap,
Face each other, draw swords from their sheaths.
Nothing can hold them back or come between them.
Nothing but death will end this enmity.   AOI   [3578]

259

King Charles of lovely France is brave and strong.   3495
Nothing scares the emir, and no one daunts him.
Up they leap. Their naked swords are drawn.
They beat and slice each other's shields. They maul
The central hides and wood shield-frames, unclaw
The nails that bind the shields, and the shields fall.   3500
They strike and scatter rivets, rawhide, cloths.
Naked to naked the two big men assault
Whatever chains the other still has on
And hack at helmets, flinging sparks aloft.
This single combat has to be prolonged   3505
Till one of the two acknowledge he is wrong.   AOI   [3588]

260

"Charles," says the emir, "you should consider something:
Repent how you've wronged me. You killed my son.
Unlawfully you overran my country.
Swear fealty to me, and you shall govern   3510
For me, from here to where the sun comes up."
King Charles replies, "That would be vile. I must
Not give a pagan fealty or trust.
No, *you* receive the law God gave to us,
Christianity, and forever have my love.   3515

Believe in God. Serve Him Who reigns above."
Baligant says, "This vow of yours is rubbish."
Swords out again, they rush against each other.   AOI   [3601]

261

The Grand Emir has courage, will, and strength.
He strikes King Charles upon his burnished helmet,   3520
Cuts it, and splits it ringing from his head.
Down through his hair the emir's blade descends
And sheers a palm-sized portion from the flesh
So that the bone remains exposed. Charles bends,
Staggers, almost buckles at the legs.   3525
God does not want him dead or overwhelmed.
Down the Angel Gabriel descends.
"What are you doing, mighty King?" he says.   [3611]

262

Hearing the angel's urgings near at hand,
Charles's fears and hesitations vanish.   3530
He gets his iron determination back
And strikes the emir with the sword of France.
The helmet, spraying shining gemstones, cracks.
The sword breaks through the skull, and the brains splash.
Through the emir's face to his white beard it slashes.   3535
The emir's dead. No cure can bring him back.
"Mountjoy!" cries Charles and shouts to God his thanks.
At that, Neïme brings Tencedor, his stallion.
Charlemagne grabs the reins and swings into the saddle.
The pagans turn. God wills them to break ranks.   3540
Now everything the French have wished is granted.   [3624]

263

The pagans flee, as God wills them to do.
The French knights and the emperor pursue.
"My lords, avenge the sorrows you've been through!
I saw you weeping in this morning's gloom.   3545
Now do your will, as your heart tells you to."
The French reply, "My lord, we'll do our duty."
Then each one does his best, hacking and hewing.
Some pagans get away, but very few.   [3632]

264

It's hot. Dust clouds kick up from the road's surface.   3550
The pagans flee. The French pursue and scourge them
All the way to Saragossa. Early,
Queen Bramimunde has climbed up to her turret,
Surrounded by canons and men of law and learning
In the false law, which God in Heaven spurns—   3555
All unordained doctors and untonsured clerks.
And when she sees the Arabians dispersed,
She cries aloud, "Mohammed, save your servants!
Noble King, our hosts are overturned.
The emir's army failed. The emir perished."   3560
When he hears this, the king goes pale; he buries
His face against the wall, his eyes tear-blurred.
At last Marsille gives up his body, burdened
With sins, to earth; his soul, to evil spirits.   AOI   [3647]

265

The pagans are killed, though some few do escape.   3565
The battle is won; the victor, Charlemagne.
He's beaten through the Saragossa gates.
Confident that no defense remains,
He takes the city, marches in, and stays
To spend the night, for this is his domain.   3570
The emperor is fierce, white beard displayed!
The queen surrenders all her royal places,
The fifty lesser towers and the ten greater.
A person does good work when God gives aid!   [3657]

266

The day is ending, and the night begins.   3575
The moon is bright. The starry sky is brilliant.
King Charles holds Saragossa in his fist.
A thousand Frenchmen search throughout the city
For synagogues and mosques and enter in them
Carrying hammers, wedges, swords, and picks   3580
And break down all the idols and false images
And cleanse the place of sorcery and wizardry.
King Charles serves God and wants to do His wishes.
To waters sanctified by Charles's bishops,
They lead the pagans, who emerge as Christians.   3585
This is the emperor's will. Whoever resists it,

He has him bound and burned, enslaved, or killed.
A hundred thousand do receive baptism.
The queen rejects the emperor's religion.
To lovely France she will be led, imprisoned,   3590
Where Charles hopes kindness will convert and win her.   [3674]

267

Night falls and fades. Here comes the light of dawn.
Charles occupies the towers and installs
A thousand knights to guard the town and walls
And govern Saragossa while he's gone.   3595
King Charlemagne and all his men set off,
Bringing the queen, whom he still holds in thrall
(Although he doesn't mean to do her wrong).
They leave the city, confident and jaunty,
Ride hard and steadily, and pass Nerbone   3600
And reach Bordeaux, the city of high crosses.
With Spanish gold he fills the Olifant
And sets it down upon St. Sevrin's altar,
Where pilgrims go to look on it with awe.
They ride beside the river of Gironde   3605
And see the tall ships docked there in the water.
At last as far as Blaye King Charles has brought
Roland his nephew, Oliver his staunch,
Noble companion, and Turpin, wise and stalwart.
In a white sarcophagus he leaves these warriors,   3610
Who lie there still inside their marble vault.
The French commend their souls to God, in all
The names of God. Charlemagne rides across
Valleys and hills. He will not sleep or pause
Until he reaches Aix, and there he halts.   3615
The king dismounts and enters his high hall.
From there he summons judges and great lawyers:
Bavarians, Saxons, Lorrainians he calls,
Frisians, Poitovans, Germans, Burgundians, also
Normans and Bretons, the wisest men of law,   3620
To meet at Aix-the-Chapel to consult,
For now begins the trial of Ganelon.   [3704]

268

King Charles has come from Spain. Now he is home
In Aix, his seat of judgment and abode.

He enters his palace, rests upon his throne.   3625
A beautiful lady, Alda, now approaches.
"Where," she asks him, "is your captain, Roland,
Who promised me that I would be his own
And he be mine?" Charles the emperor groans.
He strokes his white beard and his eyes overflow.   3630
"Dear child," he answers her, "you seek to know
About a dead man. Now instead of Roland,
You shall have Louis, my own son, most noble.[38]
No better substitute I could bestow.
He shall possess my kingdoms and my coastlands."   3635
"This," she answers, "is a strange proposal."
May God and all His angels not postpone
My time of death now Roland's life is over."
She loses color, falls dead upon the stones
At Charles's feet. May God preserve her soul!   3640
All the knights of France weep to behold her.   [3722]

269

Alda the beautiful from life has gone.
The king thinks she has fainted and he calls
With pity to her. Tears stain his cheeks with salt.
He lifts her up in both his arms and draws   3645
Her head against his shoulder, where it falls.
At last he understands that he has lost her.
He calls four countesses and has her brought
Into a convent, where with prayers and psalms
They stay awake and watch until the dawn.   3650
He has her buried underneath the altar
With honors for his nephew's fair betrothed.   AOI   [3733]

270

King Charles is back in Aix, where he has taken
Ganelon the felon. They keep the slave,
His hands with rawhide bound, his body chained   3655
To a central post inside the city square
And just outside the royal palace gates.

---

38. In terms of feudal obligation, the king can offer Alda no better substitute for
Roland than his son, but in the context of Louis' reputation for worthlessness in
other twelfth-century epics, the offer is ludicrous.

They beat him with gambrils;³⁹ they batter him with staves.
It's all the good he's earned. There he awaits
In pain the day when he will be arraigned.   3660 [3741]

271

The chronicle is there for you to read,
How Charlemagne called men from far and near,
Wise men of law, to Aix, where they convened
On St. Sylvester's Day, it is believed,
Or some high feast. There they began to hear   3665
Witnesses, arguments, details, and briefs
Concerning Ganelon, who did the treason.
The emperor has him hauled before the judgment seat. AOI   [3749]

272

"My lord barons, judge for me my claim
Against this Ganelon," says Charlemagne,   3670
"He was my vassal when I was in Spain.
He had my twenty thousand Frenchmen slain,
With them, my nephew—I'll never see his face—,
And Oliver, the courteous and brave,
And the Twelve Peers, all for the gold he craved."   3675
"To hell with excuses!" Ganelon exclaims.
"I *am* a felon if I refuse to say:
Roland cheated me in gold and gain,
So I had Roland killed, by my arrangements.
That much I did, but there was no betrayal!"   3680
The French reply, "We will deliberate."   [3761]

273

Before the king, Count Ganelon is standing,
His features beautiful, his body handsome.
If he were loyal, you would think, "What valor!"
He sees his judges and the men of France,   3685
And thirty relatives, all here to back him.
He shouts, "For God's sake, listen to me, barons!
I was there in Spain with Charles's army.
Loyally, lovingly I served my master.

---

39. A gambril [*jamel.* 3739], Jenkins tells us, is "a crooked stick upon which
carcasses are hung" (p. 335).

His nephew hated me and nursed his rancor.   3690
He judged I take a message to the Spaniards
And King Marsille, then die, sad and abandoned,
But I survived them all, by my own tactics.
I said I'd make them pay: their captain
Roland, and Oliver, all their companions.   3695
Charles heard me tell them. So did all his barons.
Vengeance there was. Betrayal never happened."
"We will deliberate," the Frenchmen answer.   [3779]

274

Ganelon watches. His great trial is beginning.
Here to support him are thirty relatives.   3700
To one of them, the other cousins listen;
He's Pinabel of Castle Soricinia,
Thoughtful, well spoken, reasonable, convincing,
Valorous in war, strong, and skillful.   AOI   [3785]
Ganelon speaks and pleads to him: "Dear kinsman,   3705
Save me from this trial. My life's at risk."
Pinabel says, "We'll get you out of this.
No Frenchman living would vote for you to swing.
And if some one of Charles's judges did,
He'd have to answer to my contradiction: 3710
With lance and sword, we'd joust before the king."
Count Ganelon in thanks kneels down to him.   [3792]

275

Saxon judges, Bavarians, Germans, Prussians,
Poitovans, Normans, French, and those Charles summoned
From scholarly Auvergne all sit in judgment.   3715
Out of respect for Pinabel, they hush
Or if they speak, whisper to each other:
"Better to let it go and not cause trouble."
"Best drop the charge." "Let's beg the king, this once,
To pardon Ganelon's offense and suffer   3720
Him to renew his loyalty and love."
"Roland is dead. The king could not recover
His nephew now for all his money." "None
But a fool fights Pinabel." "What's done is done."
Of Ganelon's trial judges, there's not one   3725
Condemns him—none but Thierry, Geoffrey's brother.   AOI   [3806]

276

Back to the king return the justice-barons
And say to Charlemagne, "My lord, we ask you:
Pardon Count Ganelon this time and grant him
Again to serve you loyally and gladly.   3730
Sire, let him live: he is a gentleman.
There's no return from death, and we can pass
No judgment that will bring your nephew back."
The emperor says, "You're all a pack of rascals!"   AOI   [3814]

277

When Charlemagne sees the judges all have failed him,   3735
His brow clouds over and his face goes gray.
Distractedly he calls them wretched cravens.
One knight stands up before the royal chair,
Duke Geoffrey of Anjou's young brother, Thierry.
He stands before the court, slender and straight.   3740
His hair is black; swarthy is his face.
He isn't short; nor is his stature great.
He speaks politely to King Charlemagne.
"My lord and king," he says, "do not despair.
I've served you often; for my forefathers' sake   3745
I will uphold the justice of your case:
If Roland wronged Ganelon, Roland remained
Your vassal still, serving within your safety.
Ganelon is a felon; he betrayed you.
He broke the vows a vassal freely makes.   3750
Therefore, I judge he hang. Let the dogs prey
Upon his body.[40] A felon he became
When he did felony. If some retainer
Of Ganelon deny my rightful claim,
I will unsheathe this sword, and with this blade   3755
Guarantee the justice of my statement."
"Thierry has spoken well," the French exclaim.   [3837]

278

Pinabel stands before the emperor,
Gigantic, strong, brave, agile, and resourceful.
Those whom he strikes do not awake next morning.   3760

---

40. A half line is missing here in the O manuscript, so we really do not know
what humiliation Thierry recommends for Ganelon's body.

He says to the king, "My lord, this trial is yours.
Order there not be so much noise in court.
This Thierry made his judgment, and he swore it,
But it is false. I will belie it with my sword.
Here is my deerskin glove." "Give me," Charles orders,   3765
"The men who stake their lives as guarantors."
Thirty kinsmen of Ganelon step forward.
"I take them," says the king. Till combat mortal
Decides their fate, the king will keep them quartered.   AOI   [3849]

279

When Thierry hears his judgment has been challenged,   3770
He gives the glove from his right hand to Charles,
Who takes and holds it up as Thierry's warrant.
Charles has four benches set on the green sward
For Pinabel and Thierry. These benches mark
The jousting zone. The people there remark   3775
How true to code and form these measures are.
The jousters listen as Ogier of Denmark
Proclaims the rules, then call for their steeds and arms.   [3857]

280

Now that the trial by combat is decreed,   AOI
The two combatants confess their sins and kneel   3780
For blessings and absolution. Each receives
Holy Communion during mass, and each
Bequeaths large holdings to the Church. They greet
King Charlemagne and put spurs on their feet,
Put hauberks on of lightly woven steel,   3785
And clamp steel helmets on. For now they keep
Their swords cinched, and their golden pommels gleam.
Down from their necks hang richly quartered shields.
In their right fists they grasp their deadly spears.
Now they are mounted on their spirited steeds.   3790
One hundred thousand Frenchmen weep. They see
Roland in Thierry and cannot hold their tears.
Only God knows what the end of this will be.   [3872]

281

Above Aix Chapel, a meadow, long and wide,
Hosts the two barons, who are judged to fight.   3795
Both of them are heroic, valiant knights.

On fiery swift horses they mount and ride,
Digging in spurs and letting go the bridles,
Faster against each other till they strike
And shatter each other's shield. The lances drive   3800
Into the hauberks, and the chain mail flies.
The horses' cinches slip, and the saddles slide.
A hundred thousand men watch them and cry.   [3882]

282

The two men fall to earth when their steeds stumble.
Up to their feet both the barons jump.   3805
Pinabel is nimble, quick, and tough.
Without their horses, they rush against each other.
With gold-encrusted swords the two knights bludgeon
Each other hard on the helmet, while a hundred
Thousand Frenchmen grieve to see the bloodshed.   3810
"O, God," says Charlemagne, "give us the judgment."   [3891]

283

"Thierry," entreats Count Pinabel, "submit.
I offer you all the money you could wish.
I'll be your man in faith. But to the king
Go first and ask for Ganelon's forgiveness."   3815
"No, I will not. That's bad advice you give,"
Says Thierry. "I'd be a felon if I did.
God will decide who has the right in this."   AOI   [3898]

284

Thierry says, "You're valiant, Pinabel,
Tall, well-proportioned, powerful, respected.   3820
In all of France your valor isn't questioned.
As for this mortal combat, let it rest.
I'll speak to Charles, and you will have his blessing.
But Ganelon—I'll serve him such a sentence
All France will talk of it and long remember."   3825
"No," says Pinabel, "May God prevent it!
I will uphold my people, not surrender
To any man alive, and I will never
Let it be said that I did not defend them."
Again they begin to strike each other's helmets,   3830
Cutting off gold and gem-starred ornaments,
Sending up sparks from steel on steel to heaven.

Such close-in fighting, nothing can sever them.
Their meeting now can only end in death.   AOI   [3914]

285

Sir Pinabel is powerful and solid.   3835
He swings his sword. It crashes through the top
Of Thierry's Provence helm. Sparks sharp and hot
From steel on steel set fire to little plots
Of dry field grass. Deflected past the forehead,
The point cuts Thierry's right cheekbone and chops   3840
The hauberk open and cuts along the body
Down to the stomach. Thierry doesn't drop.
He stands and still is living, saved by God!   AOI   [3923]

286

Thierry realizes his face is ripped
And feels blood running down his face and chin   3845
Into the grass. He lifts his sword and hits
Pinabel's helmet, splits the noseguard, sinks it
Into Pinabel's skull till the brains spill.
Thierry twists the blade inside and kicks
Pinabel's body free. The fight is finished.   3850
The Frenchmen shout, "God has accomplished this!
It's right and just that Ganelon should swing
And with him swing the men who stood by him!"[41]   AOI   [3933]

287

When Thierry's victory concludes the quarrel,
The emperor comes down to the jousting yard   3855
And with him, Duke Neïme and three more barons,
Geoffrey of Anjou, Ogier of Denmark,
William of Blaye. Tenderly King Charles
Lifts Thierry up. With his own furs of marten
He cleanses Thierry's face. These he discards   3860
And puts on others. Gently Thierry's armor
Comes off. On an Arabian mule they cart him
To the Aix square joyfully applauding.
And now the killing of the others starts.   [3946]

---

41. The author cannot have failed to notice the contrast between the reluctance
even to accuse Ganelon when Pinabel was alive and the clamor for mass and
sudden executions after Pinabel has died.

288

Charles calls his counts and dukes and asks advice: 3865
"What shall I do with those I keep confined?
They pledged themselves for Ganelon at trial.
They pledged their lives that Pinabel would triumph!"
"Not one of them should live!" the Frenchmen cry.
He tells his marshal Basbrown, "Waste no time.   3870
From a high gallows, hang Ganelon's allies.
By this white beard and every hair that's white,
You're a dead man if even one survives."
"Then what else can I do?" Basbrown replies.
A hundred guards compel the thirty knights   3875
Up to the gallows, where they hang them high.
A traitor takes his own and others' lives.   AOI   [3959]

289

Bavarian judges, German, Poitovan,
Breton, and Norman judges, too, regather;
And more than any, the ones who are from France   3880
Judge Ganelon should die in wondrous anguish.
Out on the battlefield, they tie four stallions
To Ganelon, one at each foot and hand.
These steeds are proud and powerful and fast.
Four soldiers goad them on, and the steeds stampede   3885
Toward where a creek cuts through the level land.
Ganelon breathes his last, most horrid gasps.
His joints and ligaments expand.
His bones are broken, and his sinews snap.
His watery blood makes streaks across the grass.   3890
Thus like a felon, to a felon's death they drag him.
He who betrays has nothing right to brag of.   [3974]

290

The emperor's revenge is consummated.
He tells his bishops from his French domains,
And from Bavaria, and from the German states,   3895
"I have a noble captive in my chambers.
She's heard so many sermons, lessons, prayers,
She longs for faith in God and Christian grace.
Baptize this lady so that God may claim her."
"She must have godmothers," the bishops say,   3900
"Who must be beautiful and pious ladies."

The springs are fresh and clean in the Aix square.
There bishops do baptize the Queen of Spain.
Juliana is her Christian name.
Christian she is, in knowledge and in faith.   3905 [3987]

291

The Emperor Charles's justice is administered.
He feels relief from the great rage that gripped him.
He has led Bramimunde to her baptism.
All day until the dark he has been busy.
He goes to bed beneath his vaulted windows.   3910
God sends the Angel Gabriel to visit.
"Charles!" he says, "summon your divisions!
Make a forced march to the land of Bir.
Bring help to Vivien, the King of Imphe.
A horde of pagans has besieged his city.   3915
Christians cry out and beg for your assistance!"
Charles does not want to go. "God," says the king,
"How tired I am. How weary my life is."
He weeps and tugs his white beard with his fist.
Here's where the Song runs out. Turolde is finished.[42]   3920 [4002]

---

42. The Old French is one of the most puzzling end-lines of literature: "Ci falt la geste que Turoldus declinet," which could mean "Here ends the *geste* which Turolde composes," "Here ends the *geste* which Turolde is writing down," "Here fails the *geste* because Turolde is declining," or a variety of meanings close to any of these three. By *geste* could be meant the *action,* the chronicle that may have been the author's source, or (as in this translation) the epic poem we have just finished reading, *The Song of Roland.* It would be convenient to call Turolde the author of *La Chanson de Roland,* but we know nothing about him, and we cannot tell whether he is an oral performer who composed the poem, an oral performer who received the poem from another performer and recited it for the scribe who wrote the Oxford manuscript, or the scribe himself. If he was the scribe, we do not know whether he is the author or simply the copyist, and if the copyist, whether from an oral performance or from another manuscript. The Latinization of the name, with the *-us* ending, makes it slightly more likely that Turolde was a scribe.

Notes on Editorial and Translation Decisions

78 [77]. "We have enough of these." Editors usually interpret the present-tense French, "De ço avun nus asez," as an "expression de gratitude" (William Calin, *La Chanson de Roland,* p. 20) in the future sense. Calin translates the sentence into modern French as "alors nous en aurons beaucoup" ("then we will have a lot") (p. 20), even though the sentence means literally, "Of that we have plenty." A literal translation gives more punch to the end of the *laisse* by making the Saracen nobles more human, though less subservient, and reminds us that embassies to enemy strongholds are dangerous, a reality that will be crucial when Charlemagne has to choose his own ambassador to the Saracens.

126 [126]. "He asks: 'How can salvation be attained?'" Editors sometimes add a line not in the Oxford manuscript but in ms. V⁷: "As chrestiens se voldrat asembler" ("He wants to join with Christians"). It is more interesting, however, to have Bláncandrin save the biggest promise—his king's conversion to Christianity—till last, at the end of the next *laisse.*

303–4 [307]. "You have me branded / With a false judgment": "Sur mei avez turnet false jugement"—literally: "You have turned false judgment on me." Bédier translates this interpretively into modern French: ". . . avez fait tourner sur moi cet injuste choix" (p. 29)—"you have had this unjust choice turned on me"—thus substituting the clearer, but weaker, *choice* for *judgment.* In the original Old French two *laisses* later, Charlemagne's use of the cognate verb "*jugent*" bears out Bédier's interpretation: (speaking to Ganelon) "sur vos le jugent Franc" [321] ("the French judge it on you," or, in this context, "the French choose you"). The immediate context of Ganelon's words, however, is the judgment of Roland's laughter, which makes Ganelon almost burst with anger. I prefer a reading closer to the literal than Bédier's translation, which forces a single interpretation.

750–54 [761–65]. This is the most problematic of all the *laisses.* It immediately contradicts the second line of the previous *laisse,* just nine lines back—"Dunc ad parled a lei de chevaler" [752], literally,

"Then he spoke according to law of a knight"—for there is nothing knightly about this answer. It also contradicts Roland's reluctance to admit that his stepfather has betrayed them (*laisse* 80) until the Saracens are upon them (*laisse* 90). Another problem is that Roland in this *laisse* and the next seems to have forgotten that it was the glove that Ganelon dropped, not the staff. Or was it the scribe or storyteller who forgot? For any of them, it should have been easy to remember that it was the glove, since it would be simpler and clearer for the character or author (or translator) to say, "I won't drop the glove the way you did," than "I won't drop the glove the way you dropped the staff." The fact that the author uses the more complicated phrasing in both *laisses* 60 and 61 persuades me that he intends the mistake in order to express Roland's confusion.

756 [767]. "the bow." To add to the confusion, Roland now offers to accept the *bow*—as in bow-and-arrow—which, with Neïme's advice, Charlemagne does give to Roland in the next *laisse*. Perhaps there is indeed a distinction between two symbolic sticks, the messenger's staff and the bow that betokens military command. It is, of course, possible that the scribe or author is confused by his own ignorance of chivalric symbolism dating from three centuries earlier.

1302–4 [1317–19]. Alternate translation: "Oliver stays fixed / Firm in the saddle. Márgariz rides and rings / His bugle, rallying his army's courage." Lines [1318–19] are, "Ultre s'en vait, qu'il n'i ad desturber; / Sunet sun gresle pur les soens ralier," literally, "He goes off because there is nothing to stop him. / He sounds his bugle to rally his people." The Oxford manuscript O does not make clear who rides off rallying his people, Oliver or Márgariz. Most scholars and translators think it is Márgariz, based on the St. Mark's, Venice, manuscript V⁴, which has the rider blow his bugle "for the pagans" ("por paiens"), instead of the scribe of the Oxford Digby (O) manuscript's ambiguous "for his people" ("pur les soens") (Jenkins, p. 103). I prefer Oliver as the subject because his riding off is a natural development of the previous sentences, 1301–2 [1316–17]: he is not injured, thank God; the lance breaks and does not throw him down; he rides away free to rally his people. Also, this interpretation affirms a slight distinction between the leadership qualities of the two rearguard leaders: Roland leads by heroic example, as the next *laisse* illustrates; Oliver leads by encouraging the other knights, as in *laisse* 92.

1370–71 [1388–89]. "The Gascon Peer Sir Éngeler now fells / Espérveris, the son of Count Borel." In the Oxford manuscript, line 1388 is not completely legible and does not make much sense. Line 1389 is completely illegible. I borrow Jenkins' guess at the meaning for the translation (p. 107).

1507 [1531]. In O, we are told here that Climborin gave Ganelon a sword, contradicting line 618 [629]. With support from ms. V⁴, where the gift is a helmet both times, Bedier and Jenkins emend "his sword" (*sespee*) to "his helmet" (*son elmo*) (Jenkins, p. 117). It is possible of course that the V⁴ copyist had emended the original author's mistake, but either way it is a good emendation.

1626–34 [1653–60]. In form, these lines continue and are part of the same long *laisse* (124) as lines 1612–25 [1636–52] because the assonance is the same throughout. Thematically, however, *laisse* 124 seems to conclude with the comment of the Frenchmen in line 1625 [1652], so typical of *laisse* concluding lines; while lines 1626–34 [1653–60] read like a parallel *laisse* to *laisse* 125, which follows. Bedier breaks lines [1636–60] into two absolutely distinct *laisses* by transposing lines [1653–60] to *after* the parallel *laisse* 125 so that they no longer follow a *laisse* of the same assonance. It is possible that this emendation violates the original author's intention of stretching out the *laisse* beyond "'Our Safeguard strikes good blows,' the Frenchmen say" in order to stress what a long, hard fight this was becoming. I like the notion of the poet trying a slightly unusual interplay between sound and sense this far into his poem and have followed O's order rather than Bedier's.

2905–17 [2974–86]. In the O manuscript, these lines are marked as two *laisses*, with line [2981] concluding with an AOI and line [2982] beginning with a red capital letter. However, the thirteen lines assonate as one *laisse*, emphasizing that Baligant and Charlemagne share one passion—to confront each other in battle. To emphasize a more important element of the story, Charlemagne's crucial moment of defiance, I have written lines 2913–17 as separate: *laisse* 214.

2951 [3022]. Loranz. In *laisse* 217, O has Charlemagne assign Guinemán to be in two places at once, leading two different divisions (lines [3014] and [3022]). Jenkins corrects the second Guinemán to *Loranze* on the basis of ms. V⁴ and of line [3469] in O.

GLOSSARY AND INDEX

Names are indexed according to *laisse* rather than line numbers. Where the English translation of these names is significantly different from the Old French, the Old French spelling appears in brackets after the English. The *Mal* and *Mar* that begin many of the names have an etymological whiff of evil from the French words *mal* and *mar*.

to Apollo. See footnote to line 8 as well as glossary references to Mohammed and Tervagant. 1, 32, 186, 193–94, 235, 253.

Argoilles. A people loyal to Emir Baligant. 234, 252, 255.

Armenia, Armenians [Ermines]. Although the Armenians were and are traditionally Christian, Jenkins notes that "[o]nly the small principality of Lesser Armenia, founded in 1080, was friendly to the Crusaders, nor was this friendship always to be relied upon" (p. 225). 232.

Astor. One of the leaders of the rearguard. 64, 122.

Astramarz. One of the Twelve Elite Saracens and battle-mate of Esturganz. 76, 102.

Astrimoniyees. A people loyal to Emir Baligant. 234.

Auvergne. A region of south central France. 222, 275.

Aversians [de Avers]. A people loyal to Emir Baligant. 233.

Bálaguez. An emir and one of the Twelve Elite Saracens. 72, 97.

Balbiún. The land belonging to Duke Falseron. 94.

Baldwin. Ganelon's son. 23, 27.

Balida. A fortified town loyal to Emir Baligant. 232.

Baligant. Emir of Babylon (often referred to as "the emir" and "the Grand Emir"). 187–88, 191, 193, 195–201, 213, 227–29, 231–32, 234–39, 243–45, 247–48, 251, 253–55, 257–62, 264.

Barbamouche. Literally, *Beardfly.* The Saracen Climborin's horse. 116.

Basán. A previous ambassador from Charlemagne to King Marsille's court. 14, 24, 37.

Basbrown [Basbrun]. Charlemagne's guard and executioner. 288.

Bascalese [de Bascle]. A people loyal to Emir Baligant. 252.

Basil, St. Fourth-century Christian philosopher. 172.

Básil. A previous ambassador from Charlemagne to King Marsille's court, Basán's brother. 14, 24, 37.

Bavaria, Bavarians. Same as present-day Bavaria. 171, 218, 267, 275, 289–90.

Bérenger. One of the Twelve Peers of France and a rearguard leader. 64, 102, 122, 176.

Besgun. Charlemagne's chief cook. 136.

Bevon of Dijon. A knight of the rearguard. 141.

Biterne. Possibly, made in Viterbo, a city in central Italy. 215.

Bláncandrin. The most influential of King Marsille's advisors. 2–6, 9, 10 (as "the Saracen"), 28–32, 35, 38.

Blaye. A town in southern France. 267, 287.

Blos. A land loyal to Emir Baligant. 232.

Bordeaux. A city in southern France. Because of a blank space in the manuscript, we do not know what the author meant to call Bordeaux the city *of* ("la citet de"). I take advantage of our ignorance to write "the city of high crosses" for the assonance. 100, 116, 267.

Borel. The father of Marsille's Baron Espérveris. 108.

Bramimunde (the queen). Queen to King Marsille, renamed Juliana. 50, 186–87, 194–95, 200, 264–266, 290–91.

Browns [Bruns]. A people loyal to Emir Baligant. 232.

Brownspot [Tachebrun]. Ganelon's horse. 27.

Bruise. A land loyal to Emir Baligant. 233.

Burgundy, Burgundians. Burgundy is a province of France whose people (the Burgundians) were loyal to Charlemagne. 171, 224, 267.

Butentrotiens. A people from the unknown land of Butentrot. 232.

Calif [Califerne]. A land forcibly subjected to Charlemagne's empire. 208.

Caliph. *See also* Marganice. 35, 37–38, 54, 142, 145.

Canaanites. A people loyal to Emir Baligant from the Biblical land of Canaan (Canelius). 233, 235.

Canábeus. Brother of Emir Baligant and the king of Sevre Valley. 238, 248–49, 253.

Capél. King of Cappadocia and father of Saracen captain Grandonies. 122.

Carthage. Ancient city of North Africa, here governed by the Caliph Marganice and contributing forces to the ambush at Roncevals. 142.

Charlemagne (Charles, King Charles, the king, the emperor). Emperor of France and uncle of Roland. 1–30, 32–37, 40–45, 48, 50–63, 65–70, 72–77, 79, 83–90, 92–93, 95, 105, 107, 109–12, 115–17, 124, 127–39, 141–42, 144–47, 149, 154–59, 161, 165, 168, 170–73, 175–78, 180–88, 191–92, 194–99, 201–19, 222–23, 225–30, 232, 235–39, 241–43, 246, 248–50, 253–54, 256–63, 265–80, 282–84, 287–88, 290–91.

Cheriant. Part of the land formerly belonging to King Flurit, given to Malprámis. 231.

Chernuble. Lord of Múnigre and one of the Twelve Elite Saracens. 78, 102, 104.

Chronicles of the French. Accounts of the deeds of famous Frenchmen. 111, 126, 154, 234, 271.

Ciz. The Gates of Ciz are the rock formations opening from the south into the mountain pass known as the Ports of Spain. 44, 56, 58, 66, 209.

Claren. A Syrian messenger to King Marsille from Emir Baligant and brother to Clarifan. 192, 195, 198–99.

Clarifan. A Syrian messenger to King Marsille from Emir Baligant and brother to Claren. 192.

Clarin of Balágatee. A messenger to Charlemagne from King Marsille. 5.

Clavers. A land loyal to Emir Baligant. 233.

Climborin. One of Marsille's knights. 49, 116.

Commilbury [Commibles]. An area of Spain conquered by Roland for Charlemagne. 14.

Cordoba. A city in south central Spain, recently conquered by Charlemagne and, at the beginning of the poem, the seat of his government in Spain. 5–6, 8.

Corsablix. A Berber king and one of the Twelve Elite Saracens. 71, 95.

Crazyleap [Saltperdut]. Saracen knight Grimthought's horse. 120.

Dappledeath, King of Leutzistan [Dapamort Leutiz]. One of Emir Baligant's generals. 231–32, 242.

Datliún. The land belonging to Duke Falsarun. 94.

Deadmen [Mors]. A people loyal to Emir Baligant; probably the Moors, with a pun on the French word for *dead people.* 232.

Denis, St. Bishop of Paris in the third century. 172.

Durendal. Roland's sword. 74, 78, 83–85, 88, 104, 112, 140, 158, 167, 170–73, 198, 204.

Ebro. A river in Spain. 179, 190, 195, 197, 199.

Elite Twelve Saracens. Twelve elite knights of Marsille's army organized to challenge the Twelve Peers of France at the battle of Roncevals. 70, 102.

Enfruns. A people loyal to Emir Baligant. 254.

Éngeler the Gascon of Bordeaux. One of the Twelve Peers of France and a rearguard leader. 100, 108, 116–17, 176.

Escababi. A baron in Marsille's army. 117.

Escremiz of Valterna. One of the Twelve Elite Saracens. 75, 100.

Espérveris. A baron in King Marsille's army. The line in the manuscript is badly smudged, and this is a guess at the name. 108.

Estamars. A messenger to Charlemagne from King Marsille. 5.

Esturganz. One of the Twelve Elite Saracens and battlemate of Astramarz. 76, 101.

Esturgoz. A Saracen knight. 106.

Ethiopia. Governed by the Caliph Marganice, Ethiopia contributes knights to the ambush at Roncevals. 142.

Eurropin. A messenger to Charlemagne from King Marsille. 5.

Evilgood from Oversea [Malbien d'ultremer]. A messenger to Charlemagne from King Marsille. 5.

Faldrún de Pui. A knight in Marsille's army. 140.

Falsarun. Brother to King Marsille and one of the Twelve Elite Saracens. 70, 94.

Flurit. Former king of the lands that Emir Baligant grants to his son Malprimis. 231.

Fuit Valley. A land loyal to Emir Baligant. 233.

Gaifiers. A duke and one of the rearguard leaders. 64.

Gaignun. King Marsille's horse. (A *guenon* is a female monkey.) 141.

Galaff. The emir who originally obtained Abisme's shield from the Devil. 114.

Galatan silk. The silk was probably manufactured in Galatia, the city whose Christian residents received a letter from St. Paul, or in Galata, a peninsular suburb of Constantinople. 212.

Galicia. A province of northern Spain. *See* Hamon of Galicia. 223.

Ganelon. Stepfather and bitter enemy to Roland. 12, 15–16, 20–50, 52–54, 56, 58–61, 67–68, 80, 90, 109, 112, 116, 118, 132–33, 136, 267, 270–78, 283–84, 286, 288–89.

Garlan of the Beard [Guarlan le Barbet]. A messenger to Charlemagne from King Marsille. 5.

Gascony. A province of southern France. 12, 66, 176.

Gebuin. One of Charlemagne's division commanders. 177, 212, 217, 251.

Geoffrey of Anjou. Guide-on bearer for Charlemagne and brother of Thierry of Anjou. *See* Guide-on. 8, 205, 210–11, 225, 256–57, 275, 277, 287.

Gerart of Russillon. One of the Twelve Peers of France and a rearguard leader. 64, 141, 161, 176.

Gerer. One of the Twelve Peers of France, a rearguard leader and battle-mate of Gerin. 8, 12, 64, 97, 108, 122, 161, 176.

Gerin. One of the Twelve Peers of France, a rearguard leader and battle-mate of Gerer. 8, 12, 64, 96, 108, 122, 161, 176.

Germany [Alemaigne], Germans. Germany was an important part of Charlemagne's empire. Our author considers it a separate province from Saxony and Bavaria. 219, 267, 275, 289, 290.

Giles. Saint Giles. 154.

Gironde. The river in France that flows through Bordeaux before emptying into the Atlantic. 267.

Godeselmes. A division leader of Charlemagne's army. 222.

Gramimond. The horse of Saracen knight Valdabraun. 118.

Grandonies. A Saracen captain in Marsille's army. 122, 124.

Grimálfin [Gemalfin]. The trusted lieutenant of Emir Baligant who commands the armies in the emir's absence. 200, 253.

Grimtail [Malcud]. The father of Grimthought. 120.

Grimthought [Malquiant]. A Saracen knight. 120–21.

Gros. A region loyal to Emir Baligant. 232.

Grossall [Agrossaille]. The Danish king slain at some previous time by Archbishop Turpin. 114.

Guide-on. The flag by which soldiers can locate their leaders; or, the soldier who carries the guide-on. (The guide-on for Charlemagne is Geoffrey of Anjou.) 8, 55, 68, 109, 113, 256–57.

Guinemán. One of Charlemagne's captains. 217, 240, 242, 251.

Guinemer. Ganelon's uncle. 27.

Gumalio. A land governed by the Caliph Marganice and contributing to the ambush at Roncevals. 142.

Guyun of St. Anthony. A knight of the rearguard. 122.

Hamon of Galicia. A knight in Charlemagne's army and division commander. 223.

Henry. A knight in Charlemagne's army and nephew of Richard the Old. 12.

Hungary, Huns. The fact that Roland is said to have conquered Hungary does not keep that land from supplying troops to Emir Baligant's army. 234.

Iggies [Eugiez]. A people loyal to Emir Baligant. 233.

Ivon. One of the Twelve Peers of France and a rearguard leader. 141, 176.

Jangle Oversea [Jangleu l'Ultremarin]. Emir Baligant's counselor and wizard. 253–54.

Jericho. The Biblical town, here loyal to Emir Baligant. 232.

Jouner. A messenger to Charlemagne from King Marsille. 5.

Joyeuse. Charlemagne's sword. 182, 215, 228.

Jozeran de Provence. A division commander in Charlemagne's army. 216–17, 220, 222, 224, 226, 256.

Juliana. Queen Bramimunde's baptismal name. 290.

Jurfalé. The son and heir to King Marsille. 38, 141, 193. 198. (Also, though not named yet, 37.)

Laon. The home of the abbey founded by St. Giles and one of the seats of Charlemagne's government. 154, 207.

Leu. A region loyal to Emir Baligant. 234.

Loranz. A division commander in Charlemagne's army. 217, 251 (See Notes on Editorial and Translation Decisions, line 2951.)

Machinee. A messenger to Charlemagne from King Marsille. 5.

Malatrain. A former messenger for Emir Baligant and father of Clarifan and Claren. 192.

Maldebty [Malduit]. Marsille's treasurer. 51.

Malpalin. An unidentified enemy of Charlemagne from former times. 215.

Malprámis. The son of Emir Baligant. 229–32, 243, 247, 253.

Malprese. A land loyal to Emir Baligant. 234, 236.

Málprimis Brigant. One of the Twelve Elite Saracens. 71, 96.

Malun. A Saracen knight. 106.

Marbrise. A fictional Spanish city on the Ebro River. 190.

Marbrow. Another fictional Spanish city on the Ebro River. 190.

Marchis Valley. Part of the land formerly belonging to King Flurit, given to Malprámis. 231.

Marganice. Marsille's uncle and Caliph of North Africa. 142–44.

Márgariz of Seville. One of the Twelve Elite Saracens. 77, 102–03.

Marse [Marsune]. The unknown site of a river ford in Spain. 215.

Marsille. King of the Saracens and Lord of Saragossa. 1, 2, 5–7, 9, 13–17, 19 (as "the Saracen"), 20–21, 32–48, 50–52, 54, 68–78, 90, 93–94, 111–13, 118, 125, 130, 141–42, 186–89, 192–93, 196–201, 210, 264, 273.

Maruse. A region loyal to Emir Baligant. 234.

Matthew [Maheu]. A messenger to Charlemagne from King Marsille. 5.

Micenies. A people loyal to Emir Baligant. 232.

Milon. A count in Charlemagne's army and cousin of Theobald of Reims. 12, 177, 212.

Mohammed. To pray to or adore the Prophet Mohammed is contrary to the laws of Islam. The slander that Muslims did pray to Mohammed also continued—and was probably more generally believed than the one about Apollo—throughout popular medieval Christian literature. See footnote to line 8 as well as glossary references to Apollo and Tervagant. 1, 32, 47, 68–69, 74, 104, 125, 141, 186, 193–94, 232, 235, 253, 257, 264.

Moriane. Valley where the Angel Gabriel gave the sword Durendal to Charlemagne. 171.

Mountjoy. Both the battle cry of the French forces and Charlemagne's red battle standard. The author shows some learned curiosity about the origins and use of the word. 92, 94–95, 105, 107, 115, 134, 140, 146, 159, 182, 225, 237, 258, 262.

Murgleis. Ganelon's sword. 27, 46.

Neïme. A French Duke, one of Charlemagne's foremost advisers. 16–17, 54, 62, 67, 133–34, 176–77, 205, 209, 216–17, 219–20, 222–24, 226, 247–50, 257, 262, 287.

Nerbone. Jenkins writes, "Not the larger city of Narbonne, near the Mediterranean . . . but a town in the Basque country . . . now called *Arbonne*" (p. 253). 215, 267.

Nevelin. A count in Charlemagne's army. 221.

Niger [Negres]. A people loyal to Emir Baligant. 232.

Nople. An area of Spain conquered by Roland for Charlemagne. 14, 133.

Nuble. A land loyal to Emir Baligant. 232.

Occian. A land loyal to Emir Baligant. 233, 236, 252, 255.

Oedun. A division leader in Charlemagne's army. 221.

Ogier the Dane. One of Charlemagne's foremost military leaders. 12, 58, 218, 256–57, 279, 287.

Olifant. Roland's horn, fashioned, as the etymology indicates, from a huge elephant tusk. 83–85, 87, 92, 128–29, 131–34, 137, 155, 164, 169, 173, 217, 226, 230, 237–38, 267.

Oliver. One of the Twelve Peers of France. The battle-mate of Roland, he shares leadership of the rearguard with Roland. 8, 12, 18, 24, 41–44, 54, 64, 72, 75–77, 79–83, 86–88, 90–92, 94, 97, 103, 105–8,

110, 112, 115, 117, 126–31, 139, 143–50, 162–63, 176, 183, 198–99, 212, 217, 230, 267, 272–73.

Ormalies. A people loyal to Emir Baligant. 233, 236.

Otis. One of the Twelve Peers of France and a rearguard leader. 64, 101, 176.

Oton. One of Charlemagne's knights. 177, 212, 221.

Palermese. The people of Palermo, in Sicily. 208.

Persia, Persian(s). A land and people loyal to Emir Baligant. 231–33, 241.

Peter, St. The apostle. 28, 74, 172, 215, 225.

Pinabel. The friend, kinsman, and defender of Ganelon. 27, 274–75, 278–79, 282–86, 288.

Pinceneis. Jenkins and Hemming agree that these are, in Hemming's words, the "Petchenegs, a Tartar people" (p. 177). 233.

Pineland [la terre de Pine]. An area of Spain conquered by Roland for Charlemagne. 14.

Poitou. A region of western France. 171, 222.

Ports of Spain. The mountain pass that leads up through Roncevals from Spain to France. 63, 69, 135.

Priamun. A messenger to Charlemagne from King Marsille. 5.

Rabél. One of Charlemagne's captains. 217, 240–41.

Rearguard. Roland's regiment of twenty thousand men, assigned to follow Charlemagne's main army through the Ports of Spain. 43–44, 47–49, 52, 58–59, 62–63, 67–68, 70–71, 79, 87, 91–92, 103, 198, 214.

Reinier, Duke. Oliver's father. 162.

Rembalt. A knight in Charlemagne's army and division commander. 223.

Richard the Old, Duke of Normandy. One of Charlemagne's generals. 12, 220, 251.

Roland. The nephew of Charlemagne, his most renowned military leader and foremost of the Twelve Peers of France. 8, 12, 14–15, 18, 20–22, 24, 27, 29–31, 36, 41–49, 52–55, 58–80, 83–88, 90–93, 99, 104–8, 110, 112, 115, 117, 119, 123–24, 126–43, 145–76, 179, 183, 193–94, 198–99, 203–9, 212, 214, 216–17, 226, 229–30, 267–69, 272–73, 275–77, 280.

Roncevals (literally, *Thorn Valley*, Roncevaux today). A narrow valley in the Spanish Pyrenees and the scene of the great battle. 71–78, 164, 176–77, 180, 183, 194, 199, 202–3, 216, 246.

Runer Valley. The property of Duke Reinier, Oliver's father. 162.

St. Denis. One of Charlemagne's seats of government, probably at the present St. Denis, a suburb of Paris. 77.

Samson, Duke. One of the Twelve Peers of France and a rearguard leader. 8, 98, 118–19, 161, 176.

Samuel. The ancestor of people loyal to Emir Baligant. Jenkins and Hemming believe that Czar Samuel of Bulgaria is intended. 233.

Saracens. The Arabs of Spain. 14, 18, 28, 31, 48, 79, 86, 89, 91, 95, 102, 105, 116, 122, 124–25, 133, 138, 140, 142, 154, 160, 168–69, 194, 201.

Saragossa. The last stronghold in Spain for King Marsille and the Saracens, in northeast Spain. 1–2, 14, 17–18, 23, 31, 36, 52, 54, 68, 79, 109, 116, 179, 186–88, 190, 193, 196–98, 200–201, 264–67.

Saxony. A province of Charlemagne's empire. 171.

Sevre. The valley ruled by Canábeus, Emir Baligant's brother. 238, 248.

Sevrin, St. A church in Bordeaux. 267.

Sízlorel. The sorcerer knight in Marsille's army. 108.

Slavs. The author lists the Slavs among the followers of Emir Baligant. 232.

Slingshot-Beards [Barbez de Fronde]. A people loyal to Emir Baligant. 234.

Sorbiennes. A people loyal to Emir Baligant. 232.

Soricinia [Sorence]. The home estate of Pinabel. 274.

Sorrel. Gerin's horse. 108.

Sorz. A people loyal to Emir Baligant. 232.

Stagcatcher [Passecerf]. Gerer's horse. 108.

Sultras [Solteras]. A people loyal to Emir Baligant. 233.

Swátili. A land whose king gave Marsille twelve white mules. 7.

Tencedor. Charlemagne's horse. 215, 239, 262.

Tenebrosa. A valley in Spain. Literally: *dark*. 179.

Tervagant. The third of the so-called pagan Trinity, an inaccurate parallel with the Christian Trinity. Jean Bodel, in his thirteenth-century *Play of St. Nicholas*, written to promote support for the Crusades, has a Muslim king praying to an unholy trinity of Mohammed, Apollo, and Tervagant. See footnote to line 8 as well as glossary references to Apollo and Mohammed. 47, 179, 186, 193–94, 235, 253.

Theobald of Reims. One of Charlemagne's barons and cousin of Count Milon. 12, 212, 221.

Appendix

La Chanson de Roland

Although the following text of *La Chanson de Roland* (adapted from http://www.hs-augsburg.de/~harsch/gallica/Chronologie/11siecle/ Roland/rol_ch00.html) was not one used for this translation, it is reasonably close to the editions used (see references at the end of the Translator's Introduction) and is available here for anyone wishing to peruse the Old French.

Bracketed numbers at the end of each laisse in the translation, in the footnotes, and in the Notes on Editorial and Translation Decisions refer to lines in the Old French of this text and of most other editions. At *laisse* 124, the numbering of the *laisses* in the following text begins to diverge by one from the numbering in the translation, and, at *laisse* 215, the numbering converges again. (See Notes on Editorial and Translation Decisions for lines 1626–34 [1653–60] and 2905–17 [2974–86]).

1

Carles li reis, nostre emper[er]e magnes
Set anz tuz pleins ad estet en Espaigne:
Tresqu'en la mer cunquist la tere altaigne.
N'i ad castel ki devant lui remaigne;
Mur ne citet n'i est remes a fraindre,   5
Fors Sarraguce, ki est en une muntaigne.
Li reis Marsilie la tient, ki Deu nen aimet;
Mahumet sert e Apollin recleimet:
Nes poet guarder que mals ne l'i ateignet.   AOI.

2

Li reis Marsilie esteit en Sarraguce.   10
Alez en est en un verger suz l'umbre;
Sur un perrun de marbre bloi se culchet,
Envirun lui plus de vint milie humes.
Il en apelet e ses dux e ses cuntes:
«Oëz, seignurs, quel pecchet nus encumbret: 15
Li emper[er]es Carles de France dulce

129

En cest païs nos est venuz cunfundre.
Jo nen ai ost qui bataille li dunne,
Ne n'ai tel gent ki la sue derumpet.
Cunseilez mei cume mi savie hume,   20
Si m(e) guarisez e de mort et de hunte.»
N'i ad paien ki un sul mot respundet,
Fors Blancandrins de Castel de Valfunde.

3

Blancandrins fut des plus saives paiens:
De vasselage fut asez chevaler,   25
Prozdom i out pur sun seignur aider;
E dist al rei: «Ore ne vus esmaiez!
Mandez Carlun a l'orguillus, (e) al fier,
Fedeilz servises e mult granz amistez.
Vos li durrez urs e leons e chens,   30
Set cenz camelz e mil hosturs muers,
D'or e d'argent .IIII.C. muls cargez,
Cinquante carre, qu'en ferat carier:
Ben en purrat luer ses soldeiers.
En ceste tere ad asez osteiet;   35
En France, ad Ais, s'en deit ben repairer.
Vos le sivrez a la feste seint Michel:
Si recevrez la lei de chrestiens,
Serez ses hom par honur e par ben.
S'en volt ostages, e vos l'en enveiez,   40
U dis u vint pur lui afiancer.
Enveiu[n]s i les filz de noz muillers:
Par nun d'ocire i enveierai le men.
Asez est melz qu'il i perdent le chefs,
Que nus perduns l'onur ne la deintet,   45
Ne nus seiuns cunduiz a mendeier.»   AOI.

4

Dist Blancandrins: «Pa[r] ceste meie destre
E par la barbe ki al piz me ventelet,
L'ost des Franceis verrez sempres desfere.
Francs s'en irunt en France la lur tere.   50
Quant cascuns ert a sun meillor repaire,
Carles serat ad Ais, a sa capele;
A seint Michel tendrat mult halte feste.
Vendrat li jurz, si passerat li termes,

N'orrat de nos paroles ne nuveles.   55
Li reis est fiers e sis curages pesmes:
De noz ostages ferat tre[n]cher les testes;
Asez est mielz, qu'il i perdent les testes,
Que nus perduns clere Espaigne, la bele,
Ne nus aiuns les mals ne les suffraites.»   60
Dient paien: «Issi poet il ben estre!»

5

Li reis Marsilie out sun cunseill finet:
Sin apelat Clarin (. . .) de Balaguet,
Estamarin e Eudropin, sun per,
E Priamun e Guarlan le barbet,   65
E Machiner e sun uncle, Maheu,
E Joüner e Malbien d'ultremer,
E Blancandrins, por la raisun cunter.
Des plus feluns dís en ad apelez:
«Seignurs baruns, a Carlemagnes irez;   70
Il est al siege a Cordres la citet.
Branches d'olives en voz mains porterez,
Ço senefiet pais e humilitet.
Par voz saveirs sem puez acorder,
Jo vos durrai or e argent asez,   75
Teres e fiéz tant cum vos en vuldrez.»
Dient paien: «De ço avun nus asez!»   AOI.

6

Li reis Marsilie out finet sun cunseill;
Dist a ses humes: «Seignurs, vos en ireiz;
Branches d'olive en voz mains portereiz,   80
Si me direz a Carlemagne, le rei,
Pur le soen Deu qu'il ait m(er)ercit de mei.
Ja einz ne verrat passer cest premer meis,
Que jel sivrai od mil de mes fedeilz,
Si recevrai la chrestiene lei,   85
[S]erai ses hom par amur e par feid;
S'il voelt ostages, il en avrat par veir.»
Dist Blancandrins: «Mult bon plait en avreiz.»   AOI.

7

Dis blanches mules fist amener Marsilies,
Que li tramist li reis de Suatilie;   90

Li frein sunt d'or, les seles d'argent mises.
Cil sunt muntez ki le message firent,
Enz en lur mains portent branches d'olive.
Vindrent a Charles ki France ad en baillie:
Nes poet guarder que alques ne l'engignent.   AOI.   95

8

Li empereres se fait e balz e liez,
Cordres ad prise e les murs peceiez,
Od ses cadables les turs en abatied.
Mult grant eschech en unt si chevaler
D'or e d argent e de guarnemenz chers.   100
En la citet nen ad remes paien,
Ne seit ocis, u devient chrestien.
Li empereres est en un grant verger,
Ensembl od lui Rollant et oliver
Sansun li dux e anseis li fiers   105
Gefreid d anjou le rei gunfanuner,
E si i furent e gerin et gerers,
La u cist furent, des altres i out bien:
De dulce france i ad quinze milliers.
Sur palies blancs siedent cil cevaler,   110
As tables juent pur els esbaneier
E as eschecs li plus saive e li veill,
E escremissent cil bacheler leger.
Desuz un pin delez un eglenter
Un faldestoed i unt fait tut d or mer,   115
La siet li reis, ki dulce france tient.
Blanche ad la barbe e tut flurit le chef,
Gent ad le cors e le cuntenant fier,
S'est, kil demandet, ne l estoet enseigner.
E li message descendirent a pied,   120
Sil saluerent par amur e par bien.

9

Blancandrins ad tut premereins parled,
E dist al rei: «Salvez seiez de Deu
Le glorius, que de[v]u[n]s aürer!
Iço vus mandet reis Marsilies, li bers: 125
Enquis ad mult la lei de salvetez;
De sun aveir vos voelt asez duner,
Urs e leuns e veltres enchaignez,

Set cenz cameilz e mil hosturs muez,
D'or e d'argent .IIII. cenz muls trussez,   130
Cinquante care, que carier en ferez;
Tant i avrat de besanz esmerez
Dunt bien purrez voz soldeiers luer.
En cest païs avez estet asez;
En France, ad Ais, devez bien repairer;   135
La vos sivrat, ço dit mis avoez.»
Li empereres tent (. . .) ses mains vers Deu,
Baisset sun chef, si cumencet a penser.   AOI.

10

Li empereres en tint sun chef enclin;
De sa parole ne fut mie hastifs: 140
Sa custume est qu'il parolet a leisír.
Quant se redrecet, mult par out fier lu vis;
Dist as messages: «Vus avez mult ben dit.
Li reis Marsilies est mult mis enemis.
De cez paroles que vos avez ci dit,   145
En quel mesure en purrai estre fiz?»
—«Voet par hostages,» ço dist li Sarrazins,
«Dunt vos avrez ú dis ú quinze ú vint.
Pa[r] num de ocire i metrai un mien filz,
E sin avrez, ço quid, de plus gentilz.   150
Quant vus serez el palais seignurill,
A la grant feste seint Michel del Peril,
Mis avoez la vos sivrat, ço dit;
Enz en voz bainz que Deus pur vos i fist,
La vuldrat il chrestiens devenir.»   155
Charles respunt: «Uncore purrat guarir.»   AOI.

11

Bels fut li vespres e li soleilz fut cler.
Les dis mulez fait Char[l]es establer,
El grant verger fait li reis tendre un tref,
Les dis messages ad fait enz hosteler;   160
.XII. serjanz les unt ben cunreez.
La noit demurent tresque vint al jur cler.
Li empereres est par matin levet;
Messe e matines ad li reis escultet.
Desuz un pin en est li reis alez,   165
Ses baruns mandet pur sun cunseill finer:
Par cels de France voelt il del tut errer.   AOI.

12

Li emper[er]es s'en vait desuz un pin.
Ses baruns mandet pur sun cunseill fenir:
Le duc Oger, (e) l'arcevesque Turpin,   170
Richard li Vélz e sun nev[old] Henri,
E de Gascuigne li proz quens Acelin
Tedbald de Reins e Milun, sun cusin;
E si i furent e Gerers e Gerin;
Ensembl' od els li quens Rollant i vint,   175
E Oliver, li proz e li gentilz;
Des Francs de France en i ad plus de mil.
Guenes i vint, ki la traïsun fist.
Des ore cumencet le cunseill que mal prist.   AOI.

13

«Seignurs barons,» dist li emperere Carles,   180
«Li reis Marsilie m'ad tramis ses messages;
De sun aveir me voelt duner grant masse,
Urs e leuns e veltres caeignables,
Set cenz cameilz e mil hosturs muables,
Quatre cenz mulz cargez del ór d'Arabe,   185
Avoec iço plus de cinquante care;
Mais il me mandet que en France m'en alge:
Il me sivrat ad Aís, a mun estage,
Si recevrat la nostre lei plus salve;
Chrestiens ert, de mei tendrat ses marches;   190
Mais jo ne sai quels en est sis curages.»
Dient Franceis: «Il nus i cuvent guarde!»   AOI.

14

Li empereres out sa raisun fenie.
Li quens Rollant, ki ne l'otriet mie,
En piez se drecet, si li vint cuntredire.   195
Il dist al rei: «Ja mar crerez Marsilie.
Set anz [ad] pleins, que en Espaigne venimes;
Jo vos cunquis e Noples e Commibles,
Pris ai Valterne e la tere de Pine
E Balasgued e Tuele e Sezilie.   200
Li reis Marsilie i fist mult que traïtre:
De ses pai[ens il vus] enveiat quinze,
Cha(n)cuns portout une branche d'olive;
Nuncerent vos cez paroles meïsme.

A vos Franceis un cunseill en presistes: 205
Loerent vos alques de legerie.
Dous de voz cuntes al paien tramesistes,
L'un fut Basan e li altres Basilies;
Les chef en prist es puis desuz Haltilie.
Faites la guer[re] cum vos l'avez enprise: 210
En Sarraguce menez vostre ost banie,
Metez le sege a tute vostre vie,
Si vengez cels que li fels fist ocire!»   AOI.

15

Li empe[re]re en tint sun chef enbrunc,
Si duist sa barbe, afaitad sun gernun,   215
Ne ben ne mal ne respunt sun nevuld.
Franceis se taisent ne mais que Guenelun,
En piez se drecet, si vint devant Carlun,
Mult fierement cumencet sa raisun,
E dist al rei: «Ja mar crerez bricun,   220
Ne mei ne altre, se de vostre prod nun.
Quant ço vos mandet li reis Marsiliun,
Qu'il devendrat jointes ses mains tis hom,
E tute Espaigne tendrat par vostre dun,
Puis recevrat la lei que nus tenum,   225
Ki ço vos lodet que cest plait degetuns,
Ne li chalt, sire, de quel mort nus muriuns.
Cunseill d orguill n'est dreiz que a plus munt,
Laissun les fols, as sages nus tenuns.»   AOI.

16

Apres iço i est Neimes venud;   230
Meillor vassal n'aveit en la curt nul,
E dist al rei: «Ben l'avez entendud,
Guenes li quens ço vus ad respondud,
Saveir i ad, mais qu'il seit entendud.
Li reis Marsilie est de guere vencud: 235
Vos li avez tuz ses castels toluz,
Od voz caables avez fruiset ses murs,
Ses citez arses e ses humes vencuz;
Quant il vos mandet, qu'aiez mercit de lui,
Pecchet fereit, ki dunc li fesist plus,   240
U par ostage vos (en) voelt faire soürs;
Ceste grant guerre ne deit munter a plus.»
Dient Franceis: «Ben ad parlet li dux.»   AOI.

17

—«Seignurs baruns, qui i enveieruns
En Sarraguce al rei Marsiliuns?»   245
Respunt dux Neimes: «Jo irai par vostre dun!
Livrez m'en ore le guant e le bastun.»
Respunt li reis: «Vos estes saives hom;
Par ceste barbe e par cest men gernun,
Vos n'irez pas uan de mei si luign.   250
Alez sedeir, quant nuls ne vos sumunt.»

18

—«Seignurs baruns, qui i purruns enveier
Al Sarrazin ki Sarraguce tient?»
Respunt Rollant: «Jo i puis aler mult ben!»
—«Nu ferez certes!» dist li quens Oliver;   255
«Vostre curages est mult pesmes e fiers;
Jo me crendreie, que vos vos meslisez.
Se li reis voelt, jo i puis aler ben.»
Respunt li reis: «Ambdui vos en taisez!
Ne vos ne il n'i porterez les piez.   260
Par ceste barbe que veez [blancheier],
Li duze per mar i serunt jugez!»
Franceis se taisent: as les vus aquisez.

19

Turpins de Reins en est levet del renc,
E dist al rei: «Laisez ester voz Francs!   265
En cest païs avez estet set anz;
Mult unt oüd e peines e ahans.
Dunez m'en, sire, le bastun e le guant,
E jo irai al Sarazin en Espaigne,
Sin vois vedeir alques de sun semblant.»   270
Li empereres respunt par maltalant:
«Alez sedeir desur cel palie blanc!
N'en parlez mais, se jo nel vos cumant!»   AOI.

20

—«Francs chevalers,» dist li emperere Carles,
«Car m'eslisez un barun de ma marche,   275
Qu'a Marsiliun me portast mun message.»
Ço dist Rollant: «Ço ert Guenes, mis parastre.»

Dient Franceis: «Car il le poet ben faire;
Se lui lessez, n'i trametrez plus saive.»
E li quens Guenes en fut mult anguisables;   280
De sun col getet ses grandes pels de martre,
E est remes en sun blialt de palie.
Vairs out [les oilz] e mult fier lu visage,
Gent out le cors e les costez out larges;
Tant par fut bels tuit si per l'en esguardent.   285
Dist a Rollant: «Tut fol, pur quei t'esrages?
Ço set hom ben que jo sui tis parastres;
Si as juget qu'a Marsiliun en alge!
Se Deus ço dunet que jo de la repaire,
Jo t'en muvra[i] un si grant contr[a]ire   290
Ki durerat a trestut tun edage.»
Respunt Rollant: «Orgoill ói e folage.
Ço set hom ben, n'ai cure de manace;
Mai[s] saives hom, il deit faire message:
Si li reis voelt, prez sui por vus le face.»   295

21

Guenes respunt: «Pur mei n'iras tu mie!   AOI.
Tu n'ies mes hom ne jo ne sui tis sire.
Carles comandet que face sun servise:
En Sarraguce en irai a Marsilie;
Einz i f[e]rai un poi de [le]gerie,   300
Que jo n'esclair ceste meie grant ire.»
Quant l'ot Rollant, si cumençat a rire.   AOI.

22

Quant ço veit Guenes que ore s'en rit Rollant,
Dunc ad tel doel pur poi d'ire ne fent,
A ben petit que il ne pert le sens;   305
E dit al cunte: «Jo ne vus aim nient;
Sur mei avez turnet fals jugement.
Dreiz empere, veiz me ci en present,
Ademplir voeill vostre comandement.»

23

«En Sarraguce sai ben, [qu']aler m'estoet.   AOI.   310
Hom ki la vait, repairer ne s'en poet.
Ensurquetut si ai jo vostre soer,
Sin ai un filz, ja plus bels n'en estoet:

Ço est Baldewin,» ço dit, «ki ert prozdoem.
A lui lais jo mes honurs e mes fieus. 315
Gua[r]dez le ben, ja nel verrai des oilz.»
Carles respunt: «trop avez tendre coer.
Puisquel comant, aler vus en estoet.»

24

Ço dist li reis: «Guenes venez avant.   AOI.
Si recevez le bastun e lu guant. 320
Oït l'avez, sur vos le jugent Franc.»
—«Sire,» dist Guenes, «ço ad tut fait Rollant!
Ne l'amerai a trestut mun vivant,
Ne Oliver, por ço qu'il est si cumpainz;
Li duze per, por [ço] qu'il l'aiment tant, 325
Desfi les ci, sire, vostre veiant.»
Ço dist li reis: «Trop avez maltalant.
Or irez vos certes, quant jol cumant.»
—«Jo i puis aler, mais n'i avrai guarant: AOI.
Nu l'out Basilies ne sis freres Basant.» 330

25

Li empereres li tent sun guant le destre;
Mais li quens Guenes iloec ne volsist estre:
Quant le dut prendre, si li caït a tere.
Dient Franceis: «Deus! que purrat ço estre?
De cest message nos avendrat grant perte.» 335
—«Seignurs» dist Guenes, «vos en orrez noveles!»

26

—«Sire,» dist Guenes, «dunez mei le cungied;
Quant aler dei, n'i ai plus que targer.»
Ço dist li reis: «Al Jhesu e al mien!»
De sa main destre l'ad asols e seignet, 340
Puis li livrat le bastun e le bref.

27

Guenes li quens s'en vait a sun ostel,
De guarnemenz se prent a cunreer,
De ses meillors que il pout recuvrer:
Esperuns d'or ad en ses piez fermez, 345
Ceint Murglies, s'espee, a sun costed;

En Tachebrun, sun destrer est munted;
L'estreu li tint sun uncle Guinemer.
La veïsez tant chevaler plorer,
Ki tuit li dient «Tant mare fustes, ber!   350
En (la) cort al rei mult i avez ested,
Noble vassal vos i solt hom clamer.
Ki ço jugat, que doüsez aler
Par Charlemagne n'er(cs) guariz ne tensez.
Li quens Rollant nel se doüst penser,   355
Que estrait estes de mult grant pared.»
Enpres li dient: «Sire, car nos menez!»
Ço respunt Guenes: «Ne placet Damnedeu!
Mielz est que sul moerge que tant bon chevaler.
En dulce France, seignurs, vos en irez: 360
De meie part ma muiller saluez,
E Pinabel, mun ami e mun per,
E Baldewin, mun filz que vos savez,
E lui aidez e pur seignur le tenez.»
Entret en sa veie, si s'est achiminez.   AOI.   365

                    28
Guenes chevalchet suz une olive halte,
Asemblet s'est as sarrazins messag[es].
Mais Blancandrins ki envers lu s'atarget;
Par grant saveir parolet li uns a l'altre.
Dist Blancandrins: «Merveilus hom est Charles,   370
Ki cunquist Puille e trestute Calabre;
Vers Engletere passat il la mer salse,
Ad oes seint Perre en cunquist le chevage:
Que nus requert ça en la nostre marche?»
Guenes respunt: «Itels est sis curages,   375
Jamais n'ert hume ki encuntre lui vaille.»   AOI.

                    29
Dist Blancandrins: «Francs sunt mult gentilz home;
Mult grant mal funt e [cil] duc e cil cunte
A lur seignur, ki tel cunseill li dunent:
Lui e altrui travaillent, e cunfundent.»   380
Guenes respunt: «Jo ne sai veirs nul hume,
Ne mes Rollant, ki uncore en avrat hunte.
Er matin sedeit li emperere suz l'umbre;
Vint i ses nies, out vestue sa brunie,

E out predet dejuste Carcasonie;   385
En sa main tint une vermeille pume:
«Tenez bel sire,» dist Rollant a sun uncle,
«De trestuz reis vos present les curunes.»
Li soens orgoilz le devreit ben cunfundre,
Kar chascun jur de mort [il] s'abandunet.   390
Seit, ki l'ociet, tute pais puis avriúmes.»   AOI.

30

Dist Blancandrins: «Mult est pesmes Rollant,
Ki tute gent voelt faire recreant,
E tutes teres met en chalengement!
Par quele gent quiet il espleiter tant?»   395
Guenes respunt: «Par la franceise gent.
Il l'a[i]ment tant ne li faldrunt nient;
Or e argent lur met tant en present,
Muls e destrers, e palies e guarnemenz;
L'emperere meïsmes ad tut a sun talent.   400
Cunquerrat li les teres d'ici qu'en Orient.»   AOI.

31

Tant chevalcherent Guenes e Blancandrins,
Que l'un a l'altre la sue feit plevit,
Que il querreient, que Rollant fust ocis.
Tant chevalcherent e veies e chemins,   405
Que en Sarraguce descendent suz un if.
Un faldestoet out suz l'umbre d'un pin;
Esvolupet fut d'un palie alexandrin:
La fut li reis ki tute Espaigne tint;
Tut entur lui vint milie Sarrazins.   410
N'i ad celoi ki mot sunt ne mot tint,
Pur les nuveles qu'il vuldreient oïr.
Atant as vos Guenes e Blanchandrins.

32

Blancandrins vint devant l'empereür;
Par le puig[n] tint le cunte Guenelun,   415
E dist al rei: «Salvez seiez de Mahun
E d'Apollin, qui seintes leis tenuns!
Vostre message fesime[s] a Charlun.
Ambes ses mains en levat cuntre munt,
Loat sun Deu, ne fist altre respuns.   420

Ci vos enveiet un sun noble barun,
Ki est de France, si est mult riches hom:
Par lui orrez si avrez pais u nun.»
Respunt Marsilie: «Or diet, nus l'orrum!»   AOI.

33

Mais li quens Guenes se fut ben purpenset.   425
Par grant saver cumencet a parler
Cume celui ki ben faire le set,
E dist al rei: «Salvez seiez de Deu
Li Glorius, qui devum aürer!
Iço vus mandet Carlemagnes, li ber,   430
Que recevez seinte chrestientet;
Demi Espaigne vos voelt en fiu duner.
Se cest acorde ne vulez otrier,
Pris e liez serez par poested;
Al siege ad Ais en serez amenet,   435
Par jugement serez iloec finet;
La murrez vus a hunte e a viltet.»
Li reis Marsilies en fut mult esfreed.
Un algier tint, ki d'or fut enpenet,
Ferir l'en volt, se n'en fust desturnet.   AOI.   440

34

Li reis Marsilies ad la culur muee;
De sun algeir ad la hanste crollee.
Quant le vit Guenes, mist la main a l'espee,
Cuntre dous deie l'ad del furrer getee,
Si li ad dit: «Mult estes bele e clere!   445
Tant vus avrai en curt a rei portee!
Ja nel dirat de France li emperere,
Que suls i moerge en l'estrange cuntree,
Einz vos avrunt li meillor comperee.»
Dient paien: «Desfaimes la mellee!»   450

35

Tuit li preierent li meillor Sarrazin,
Qu'el faldestoed s'es[t] Marsilies asis.
Dist l'algalifes: «Mal nos avez baillit,
Que li Franceis asmastes a ferir;
Vos le doüssez esculter e oïr.»   455
—«Sire,» dist Guenes, «mei l'avent a suffrir;

Jo ne lerreie, por l'or que Deus fist
Ne por tut l'aveir, ki seit en cest païs,
Que jo ne li die, se tant ai de leisir,
Que Charles li mandet, li reis poesteïfs,   460
Par mei li mandet, sun mortel enemi.»
Afublez est d'un mantel sabelin,
Ki fut cuvert d'une palie alexandrin.
Getet le a tere, sil receit Blancandrin;
Mais de s'espee ne volt mie guerpir;   465
En sun puign destre par l'orie punt la tint.
Dient paien: «Noble baron ad ci!»   AOI.

36

Envers le rei s'est Guenes aproismet,
Si li ad dit: «A tort vos curuciez,
Quar ço vos mandet Carles, ki France tient,   470
Que recevez la lei de chrestiens;
Demi Espaigne vus durat il en fiet.
L'altre meitet avrat Rollant, sis nies:
Mulz orguillos parçuner i avrez!
Si ceste acorde ne volez otrier,   475
En Sarraguce vus vendrat aseger;
Par poestet serez pris e liez;
Menet serez . . . [tut] dreit ad Ais le siet:
Vus n'i avrez palefreid ne destrer,
Ne mul ne mule que puissez chevalcher;   480
Getet serez sur un malvais sumer.
Par jugement iloec perdrez le chef.
Nostre emperere vus enveiet cest bref.»
El destre poign al paien l'ad liv(e)ret.

37

Marsilies fut esculurez de l'ire;   485
Freint le seel, getet en ad la cire,
Guardet al bref, vit la raisun escrite:
«Carle me mandet, ki France ad en baillie,
Que me remembre de la dolur e (de) l'ire,
Ço est de Basan e de sun frere Basilie,   490
Dunt pris les chefs as puis de Haltoíe;
Se de mun cors voeil aquiter la vie,
Dunc li envei mun uncle, l'algalife;
Altrement ne m'amerat il mie.»

Apres parlat ses filz envers Marsilies,   495
E dist al rei: «Guenes ad dit folie;
Tant ad erret nen est dreiz que plus vivet.
Livrez le mei, jo en ferai la justise.»
Quant l'oït Guenes, l'espee en ad branlie;
Vait s'apuier suz le pin a la tige.   500

38

Enz el verger s'en est alez li reis,
Ses meillors humes enmeinet ensembl'od sei:
E Blancandrins i vint, al canud peil,
E Jurfaret, ki est ses filz e ses heirs,
E l'algalifes, sun uncle e sis fedeilz.   505
Dist Blancandrins: «Apelez le Franceis,
De nostre prod m'ad plevie sa feid.»
Ço dist li reis: «E vos l'i ameneiz.»
E Guenes (l')ad pris par la main destre ad deiz,
Enz el verger l'en meinet josqu'al rei.   510
La purparolent la traïson seinz dreit.   AOI.

39

«Bel sire Guenes,» ço li ad dit Marsilie,
«Jo vos ai fait alques de legerie,
Quant por ferir vus demustrai grant ire.
Guaz vos en dreit par cez pels sabelines;   515
Melz en valt l'or que ne funt cinc cenz livres:
Einz demain noit en iert bele l'amendise.»
Guenes respunt: «Jo nel desotrei mie.
Deus se lui plaist, a bien le vos mercie!»   AOI.

40

Ço dist Marsilies: «Guenes par veir sacez,   520
En talant ai que mult vos voeill amer,
De Carlemagne vos voeill oïr parler.
Il est mult vielz, si ad sun tens uset;
Men escient dous cenz anz ad passet.
Par tantes teres ad sun cors demened,   525
Tanz [colps] ad pris sur sun escut bucler,
Tanz riches reis cunduit a mendisted:
Quant ert il mais recreanz d'osteier?»
Guenes respunt: «Carles n'est mie tels.
N'est hom kil veit e conuistre le set   530

Que ço ne diet que l'emperere est ber.
Tant nel vos sai ne preiser ne loer
Que plus n'i ad d'onur e de bontet.
Sa grant valor, kil purreit acunter?
De tel barnage l'ad Deus enluminet,   535
Meilz voelt murir que guerpir sun barnet.»

41

Dist li paiens: «Mult me puis merveiller
De Carlemagne, ki est canuz e vielz!
Men escientre dous cenz anz ad e mielz.
Par tantes teres ad sun cors traveillet,   540
Tanz colz ad pris de lances e d'espiet,
Tanz riches reis cunduiz a mendistiet:
Quant ert il mais recreanz d'osteier?»
—«Ço n'iert,» dist Guenes: «tant cum vivet sis niés:
N'at tel vassal suz la cape del ciel.   545
Mult par est proz sis cumpainz Oliver.
Les .XII. pers, que Carles ad tant chers,
Funt les enguardes a .XX. milie chevalers.
Soürs est Carles, que nuls home ne crent.»   AOI.

42

Dist li Sarrazins: «Merveille en ai grant   550
De Carlemagne, ki est canuz e blancs!
Mien escientre plus ad de .II.C. anz.
Par tantes teres est alet cunquerant,
Tanz colps ad pris de bons espiez trenchanz,
Tanz riches reis morz e vencuz en champ: 555
Quant ier il mais d'osteier recreant?»
—«Ço n'iert,» dist Guenes, «tant cum vivet Rollant:
N'ad tel vassal d'ici qu en Orient.
Mult par est proz Oliver, sis cumpainz;
Li .XII. per, que Carles aimet tant,   560
Funt les enguardes a .XX. milie de Francs,
Soürs est Carlles, ne (cre) crent hume vivant.»   AOI.

43

—«Bel sire Guenes» dist marsilies li reis,
«Jo ai tel gent, plus bele ne verreiz;
Quarte cenz milie chevalers puis aveir.   565

Puis m'en cumbatre a Carlles e a Franceis?»
Guenes respunt: «Ne vus a ceste feiz!
De voz paiens mult grant perte i avreiz.
Lessez (la) folie, tenez vos al saveir.
L'empereür tant li dunez aveir,   570
N'i ait Franceis ki tot ne s'en merveilt.
Par .XX. hostages que li enveiereiz
En dulce France s'en repairerat li reis;
Sa rereguarde lerrat derere sei:
Iert i sis nies, li quens Rollant, (. . .) ço crei,   575
E Oliver, li proz e li curteis.
Mort sunt li cunte, se est ki mei en creit.
Carlles verrat sun grant orguill cadeir;
N'avrat talent, que ja mais vus guerreit.»   AOI.

                          44
—«Bel sire Guenes,[» ço dist li reis Marsilies,]   580
«Cum faitement purrai Rollant ocire?»
Guenes respont: «Ço vos sai jo ben dire.
Li reis serat as meillors porz de Sizer;
Sa rereguarde avrat detres sei mise;
Iert i sis nies, li quens Rollant, li riches,   585
E Oliver, en qui il tant se fiet;
.XX. milie Francs unt en lur cumpaignie.
De voz paiens lur enveiez .C. milie:
Une bataille lur i rendent cil primes;
La gent de France iert blecee e blesmie;   590
Nel di por ço, des voz iert la martirie.
Altre bataille lur livrez de meïsme:
De quel que seit Rollant n'estuertrat mie.
Dunc avrez faite gente chevalerie;
N'avrez mais guere en tute vostre vie.»   AOI.   595

                          45
—«Chi purreit faire, que Rollant i fust mort,
Dunc perdreit Carles le destre braz del cors,
Si remeindreient les merveilluses óz;
N'asemblereit jamais Carles si grant esforz;
Tere Major remeindreit en repos.»   600
Quan l'ot Marsilie, si l'ad baiset el col,
Puis si cumencet a venir ses tresors.   AOI.

46

Ço dist Marsilies: «Qu'en parlereient il plus?
Cunseill n'est proz dunt hume n'est sevus.
La traïsun me jurrez de Rollant si illi est.»   605
Ço respunt Guenes: «Issi seit cum vos plaist!»
Sur les reliques de s'espee Murgleis,
La traïsun jurat, e si s'en est forsfait.   AOI.

47

Un faldestoed i out d'un olifant;
Marsilies fait porter un livre avant: 610
La lei i fut Mahum e Tervagan.
Ço ad juret li Sarrazins espans:
Se en rereguarde troevet le cors Rollant,
Cumbatrat sei a trestute sa gent,
E, se il poet, murrat i veirement.   615
Guenes respunt: «Ben seit vostre comant!»   AOI.

48

A tant i vint uns paiens, Valdabruns:
Icil en vait al rei Marsiliun;
Cler en riant l'ad dit a Guenelun:
«Tenez m'espee, meillur n'en at nuls hom;   620
Entre les helz ad plus de mil manguns.
Par amistiez, bel sire, la vos duins,
Que (v)[n]os aidez de Rollant le barun,
Qu'en rereguarde trover le poüsum.»
—«Ben serat fait,» li quens Guenes respunt.   625
Puis se baiserent es vis e es mentuns.

49

Apres i vint un paien, Climorins.
Cler en riant a Guenelun l'ad dit:
«Tenez mun helme, unches meillor ne vi.
Si nos aidez de Rollant li marchis,   630
Par quel mesure le poüssum hunir.»
—«Ben serat fait,» Guenes respundit.
Puis se baiserent es buches e es vis.   AOI.

50

A tant i vint la reine Bramimunde.
«Jo vos aim mult, sire,» dist ele al cunte,   635
«Car mult vos priset mi sire e tuit si hume.
A vostre femme enveierai dous nusches;
Bien i ad or, matices e jacunces:
Eles valent mielz que tut l'aveir de Rume,
Vostre emperere si bones n'en out unches.»   640
Il les ad prises, en sa hoese les butet.   AOI.

51

Li reis apelet Malduit sun tresorer:
«L'aveir Carlun est il apareillez?»
E cil respunt: «Oïl, sire, asez bien:
.VII.C. cameilz, d'or e argent cargiez,   645
E .XX. hostages, des plus gentilz desuz cel.»   AOI.

52

Marsilies tint Guen[elun] par l'espalle;
Si li ad dit: «Mult par ies ber e sage.
Par cele lei que vos tenez plus salve,
Guardez de nos ne turnez le curage.   650
De mun aveir vos voeill dunner grant masse:
.X. muls cargez del plus fin or d'Arabe;
Jamais n'iert an, altretel ne vos face.
Tenez les clefs de ceste citet large,
Le grant aveir en presentez al rei Carles,   655
Pois me jugez Rollant a rereguarde.
Sel pois trover a port ne a passage,
Liverrai lui une mortel bataille.»
Guenes respunt: «Mei est vis que trop targe!»
Pois est munted, entret en sun veiage.   AOI.   660

53

Li empereres aproismet sun repaire.
Venuz en est a la citet de Galne.
Li quens Rollant il l'ad e prise e fraite;
Puis icel jur en fut cent anz deserte.
De Guenelun atent li reis nuveles,   665
E le treüd d'Espaigne, la grant tere.
Par main en l'albe, si cum li jurz esclairet,
Guenes li quens est venuz as herberges.   AOI.

54

Li empereres est par matin levet;
Messe e matines ad li reis escultet.   670
Sur l'erbe verte estut devant sun tref.
Rollant i fut e Oliver li ber,
Neimes li dux e des altres asez.
Guenes i vint, li fels, li parjurez.
Par grant veisdie cumencet a parler,   675
E dist al rei: «Salvez seiez de Deu!
De Sarraguce ci vos aport les clefs;
Mult grant aveir vos en faz amener,
E .XX. hostages; faites les ben guarder!
E si vos mandet reis Marsilies li ber,   680
De l'algalifes nel devez pas blasmer,
Kar a mes oilz vi .IIII.C. milie armez,
Halbers vestuz, alquanz healmes fermez,
Ceintes espees as punz d'or neielez,
Ki l'en cunduistrent tresqu'en la mer: 685
De Marcilie s'en fuient por la chrestientet,
Que il ne voelent ne tenir ne guarder.
Einz qu'il oüssent .IIII. liues siglet,
Sis aquillit e tempeste e ored:
La sunt neiez, jamais nes en verrez;   690
Se il fust vif, jo l'oüsse amenet.
Del rei paien, sire, par veir creez,
Ja ne verrez cest premer meis passet
Qu'il vos sivrat en France le regnet,
Si recevrat la lei que vos tenez,   695
Jointes ses mains iert vostre comandet;
De vos tendrat Espaigne le regnet.»
Ço dist li reis: «Graciet en seit Deus!
Ben l'avez fait, mult grant prod i avrez.»
Par mi cel ost funt mil grailles suner;   700
Franc desherbergent, funt lur sumers trosser:
Vers dulce France tuit sunt achiminez.   AOI.

55

Carles li magnes ad Espaigne guastede
Les castels pris, (. . .) les citez violees.
Ço dit li reis que sa guere out finee.   705
Vers dulce France chevalchet l'emperere.
Li quens Rollant ad l'enseigne fermee
En sur un tertre cuntre le ciel levee.

Franc se herbergent par tute la cuntree.
Paien chevalchent par cez greignurs valees,   710
Halbercs vestuz e tres bien fermeez
Healmes lacez e ceintes lur espees,
Escuz as cols e lances adubees.
En un bruill par sum les puis remestrent,
.IIII.C. milie atendent l'ajurnee.   715
Deus! quel dulur que li Franceis nel sevent!   AOI.

56

Tresvait le jur, la noit est aserie.
Carles se dort, li empereres riches.
Sunjat qu'il eret al greignurs porz de Sizer,
Entre ses poinz teneit sa hanste fraisnine.   720
Guenes li quens l'ad sur lui saisie;
Par tel air l'at estrussee e brandie,
Qu'envers le cel en volent les escicles.
Carles se dort, qu'il ne s'esveillet mie.

57

Apres iceste altre avisiun sunjat: 725
Qu'il en France ert, a sa capele, ad Ais,
El destre braz li morst uns vers si mals.
Devers Ardene vit venir uns leuparz,
Sun cors demenie mult fierement asalt.
D'enz de la sale uns veltres avalat,   730
Que vint a Carles le galops e les salz,
La destre oreille al premer uer trenchat,
Ireement se cumbat al lepart.
Dient Franceis, que grant bataille i ad;
Il ne sevent, liquels d'els la veintrat.   735
Carles se dort, mie ne s'esveillat.   AOI.

58

Tresvait la noit, e apert la clere albe.
Par mi cel host suvent e menu reguarded:.
Li empereres mult fierement chevalchet.
«Seignurs barons,» dist li empere Carles,   740
«Veez les porz e les destreiz passages:
Kar me jugez, ki ert en la rereguarde.»
Guenes respunt: «Rollant cist miens fillastre:
N'avez baron de si grant vasselage.»

Quant l'ot li reis, fierement le reguardet,   745
Si li ad dit: «Vos estes vifs diables.
El cors vos est entree mortel rage.
E ki serat devant mei en l'ansguarde?»
Guenes respunt: «Oger de Denemarche:
N'avez barun, ki mielz de lui la facet.»   750

59

Li quens Rollant quant il s'oït juger,   AOI.
Dunc ad parled a lei de chevaler:
«Sire parastre, mult vos dei aveir cher:
La rereguarde avez sur mei jugiet.
N'i perdrat Carles, li reis ki France tient,   755
Men escientre palefreid ne destrer,
Ne mul ne mule que deiet chevalcher,
Ne n'i perdrat ne runcin ne sumer,
Que as espees ne seit einz eslegiet.»
Guenes respunt: «Veir dites, jol sai bien.»   AOI.   760

60

Quant ot Rollant, qu'il ert en la rereguarde,
Ireement parlat a sun parastre:
«Ahi! culvert, malvais hom de put aire,
Qui[d]ás, le guant me caïst en la place,
Cume fist a tei le bastun devant Carle?»   AOI.   765

61

—«Dreiz emperere,» dist Rollant le barun,
«Dunez mei l'arc, que vos tenez el poign.
Men escientre nel me reproverunt
Que il me chedet, cum fist a Guenelun
De sa main destre, quant reçut le bastun.»   770
Li empereres en tint sun chef enbrunc,
Si duist sa barbe, e detoerst sun gernun;
Ne poet muer que des oilz ne plurt.

62

Anpres iço i est Neimes venud:
Meillor vassal n'out en la curt de lui;   775
E dist al rei: «Ben l'avez entendut;
Li quens Rollant, il est mult irascut.

La rereguarde est jugee (. . .) sur lui:
N'avez baron ki jamais la remut.
Dunez li l'arc que vos avez tendut,   780
Si li truvez ki tres bien li aiut!»
Li reis li dunet, e Rollant l'a reçut.

63

Li empereres apelet ses nies Rollant:
«Bel sire nies, or savez veirement,
Demi mun host vos lerrai en present.   785
Retenez les, ço est vostre salvement.»
Ço dit li quens: «Jo n'en ferai nient;
Deus me cunfunde, se la geste en desment!
.XX. milie Francs retendrai ben vaillanz.
Passez les porz trestut soürement: 790
Ja mar crendrez nul hume a mun vivant!»

64

Li quens Rollant est muntet el destrer.   AOI.
Cuntre lui vient sis cumpainz Oliver;
Vint i Gerins e li proz quens Gerers,
E vint i Otes, si i vint Berengers,   795
E vint i Astors e Anseïs li veillz;
Vint i Gerart de Rossillon li fiers;
Venuz i est li riches dux Gaifiers.
Dist l'arcevesque: «Jo irai, par mun chef!»
—«E jo od vos,» ço dist li quens Gualters;   800
«Hom sui Rollant, jo ne li dei faillir.»
Entr'e[l]s eslisent .XX. milie chevalers.   AOI.

65

Li quens Rollant Gualter de l'Húm apelet:
«Pernez mil Francs de France, nostre tere,
Si purpernez les deserz e les tertres,   805
Que l'empere nis un des soens n'i perdet.»   AOI.
Respunt gualter: «Pur vos le dei ben faire.»
Od mil Franceis de France, la lur tere,
Gualter desrenget les destreiz e les tertres,
N'en descendrat pur malvaises nuveles,   810
Enceis qu'en seient. VII.C. espees traites.
Reis Almaris, del regne de Belferne
Une bataille lur livrat le jur pesme.

66

Halt sunt li pui e li val tenebrus,
Les roches bises, les destreiz merveillus.   815
Le jur passerent Franceis a grant dulur;
De .XV. lius en ot hom la rimur.
Puis que il venent a la Tere Majur,
Virent Guascuigne, la tere lur seignur.
Dunc le remembret des fius e des honurs,   820
E des pulcele e des gentilz oixurs:
Cel nen i ad ki de pitet ne plurt.
Sur tuz les altres est Carles anguissus:
As porz d'Espaigne ad lesset sun nevold.
Pitet l'en prent, ne poet muer n'en plurt.   AOI.   825

67

Li .XII. per sunt remes en Espaigne.
.XX. milie F(r)rancs unt en lur cumpaigne,
N'en unt poür ne de murir dutance.
Li emperere s'en repairet en France;
Suz sun mantel en fait la cuntenance.   830
Dejuste lui li dux Neimes chevalchet
E dit al rei: «De quei avez pesance?»
Carles respunt: «Tort fait kil me demandet!
Si grant doel ai ne puis muer nel pleigne.
Par Guenelun serat destruite France,   835
Enoit m'avint un avisiun d'angele,
Que entre mes puinz me depeçout ma hanste,
Chi ad juget mis nes a (la) rereguarde.
Jo l'ai lesset en une estrange marche!
Deus! se jol pert, ja n'en avrai escange!»   AOI.   840

68

Carles li magnes ne poet muer n'en plurt.
.C. milie Francs pur lui unt grant tendrur,
E de Rollant merveilluse poür.
Guen[e]s li fels en ad fait traïsun:
Del rei paien en ad oüd granz duns,   845
Or e argent, palies e ciclatuns,
Muls e chevals e cameilz e leuns.
Marsilies mandet d'Espaigne les baruns,
Cuntes, vezcuntes e dux e almaçurs,
Les amirafles e les filz as cunturs: 850

.IIII.C. milie en ajustet en .III. jurz.
En Sarraguce fait suner ses taburs;
Mahumet levent en la plus halte tur.
N'i ad paien nel prit e nel aort.
Puis si chevalchent, par mult grant cuntençun,   855
La Tere Certeine e les vals e les munz:
De cels de France virent les gunfanuns.
La rereguarde des .XII. cumpaignuns
Ne lesserat bataille ne lur dunt.

69

Li nies Marsilie, il est venuz avant,   860
Sur un mulet od un bastun tuchant.
Dist a sun uncle belement en riant:
«Bel sire reis, jo vos ai servit tant,
Sin ai oüt e peines e ahans,
Faites batailles e vencues en champ!   865
Dunez m'un feu, ço est le colp de Rollant;
Jo l'ocirai a mun espiet trenchant.
Se Mahumet me voelt estre guarant,
De tute Espaigne aquiterai les pans
Des porz d'Espaigne entresqu'a Durestant.   870
Las serat Carles, si recrerrunt si Franc;
Ja n'avrez mais guere en tut vostre vivant.»
Li reis Marsilie l'en ad dunet le guant.   AOI.

70

Li nies Marsilies tient le guant en sun poign,
Sun uncle apelet de mult fiere raisun: 875
«Bel sire reis, fait m'avez un grant dun.
Eslisez mei .XII. de voz baruns,
Sim cumbatrai as .XII. cumpaignuns.»
Tut premerein l'en respunt Falsaron,
Icil ert frere al rei Marsiliun: 880
«Bel sires nies, e jo e vos [í]irum.
Ceste bataille veirement la ferum:
La rereguarde de la grant host Carlun,
Il est juget que nus les ocirum.»   AOI.

71

Reis Corsalis, il est de l'altre part: 885
Barbarins est e mult de males arz.

Cil ad parlet a lei de bon vassal:
Pur tut l'or Deu ne volt estre cuard [. . .]
As vos poignant Malprimis de Brigant:
Plus curt a piet que ne fait un cheval.   890
Devant Marsilie cil s'escriet mult halt:
«Jo cunduirai mun cors en Rencesvals;
Se truis Rollant, ne lerrai que nel mat!»

72

Uns amurafles i ad de Balaguez:
Cors ad mult gent e le vis fier e cler;   895
Puis que il est sur un cheval muntet,
Mult se fait fiers de ses armes porter;
De vasselage est il ben alosez;
Fust chrestiens, asez oüst barnet.
Devant Marsilie cil en est escriet: 900
«En Rencesvals irai mun cors juer!
Se truis Rollant, de mort serat finet,
E Oliver e tuz les .XII. pers.
Franceis murrunt a doel e a viltiet.
Carles li magnes velz est e redotez: 905
Recreanz ert de sa guerre mener,
Si nus remeindrat Espaigne en quitedet.»
Li reis Marsilie mult l'en ad merciet.   AOI.

73

Uns almaçurs i ad de Moriane;
N'ad plus felun en la tere d'Espaigne.   910
Devant Marsilie ad faite sa vantance:
«En Rencesvals guierai ma cumpaigne,
.XX. milie ad escuz e a lances.
Se trois Rollant, de mort li duins fiance.
Jamais n'ert jor que Carles ne se pleignet.»   AOI.   915

74

D'altre part est Turgis de Turteluse:
Cil est uns quens, si est la citet sue.
De chrestiens voelt faire male vode.
Devant Marsilie as altres si s'ajust,
Ço dist al rei: «Ne vos esmaiez unches!   920
Plus valt Mahum que seint Perre de Rume!
Se lui servez, l'onur del camp ert nostre.

En Rencesvals a Rollant irai juindre,
De mort n'avrat guarantisun pur hume.
Veez m'espee, ki est e bone e lunge: 925
A Durendal jo la metrai encuntre;
Asez orrez, laquele irat desure.
Franceis murrunt, si a nus s'abandunent;
Carles li velz avrat e deol e hunte:
Jamais en tere ne portera curone.»   930

                    75
De l'altre part est Escremiz de Valterne:
Sarrazins est, si est sue la tere.
Devant Marsilie s'escriet en la presse,
«En Rencesvals irai l'orgoill desfaire.
Se trois Rollant, n'en porterat la teste,   935
Ne Oliver, ki les altres cadelet;
Li .XII. per tuit sunt jugez a perdre;
Franceis murrunt e France en ert deserte,
De bons vassals avrat Carles suffraite.»   AOI.

                    76
D'altre part est uns paiens, Esturganz;   940
Estramariz i est, un soens cumpainz:
Cil sunt felun, traïtur suduiant.
Ço dist Marsilie: «Seignurs, venez avant!
En Rencesvals irez as porz passant,
Si aiderez a cunduire ma gent.»   945
E cil respundent: «(Sire,) a vostre comandement!
Nus asaldrum Oliver e Rollant;
Li .XII. per n'avrunt de mort guarant.
Noz espees sunt bones e trenchant;
Nus les feruns vermeilles de chald sanc.   950
Franceis murrunt, Carles en ert dolent.
Tere Majur vos metrum en present.
Venez i, reis, sil verrez veirement:
L'empereor vos metrum en present.»

                    77
Curant i vint Margariz de Sibilie;   955
Cil tient la tere entre[s]qu'as Cazmarine.
Pur sa beltet dames li sunt amies:
Cele nel veit vers lui ne s'esclargisset;

Quant ele le veit, ne poet muer ne riet;
N'i ad paien de tel chevalerie.   960
Vint en la presse, sur les altres s'escriet
E dist al rei: «Ne vos esmaiez mie!
En Rencesvals irai Rollant ocire,
Ne Oliver n'en porterat la vie;
Li .XII. per sunt remes en martirie.   965
Veez m'espee, ki d'or est enheldie:
Si la tramist li amiralz de Primes.
Jo vos plevis qu'en vermeill sanc ert mise.
Franceis murrunt e France en ert hunie;
Carles li velz a la barbe flurie,   970
Jamais n'ert jurn qu'il n'en ait doel e ire.
Jusqu'a un an avrum France saisie;
Gesir porrum el burc de seint Denise.»
Li reis paiens parfundement l'enclinet.   AOI.

78

De l'altre part est Chernubles de Munigre;   975
Jusqu'a la tere si chevoel li balient;
Greignor fais portet par giu, quant il s'enveiset,
Que .IIII. mulez ne funt, quant il sumeient.
Icele tere, ço dit, dun il esteit,
Soleill n'i luist, ne blet n'i poet pas creistre,   980
Pluie n'i chet, rusee n'i adeiset,
Piere n'i ad que tute ne seit neire.
Dient alquanz que diables i meignent.
Ce dist Chernubles: «Ma bone espee ai ceinte;
En Rencesvals jo la teindrai vermeille.   985
Se trois Rollant li proz enmi ma veie,
Se ne l'asaill, dunc ne faz jo que creire,
Si cunquerrai Durendal od la meie.
Franceis murrunt e France en ert deserte.»
A icez moz li .XII. [per] s'alient;   990
Itels .C. milie Sarrazins od els meinent,
Ki de bataille s'argüent,e hasteient:
Vunt s'aduber desuz une sapide.

79

Paien s'adubent des osbercs sarazineis,
Tuit li plusur en sunt (saraguzeis) dublez en treis,   995
Lacent lor elmes mult bons sarraguzeis,

Ceignent espees de l'acer vianeis;
Escuz unt genz, espiez valentineis,
E gunfanuns blancs e blois e vermeilz.
Laissent les mulz e tuz les palefreiz,   1000
Es destrers muntent, si chevalchent estreiz.
Clers fut li jurz e bels fut li soleilz:
N'unt guarnement que tut ne reflambeit.
Sunent mil grailles por ço que plus bel seit:
Granz est la noise, si l'oïrent Franceis.   1005
Dist Oliver: «Sire cumpainz, ce crei,
De Sarrazins purum bataille aveir.»
Respont Rollant: «E! Deus la nus otreit!
Ben devuns ci estre pur nostre rei:
Pur sun seignor deit hom susfrir destreiz   1010
E endurer e granz chalz e granz freiz,
Sin deit hom perdre e del quir e del peil.
Or guart chascuns que granz colps (l')[i] empleit,
Que malvaise cançun de nus chantet ne seit!
Paien unt tort e chrestiens unt dreit;   1015
Malvaise essample n'en serat, ja de mei.»   AOI.

80

Oliver est desur un pui haut muntez,
Guardet su destre par mi un val herbus,
Si veit venir cele gent paienur,
Sin apelat Rollant, sun cumpaignun: 1020
«Devers Espaigne vei venir tel bruur,
Tanz blancs osbercs, tanz elmes flambius!
Icist ferunt nos Franceis grant irur.
Guenes le sout, li fel, li traïtur,
Ki nus jugat devant l'empereür.»   1025
—«Tais Oliver,» li quens Rollant respunt,
«Mis parrastre est, ne voeill que mot en suns.»

81

Oliver est desur un pui muntet;
Or veit il ben d'Espaigne le regnet
E Sarrazins, ki tant sunt asemblez.   1030
Luisent cil elme, ki ad or sunt gemmez,
E cil escuz e cil osbercs safrez
E cil espiez, cil gunfanun fermez.
Sul les escheles ne poet il acunter;

Tant en i ad que mesure n'en set.   1035
E lui meïsme en est mult esguaret.
Cum il einz pout, del pui est avalet,
Vint as Franceis, tut lur ad acuntet.

82

Dist Oliver: «Jo ai paiens veüz:
Unc mais nuls hom en tere n'en vit plus.   1040
Cil devant sunt .C. milie ad escuz
Helmes laciez e blancs osbercs vestuz
Dreites cez hanstes, luisent cil espiet brun.
Bataille avrez, unches mais tel ne fut.
Seignurs Franceis, de Deu aiez vertut!   1045
El camp estez, que ne seium vencuz!»
Dient Franceis: «Dehet ait ki s'en fuit!
Ja pur murir ne vus en faldrat uns.»   AOI.

83

Dist Oliver: «Paien unt grant esforz,
De noz Franceis m'i semblet aveir mult poi!   1050
Cumpaign Rollant, kar sunez vostre corn:
Si l'orrat Carles, si returnerat l'ost.»
Respunt Rollant: «Jo fereie que fols!
En dulce France en perdreie mun los.
Sempres ferrai de Durendal granz colps;   1055
Sanglant en ert li branz entresqu'a l'or.
Felun paien mar i vindrent as porz:
Jo vos plevis, tuz sunt jugez a mort.»   AOI.

84

—«Cumpainz Rollant l'olifan car sunez:
Si l'orrat Carles, ferat l'ost returner,   1060
Succurrat nos li reis od tut sun barnet.»
Respont Rollant: «Ne placet Damnedeu
Que mi parent pur mei seient blasmet
Ne France dulce ja cheet en viltet!
Einz i ferrai de Durendal asez,   1065
Ma bone espee que ai ceint al costet:
Tut en verrez le brant ensanglentet.
Felun paien mar i sunt asemblez:
Jo vos plevis, tuz sunt a mort livrez.»   AOI.

85

—«Cumpainz Rollant, sunez vostre olifan: 1070
Si l'orrat Carles, ki est as porz passant.
Je vos plevis, ja returnerunt Franc.»
—«Ne placet Deu,» ço li respunt Rollant,
«Que ço seit dit de nul hume vivant,
Ne pur paien, que ja seie cornant!   1075
Ja n'en avrunt reproece mi parent!
Quant jo serai en la bataille grant
E jo ferrai e mil colps e .VII. cenz,
De Durendal verrez l'acer sanglent.
Franceis sunt bon, si ferrunt vassalment,   1080
Ja cil d'Espaigne n'avrunt de mort guarant.»

86

Dist Oliver: «D'iço ne sai jo blasme?
Jo ai veüt les Sarrazins d'Espaigne,
Cuverz en sunt li val e les muntaignes
E li lariz e trestutes les plaignes.   1085
Granz sunt les oz de cele gent estrange;
Nus i avum mult petite cumpaigne.»
Respunt Rollant: «Mis talenz en est graigne.
Ne placet Damnedeu ne ses angles
Que ja pur mei perdet sa valur France!   1090
Melz voeill murir que huntage me venget.
Pur ben ferir l'empereere plus nos aimet.»

87

Rollant est proz e Oliver est sage;
Ambedui unt me[r]veillus vasselage.
Puis que il sunt as chevals e as armes,   1095
Ja pur murir n'eschiverunt bataille.
Bon sunt li cunte e lur paroles haltes.
Felun paien par grant irur chevalchent.
Dist Oliver: «Rollant, veez en alques!
Cist nus sunt pres, mais trop nus est loinz Carles.   1100
Vostre olifan, suner vos nel deignastes;
Fust i li reis, n'i oüssum damage.
Guardez amunt devers les porz d'Espaigne:
Veeir poez, dolente est la rereguarde;
Ki ceste fait, jamais n'en ferat altre.»   1105
Respunt Rollant: «Ne dites tel ultrage!

Mal seit del coer ki el piz se cuardet!
Nus remeindrum en estal en la place;
Par nos í ert e li colps e li caples.»   AOI.

88

Quant Rollant veit que la bataille serat,   1110
Plus se fait fiers que leon ne leupart.
Franceis escriet, Oliver apelat:
«Sire cumpainz, amis, nel dire ja!
Li emperere, ki Franceis nos laisat,
Itels .XX. milie en mist a une part   1115
Sun escientre n'en i out un cuard.
Pur sun seignur deit hom susfrir granz mals
E endurer e forz freiz e granz chalz,
Sin deit hom perdre del sanc e de la char.
Fier de [ta] lance e jo de Durendal,   1120
Ma bone espee, que li reis me dunat.
Se jo i moert, dire poet ki l'avrat
(E purrunt dire) que ele fut a noble vassal.»

89

D'altre part est li arcevesques Turpin,
Sun cheval broche e muntet un lariz,   1125
Franceis apelet, un sermun lur ad dit:
«Seignurs baruns, Carles nus laissat ci;
Pur nostre rei devum nus ben murir.
Chrestientet aidez a sustenir!
Bataille avrez, vos en estes tuz fiz,   1130
Kar a voz oilz veez les Sarrazins.
Clamez vos culpes, si preiez Deu mercit!
Asoldrai vos pur voz anmes guarir.
Se vos murez, esterez seinz martirs,
Sieges avrez el greignor pareïs.»   1135
Franceis de[s]cendent, a tere se sunt mis,
E l'arcevesque de Deu les beneïst:
Par penitence les cumandet a ferir.

90

Franceis se drecent, si se metent sur piez.
Ben sunt asols e quites de lur pecchez,   1140
E l'arcevesque de Deu les ad seignez;
Puis sunt muntez sur lur curanz destrers.

Adobez sunt a lei de chevalers
E de bataille sunt tuit apareillez.
Li quens Rollant apelet Oliver: 1145
«Sire cumpainz, mult ben le saviez
Que Guenelun nos ad tuz espiez;
Pris en ad or e aveir e deners.
Li emperere nos devreit ben venger.
Li reis Marsilie de nos ad fait marchet;   1150
Mais as espees l'estuvrat esleger.»   AOI.

91

As porz d'Espaigne en est passet Rollant
Sur Veillantif, sun bun cheval curant.
Portet ses armes, mult li sunt avenanz,
Mais sun espiet vait li bers palmeiant,   1155
Cuntre le ciel vait la mure turnant,
Laciet en su un gunfanun tut blanc;
Les renges li batent josqu'as mains.
Cors ad mult gent, le vis cler e riant.
Sun cumpaignun apres le vait sivant,   1160
E cil de France le cleiment a guarant.
Vers Sarrazins reguardet fierement
E vers Franceis humeles e dulcement,
Si lur ad dit un mot curteisement:
«Seignurs barons, suef pas alez tenant!   1165
Cist paien vont grant martirie querant.
Encoi avrum un eschec bel e gent:
Nuls reis de France n'out unkes si vaillant.»
A cez paroles vunt les oz ajustant.   AOI.

92

Dist Oliver: «N'ai cure de parler.   1170
Vostre olifan ne deignastes suner,
Ne de Carlun mie vos n'en avez.
Il n'en set mot, n'i ad culpes li bers.
Cil ki la sunt ne funt mie a blasmer.
Kar chevalchez a quanque vos puez!   1175
Seignors baruns, el camp vos retenez!
Pur deu vos pri, ben seiez purpensez
De colps ferir, de receivre e (de) duner!
L'enseigne Carle n'i devum ublier.»
A icest mot sunt Franceis escriet.   1180

Ki dunc oïst «Munjoie» demander,
De vasselage li poüst remembrer.
Puis si chevalchent, Deus! par si grant fiertet!
Brochent ad ait pur le plus tost aler,
Si vunt ferir, que fereient il el?   1185
E Sarrazins nes unt mie dutez;
Francs e paiens, as les vus ajustez.

93

Li nies Marsilie, il ad a num Aelroth;
Tut premereins chevalchet devant l'ost.
De noz Franceis vait disant si mals moz: 1190
«Feluns Franceis, hoi justerez as noz,
Traït vos ad ki a guarder vos out.
Fols est li reis ki vos laissat as porz.
Enquoi perdrat France dulce sun los,
Charles li magnes le destre braz del cors.»   1195
Quant l'ot Rollant, Deus! si grant doel en out!
Sun cheval brochet, laiset curre a esforz,
Vait le ferir li quens quanque il pout.
L'escut li freint e l'osberc li desclot,
Trenchet le piz, si li briset les os,   1200
Tute l'eschine li desevret del dos,
Od sun espiet l'anme li getet fors,
Enpeint le ben, fait li brandir le cors,
Pleine sa hanste del cheval l'abat mort,
En dous meitiez li ad briset le col;   1205
Ne leserat, ço dit, que n'i parolt:
«Ultre culvert! Carles n'est mie fol,
Ne traïsun unkes amer ne volt.
Il fist que proz qu'il nus laisad as porz:
Oí n'en perdrat France dulce sun los.   1210
Ferez i, Francs, nostre est li premers colps!
Nos avum dreit, mais cist glutun unt tort.»   AOI.

94

Un duc i est, si ad num Falsaron:
Icil er[t] frere al rei Marsiliun;
Il tint la tere Datliun e Balbiun.   1215
Suz cel nen at plus encrisme felun.
Entre les dous oilz mult out large le front,
Grant demi pied mesurer i pout hom.

Asez ad doel quant vit mort sun nevold,
Ist de la prese, si se met en bandun,   1220
E se s'escriet l'enseigne paienor;
Envers Franceis est mult cuntrarius:
«Enquoi perdrat France dulce s'onur!»
Ot le Oliver, sin ad mult grant irur;
Le cheval brochet des oriez esperuns,   1225
Vait le ferir en guise de baron.
L'escut li freint e l'osberc li derumpt,
El cors li met les pans del gunfanun,
Pleine sa hanste l'abat mort des arçuns;
Guardet a tere, veit gesir le glutun,   1230
Si li ad dit par mult fiere raison:
«De voz manaces, culvert, jo n'ai essoign.
Ferez i, Francs, kar tres ben les veincrum!»
—«Munjoie!» escriet, ço est l'enseigne Carlun.   AOI.

95

Uns reis i est, si ad num Corsablix: 1235
Barbarins est, d'un estra[n]ge païs.
Si apelad les altres Sarrazins:
«Ceste bataille ben la puum tenir,
Kar de Franceis i ad asez petit.
Cels ki ci sunt devum aveir mult vil;   1240
Ja pur Charles n'i ert un sul guarit:
Or est le jur qu'els estuvrat murir.»
Ben l'entendit li arc[e]vesques Turpin.
Suz ciel n'at hume que [tant] voeillet haïr;
Sun cheval brochet des esperuns d'or fin,   1245
Par grant vertut si l'est alet ferir.
L'escut li freinst, l'osberc li descumfist,
Sun grant espiet par mi le cors li mist,
Empeint le ben, que mort le fait brandir,
Pleine sa hanste l'abat mort el chemin.   1250
Guardet arere, veit le glutun gesir,
Ne laisserat que n'i parolt, ço dit:
«Culvert paien, vos i avez mentit!
Carles, mi sire, nus est guarant tuz dis;
Nostre Franceis n'unt talent de fuïr.   1255
Voz cumpaignuns feruns trestuz restifs;
Nuveles vos di: mort vos estoet susfrir.
Ferez, Franceis! Nul de vus ne s'ublit!

Cist premer colp est nostre, Deu mercit!»
—«Munjoie!» escriet por le camp retenir.   1260

96

Engelers fiert Malprimis de Brigal;
Sis bons escuz un dener ne li valt:
Tute li freint la bucle de cristal,
L'une meitiet li turnet cuntreval;
L'osberc li rumpt entresque a la charn,   1265
Sun bon espiet enz el cors li enbat.
Li paiens chet cuntreval a un quat;
L'anme de lui en portet Sathanas.   AOI.

97

E sis cumpainz Gerers fiert l'amurafle:
L'escut li freint e l'osberc li desmailet,   1270
Sun bon espiet li me(n)t en la curaille,
Empeint le bien, par mi le cors li passet,
Que mort l'abat el camp, pleine sa hanste.
Dist Oliver: «Gente est nostre bataille!»

98

Sansun li dux, (il) vait ferir l'almaçur: 1275
L'escut li freinst, ki est a flurs e ad ór,
Li bons osbercs ne li est guarant prod,
Trenchet li le coer, le firie e le pulmun,
Que l'abat [mort], qui qu'en peist u qui nun.
Dist l'arcevesque: «Cist colp est de baron!»   1280

99

E Anseïs laiset le cheval curre,
Si vait ferir Turgis de Turteluse;
L'escut li freint desuz l'oree bucle,
De sun osberc li derumpit les dubles,
Del bon espiet el cors li met la mure,   1285
Empeinst le ben, tut le fer li mist ultre,
Pleine sa hanste el camp mort le tresturnet.
Ço dist Rollant: «Cist colp est de produme!»

100

Et Engelers li Guascuinz de Burdele
Sun cheval (. . .) brochet, si li laschet la resne,   1290
Si vait ferir Escremiz de Valterne:
L'escut del col li freint e escantelet,
De sun osberc li rumpit la ventaille,
Sil fiert el piz entre les dous furceles,
Pleine sa hanste l'abat mort de la sele;   1295
Apres li dist: «Turnet estes a perdre!»   AOI.

101

E Gualter fie[r]t un paien, Estorgans,
Sur sun escut en la pene devant,
Que tut li trenchet le vermeill e le blanc;
De sun osberc li ad rumput les pans,   1300
El cors li met sun bon espiet tre[n]chant,
Que mort l'abat de sun cheval curant.
Apres li dist: «Ja n'i avrez guarant!»

102

E Berenger, il fiert Astramariz:
L'escut li freinst, l'osberc li descumfist,   1305
Sun fort escut par mi le cors li mist,
Que mort l'abat entre mil Sarrazins.
Des .XII. pers li .X. en sunt ocis;
Ne mes que dous n'en i ad remes vifs;
Ço est Chernubles e li quens Margariz.   1310

103

Margariz est mult vaillant chevalers,
E bels e forz e isnels e legers.
Le cheval brochet, vait ferir Oliver:
L'escut li freint suz la bucle d'or mer,
Lez le costet li conduist sun espiet.   1315
Deus le guarit, qu'el(l) cors ne l'ad tuchet.
La hanste fruisset, mie n'en a(d)[b]atiet.
Ultre s'en vait, qu'il n'i ad desturber;
Sunet sun gresle pur les soens ralier.

104

La bataille est merveilluse e cumune.   1320
Li quens Rollant mie ne s'asoüret,
Fiert de l'espiet tant cume hanste li duret;
A .XV. cols l'ad fraite e [. . .] perdue,
Trait Durendal, sa bone espee nue,
Sun cheval brochet, si vait ferir Chernuble: 1325
L'elme li freint u li carbuncle luisent,
Trenchet la cors e la cheveleüre,
Si li trenchat les oilz e la faiture,
Le blanc osberc, dunt la maile est menue,
E tut le cors tresqu'en la furcheüre,   1330
Enz en la sele, ki est a or batue;
El cheval est l'espee aresteüe,
Trenchet l'eschine, hunc n'i out quis [joi]nture,
Tut abat mort el pred sur l'erbe drue;
Apres li dist: «Culvert, mar i moüstes!   1335
De Mahumet ja n'i avrez aiude.
Par tel glutun n'ert bataille oi vencue.»

105

Li quens Rollant par mi le champ chevalchet,
Tient Durendal, ki ben trenchet e taillet,
Des Sarrazins lur fait mult grant damage.   1340
Ki lui veïst l'un geter mort su[r] l'altre,
Li sanc tuz clers gesir par cele place!
Sanglant en ad e l'osberc e [la] brace,
Sun bon cheval le col e les [es]palles.
E Oliver de ferir ne se target,   1345
Li .XII. per n'en deivent aveir blasme,
E li Franceis i fierent e si caplent.
Moerent paien e alquanz en i pasment.
Dist l'arcevesque: «Ben ait nostre barnage!»
—«Munjoie!» escriet, ço est l'enseigne Carle.   AOI.   1350

106

E Oliver chevalchet par l'estor,
Sa hanste est frait, n'en ad que un trunçun,
E vait fer(en)[ir] un paien, Malun:
L'escut li freint, ki est ad or e a flur,
Fors de la teste li met les oilz ansdous,   1355
E la cervele li chet as piez desuz;

Mort le tresturnet od tut .VII.C. des lur.
Pois ad ocis Turgis e Esturguz;
La hanste briset e esclicet josqu'as poinz.
Ço dist Rollant: «Cumpainz, que faites vos?   1360
En tel bataille n'ai cure de bastun;
Fers e acers i deit aveir valor.
U est vostre espee, ki Halteclere ad num?
D'or est li helz e de cristal li punz.»
—«Ne la poi traire,» Oliver li respunt,   1365
«Kar de ferir oi jo si grant bosoign.»   AOI.

107

Danz Oliver trait ad sa bone espee,
Que ses cumpainz Rollant li ad tant demandee,
E il li ad cum chevaler mustree.
Fiert un paien, Justin de Val Ferree: 1370
Tute la teste li ad par mi sevree,
Trenchet le cors e [la] bronie safree,
La bone sele, ki a ór est gemmee,
E al ceval a l'eschine trenchee;
Tut abat mort devant loi en la pree.   1375
Ço dist Rollant: «Vos receif jo, frere!
Por itels colps nos eimet li emperere.»
De tutes parz est «Munjo[i]e» escriee.   AOI.

108

Li quens Gerins set el ceval Sorel
E sis cumpainz Gerers en Passecerf,   1380
Laschent lor reisnes, brochent amdui a ait,
E vunt ferir un paien, Timozel,
L'un en l'escut e li altre en l'osberc,
Lur dous espiez enz el cors li unt frait,
Mort le tresturnent tres enmi un guaret,   1385
Ne l'oï dire ne jo mie nel sai
Liquels d'els dous en fut li plus isnels.
Esprieres icil fut filz Burdel,
. . . .
E l'arcevesque lor ocist Siglorel,   1390
L'encanteür ki ja fut en enfer:
Par artimal l'i cundoist Jupiter.
Ço dist Turpin: «Icist nos ert forsfait.»
Respunt Rollant: «Vencut est le culvert.
Oliver, frere, itels colps me sunt bel!»   1395

109

La bataille est aduree endementres.
Franc e paien merveilus colps i rendent.
Fierent li un, li altre se defendent.
Tant hanste i ad e fraite e sanglente,
Tant gunfanun rumpu e tant enseigne!   1400
Tant bon Franceis i perdent lor juvente!
Ne reverrunt lor meres ne lor femmes,
Ne cels de France ki as porz les atendent.   AOI.
Karles li magnes en pluret, si se demente.
De ço qui calt? N'en avrunt sucurance.   1405
Malvais servis[e] le jur li rendit Guenes,
Qu'en Sarraguce sa maisnee alat vendre;
Puis cn perdit e sa vie e ses membres;
El plait ad Ais en fut juget a prendre,
De ses parenz ensembl'od lui tels trente   1410
Ki de murir nen ourent esperance.   AOI.

110

La bataille est merveilluse e pesant;
Mult ben i fiert Oliver e Rollant,
Li arcevesques plus de mil colps i rent,
Li .XII. per ne s'en targent nient,   1415
E li Franceis i fierent cumunement.
Moerent paien a miller(e)[s] e a cent;
Ki ne s'en fuit de mort n'i ad guarent;
Voillet o nun, tut i laisset sun tens.
Franceis i perdent lor meillors guarnemenz;   1420
Ne reverrunt lor peres ne lor parenz
Ne Carlemagne, ki as porz les atent.
En France en ad mult merveillus turment;
Orez i ad de tuneire e de vent,
Pluies e gresilz desmesureement;   1425
Chiedent i fuildres e menut e suvent,
E terremoete ço i ad veirement.
De seint Michel de(l) P(aris)[eril] josqu'as Seinz
Des Besençun tresqu'as [port] de Guitsand
N'en ad recet dunt del mur ne cravent.   1430
Cuntre midi tenebres i ad granz;
N'i ad clartet, se li ciels nen i fent.
Hume nel veit,ki mult ne s espaent.
Dient plusor: «Ço est li definement,

La fin del secle ki nus est en present.»   1435
Il nel sevent, ne dient veir nient:
Ço est li granz dulors por la mort de Rollant.

111

Franceis i unt ferut de coer e de vigur;
Paien sunt morz a millers e a fuls:
De cent millers n'en poent guarir dous.   1440
Rollant dist: «Nostre hume sunt mult proz:
Suz ciel n'ad home plus en ait de meillors.»
Il est escrit en la Geste Francor
Que vassals ad li nostre empereür.
Vunt par le camp, si requerent les lor,   1445
Plurent des oilz de doel e de tendrur
Por lor parenz par coer e par amor.
Li reis Marsilie od sa grant ost lor surt.   AOI.

112

Marsilie vient par mi une valee
Od sa grant ost que il out asemblee.   1450
.XX. escheles ad li reis anumbrees.
Lacent cil'elme as perres d'or gemmees,
E cil escuz e cez bronies sasfrees;
.VII. milie graisles i sunent la menee:
Grant est la noise par tute la contree.   1455
Ço dist Rollant: «Oliver, compaign, frere,
Guenes li fels ad nostre mort juree;
La traïsun ne poet estre celee;
Mult grant venjance en prendrat l'emperere.
Bataille avrum e forte [e] aduree,   1460
Unches mais hom tel ne vit ajustee.
Jo i ferrai de Durendal, m'espee,
E vos, compainz, ferrez de Halteclere.
En tanz lius les avum nos portees!
Tantes batailles en avum afinees!   1465
Male chançun n'en deit estre cantee.»   AOI.

113

Marsilies veit de sa gent le martirie,
Si fait suner ses cors e ses buisines,
Puis si chevalchet od sa grant ost banie.

Devant chevalchet un Sarrasin, Abisme: 1470
Plus fel de lui n'out en sa cumpagnie.
Te(t)ches ad males e mult granz felonies;
Ne creit en Deu, le filz sainte Marie;
Issi est neirs cume peiz ki est demise;
Plus aimet il traïsun e murdrie   1475
Qu'(e) il ne fesist trestut l'or de Galice;
Unches nuls hom nel vit juer ne rire.
Vasselage ad e mult grant estultie:
Por ço est drud al felun rei Marsilie;
Sun dragun portet a qui sa gent s'alient.   1480
Li arcevesque ne l'amerat ja mie;
Cum il le vit, a ferir le desiret.
Mult quiement le dit a sei meïsme:
«Cel Sarraz[in] me semblet mult herite:
Mielz est mult que jo l'alge ocire.   1485
Unches n'amai cuard ne cuardie.»   AOI.

                          114
Li arcevesque cumencet la bataille.
Siet el cheval qu'il tolit a Grossaille,
Ço ert uns reis qu'l ocist en Denemarche.
Li destrers est e curanz e aates,   1490
Piez ad copiez e les gambes ad plates,
Curte la quisse e la crupe bien large,
Lungs les costez e l'eschine ad ben halte,
Blanche la cue e la crignete jalne
Petites les oreilles, la teste tute falve;   1495
Beste nen est nule ki encontre lui alge.
Li arcevesque brochet par tant grant vasselage:
Ne laisserat qu'Abisme nen asaillet;
Vait le ferir en l'escut amiracle:
Pierres i ad, ametistes e topazes,   1500
Esterminals e carbuncles ki ardent;
En Val Metas li dunat uns diables,
Si li tramist li amiralz Galafes.
Turpins i fiert, ki nient ne l'esparignet,
Enpres sun colp ne quid que un dener vaillet,   1505
Le cors li trenchet tres l'un costet qu'a l'altre,
Que mort l'abat en une voide place.
Dient Franceis: «Ci ad grant vasselage!
En l'arcevesque est ben la croce salve.»

115

Franceis veient que paiens i ad tant,   1510
De tutes parz en sunt cuvert li camp;
Suvent regretent Oliver e Rollant
Les .XII. pers, qu'il lor seient guarant.
E l'arcevesque lur dist de sun semblant:
«Seignors barons, n'en alez mespensant!   1515
Pur Deu vos pri que ne seiez fuiant,
Que nuls prozdom malvaisement n'en chant.
Asez est mielz que moerium cumbatant.
Pramis nus est, fin prendrum a itant,
Ultre cest jurn ne serum plus vivant;   1520
Mais d'une chose vos soi jo ben guarant:
Seint pareïs vos est abandunant;
As Innocenz vos en serez seant.»
A icest mot si s'esbaldissent Franc,
Cel nen i ad «Munjoie!» ne demant.   AOI.   1525

116

Un Sarrazin i out de Sarraguce,
De la citet l'une meitet est sue:
Ço est Climborins, ki pas ne fut produme.
Fiance prist de Guenelun le cunte,
Par amistiet l'en baisat en la buche,   1530
Si l'en dunat s'espee e s'escarbuncle.
Tere Major ço dit, metrat a hunte,
A l'emperere si toldrat la curone.
Siet el ceval qu'il cleimet Barbamusche,
Plus est isnels que esprever ne arunde.   1535
Brochet le bien, le frein li abandunet,
Si vait ferir Engeler de Guascoigne.
Nel poet guarir sun escut ne sa bronie:
De sun espiet el cors li met la mure,
Empeint le ben, tut le fer li mist ultre,   1540
Pleine sa hanste el camp mort le tresturnet.
Apres escriet: «Cist sunt bon a (o)[c]unfundre!
Ferez, paien, pur la presse derumpre!»
Dient Franceis: «Deus quel doel de prodome!»   AOI.

117

Li quens Rollant en apelet Oliver: 1545
«Sire cumpainz, ja est morz Engeler;

Nus n'avium plus vaillant chevaler.»
Respont li quens: «Deus le me doinst venger!»
Sun cheval brochet des esperuns d'or mier,
Tient Halteclere, sanglent en est l'acer,   1550
Par grant vertut vait ferir le paien.
Brandist sun colp e li Sarrazins chiet;
L'anme de lui en portent aversers.
Puis ad ocis le duc Alphaïen;
Escababi i ad le chef trenchet;   1555
.VII. Arrabiz i ad deschevalcet:
Cil ne sunt proz ja mais pur guerreier.
Ço dist Rollant: «Mis cumpainz est irez!
Encuntre mei fait asez a preiser.
Pur itels colps nos ad Charles plus chcr.»   1560
A voiz escriet: «Ferez i, chevaler!»   AOI.

118

D'altre part est un paien, Valdabrun:
Celoi levat le rei Marsiliun,
Sire est par mer de .IIII.C. drodmunz;
N'i ad eschipre quis cleim se par loi nun.   1565
Jerusalem prist ja par traïsun,
Si violat le temple Salomon,
Le patriarche ocist devant les funz.
Cil ot fiance del cunte Guenelon:
Il li dunat s'espee e mil manguns.   1570
Siet el cheval qu'il cleimet Gramimund,
Plus est isnels que nen est uns falcuns.
Brochet le bien des aguz esperuns,
Si vait ferir li riche duc Sansun,
L'escut li freint e l'osberc li derumpt,   1575
El cors li met les pans del gunfanun,
Pleine sa hanste l'abat mort des arçuns:
«Ferez paien, car tres ben les veintrum!»
Dient Franceis: «Deus quel doel de baron.!»   AOI.

119

Li quens Rollant, quant il veit Sansun mort,   1580
Poez saveir que mult grant doel en out.
Sun ceval brochet, si li curt ad esforz;
Tient Durendal, qui plus valt que fin ór.
Vait le ferir li bers, quanque il pout,

Desur sun elme, ki gemmet fut ad or: 1585
Trenchet la teste e la bronie e le cors,
La bone sele, ki est gemmet ad or,
E al cheval parfundement le dos;
Ambure ocit, ki quel blasme ne quil lot.
Dient paien(t) [. . .]: «Cist colp nus est mult fort!»   1590
Respont Rollant: «Ne pois amer les voz;
Devers vos est li orguilz e li torz.»   AOI.

120

D'Affrike i ad un Affrican venut,
Ço est Malquiant, le filz al rei Malcud.
Si guarnement sunt tut a or batud;   1595
Cuntre le ciel sur tuz les altres luist.
Siet el ceval qu'il cleimet Salt Perdut:
Beste nen est ki poisset curre a lui.
Il vait ferir Anseïs en l'escut:
Tut li trenchat le vermeill e l'azur;   1600
De sun osberc li ad les pans rumput,
El cors li met e le fer e le fust;
Morz est li quens, de sun tens n'i ad plus.
Dient Franceis: «Barun, tant mare fus!»

121

Par le camp vait Turpin li arcevesque;   1605
Tel coronet ne chantat unches messe
Ki de sun cors feïst [. . .] tantes proecces.
Dist al paien: «Deus tut mal te tramette!
Tel ad ocis dunt al coer me regrette.»
Sun bon ceval i ad fait esdemetre,   1610
Si l'ad ferut sur l'escut de Tulette,
Que mort l'abat desur le herbe verte.

122

De l'altre part est un paien, Grandonies,
Filz Capuel, le rei de Capadoce(neez).
Siet el cheval que il cleimet Marmorie,   1615
Plus est isnels que n'est oisel ki volet;
Laschet la resne, des esperuns le brochet,
Si vait ferir Gerin par sa grant force.
L'escut vermeill li freint, de col li portet;
Aprof li ad sa bronie desclose,   1620

El cors li met tute l'enseingne bloie,
Que mort l'abat en une halte roche.
Sun cumpaignun Gerers ocit uncore
E Berenger e Guiun de Seint Antonie;
Puis vait ferir un riche duc Austorje,   1625
Ki tint Valeri e envers sur le Rosne.
Il l'abat mort; paien en unt grant joie.
Dient Franceis: «Mult decheent li nostre!»

123

[L]i quens Rollant tint s'espee sanglente.
Ben ad oït que Franceis se dementent;   1630
Si grant doel ad que par mi quiet fendre;
Dist al paien: «Deus tut mal te consente!
Tel as ocis que mult cher te quid vendre!»
Sun ceval brochet, ki oït del cuntence.
Ki quel cumpert, venuz en sunt ensemble.   1635

124

Grandonie fut e prozdom e vaillant
E vertuus e vassal cumbatant.
Enmi sa veie ad encuntret Rollant.
Enceis nel vit, sil recunut veirement,
Al fier visage e al cors qu'il out gent   1640
E al reguart e al contenement:
Ne poet muer qu'il ne s'en espoent,
Fuïr s'en voel, mais ne li valt nient:
Li quens le fiert tant vertuusement
Tresqu'al nasel tut le elme li fent,   1645
Trenchet le nes e la buche e les denz,
Trestut le cors e l'osberc jazerenc
De l'oree sele (se)[les] dous alves d'argent
E al ceval le dos parfundement;
Ambure ocist seinz nul recoevrement,   1650
E cil d'Espaigne s'en cleiment tuit dolent.
Dient Franceis: «Ben fiert nostre guarent!»

125

La bataille est e merveillose e grant.
Franceis i ferent des espiez brunisant.
La veïssez si grant dulor de gent,   1655
Tant hume mort e nasfret e sanglent!

L'un gist sur l'altre e envers e adenz.
Li Sarrazin nel poent susfrir tant:
Voelent u nun, si guerpissent le camp.
Par vive force les encacerent Franc.   AOI.   1660

126

La (la) b[at]aille est m[erv]eilluse e hastive.
Franceis i ferent par vigur e par ire,
Tren[chen]t cez poinz, cez costez, cez eschines,
Cez vestemenz entresque as chars vives.
Sur l'erbe verte li cler sancs s'en afilet.   1665
. . . .
«Tere Major, Mahummet te maldie!
Sur tute gent est la tue hardie.»
Cel nen i ad ki ne criet: «Marsilie!
Cevalche, rei! Bosuign avum d'aïe!»   1670

127

Li quens Rollant apelet Oliver:
«Sire cumpaign, sel volez otrier,
Li arcevesque est mult bon chevaler,
Nen ad meillor en tere ne suz cel;
Ben set ferir e de lance e d'espiet.»   1675
Respunt li quens: «Kar li aluns aider!»
A icest mot l'unt Francs recumencet.
Dur sunt li colps e li caples est grefs;
Mu(n)lt grant dulor i ad de chrestiens.
Ki puis veïst Rollant e Oliver   1680
De lur espees e ferir e capler!
Li arcevesque i fiert de sun espiet,
Cels qu'il unt mort, ben les poet hom preiser;
Il est escrit es cartres e es brefs,
Ço dit la Geste, plus de .IIII. milliers.   1685
As quatre [es]turs lor est avenut ben;
Li quint apres lor est pesant e gref.
Tuz sunt ocis cist Franceis chevalers,
Ne mes seisante, que Deus i ad esparniez:
Einz que il moergent, se vendrunt mult cher.   AOI.   1690

128

Li quens Rollant des soens i veit grant perte;
Sun cumpaignun Oliver en apelet:

«Bel sire, chers cumpainz, pur Deu, que vos enhaitet?
Tanz bons vassals veez gesir par tere!
Pleindre poüms France dulce, la bele: 1695
De tels barons cum or remeint deserte!
E! reis, amis, que vos ici nen estes?
Oliver, frere, cumment le purrum nus faire?
Cum faitement li manderum nuveles?»
Dist Oliver: «Jo nel sai cument quere.   1700
Mielz voeill murir que hunte nus seit retraite.»   AOI.

                        129
Ço dist Rollant: «Cornerai l'olifant,
Si l'orrat Carles, ki est as porz passant.
Jo vos plevis ja returnerunt Franc.»
Dist Oliver: «Vergoigne sereit grant   1705
E reprover a trestuz voz parenz;
Iceste hunte dureit al lur vivant!
Quant jel vos dis, n'en feïstes nient;
Mais nel ferez par le men loement.
Se vos cornez, n'ert mie hardement.   1710
Ja avez vos ambsdous les braz sanglanz!»
Respont li quens: «Colps i ai fait mult genz!»   AOI.

                        131
Ço dit Rollant: «Forz est nostre bataille;
Jo cornerai, si l'orrat li reis Karles.»
Dist Oliver: «Ne sereit vasselage!   1715
Quant jel vos dis, cumpainz, vos ne deignastes.
Si fust li reis, n'i oüsum damage.
Cil ki la sunt n'en deivent aveir blasme.»
Dist Oliver: «Par ceste meie barbe,
Se puis veeir ma gente sorur Alde,   1720
Ne jerrei(e)z ja mais entre sa brace!»   AOI.

                        131
Ço dist Rollant: «Por quei me portez ire?»
(E cil) E il respont: «Cumpainz, vos le feïstes,
Kar vasselage par sens nen est folie;
Mielz valt mesure que ne fait estultie.   1725
Franceis sunt morz par vostre legerie.
Jamais Karlon de nus n'avrat servise.
Sem(e) creïsez, venuz i fust mi sire;

Ceste bataille oüsum faite u prise;
U pris ú mort i fust li reis Marsilie.   1730
Vostre proecce, Rollant, mar la ve[ï]mes!
Karles li Magnes de nos n'avrat aïe.
N'ert mais tel home des qu'a Deu juïse.
Vos i murrez e France en ert (. . .) hun íe.
Oi nus defalt la leial cumpaignie: 1735
Einz le vesp(e)re mult ert gref la departie.»   AOI.

132

Li arceves[ques] les ót cuntrarier,
Le cheval brochet des esperuns d'or mer,
Vint tresqu'a els, sis prist a castier:
«Sire Rollant, e vos, sire Oliver,   1740
Pur Deu vos pri, ne vos cuntraliez!
Ja li corners ne nos avreit mester,
Mais nepurquant si est il asez melz:
Venget li reis, si nus purrat venger;
Ja cil d'Espaigne ne s'en deivent turner liez.   1745
Nostre Franceis i descendrunt a pied,
Truverunt nos e morz e detrenchez,
Leverunt nos en bieres sur sumers,
Si nus plurrunt de doel e de pitet,
Enfuerunt [nos] en aitres de musters;   1750
N'en mangerunt ne lu ne porc ne chen.»
Respunt Rollant: «Sire, mult dites bien.»   AOI.

133

Rollant ad mis l'olifan a sa buche,
Empeint le ben, par grant vertut le sunet.
Halt sunt li pui e la voiz est mult lunge,   1755
Granz .XXX. liwes l'oïrent il respundre.
Karles l'oït e ses cumpaignes tutes.
Ço dit li reis: «Bataille funt nostre hume!»
E Guenelun li respundit encuntre:
«S'altre le desist, ja semblast grant mençunge!»   AOI.   1760

134

Li quens Rollant, par peine e par ahans,
Par grant dulor sunet sun olifan.
Par mi la buche en salt fors li cler sancs.
De sun cervel le temple en est rumpant.

Del corn qu'il tient l'oïïe en est mult grant: 1765
Karles l'entent, ki est as porz passant.
Naimes li duc l'oïd, si l'escultent li Franc.
Ce dist li reis: «Jo oi le corn Rollant!
Unc nel sunast se ne fust (cu)cumbatant.»
Guenes respunt: «De bataille est il nient!   1770
Ja estes veilz e fluriz e blancs;
Par tels paroles vus resemblez enfant.
Asez savez le grant orgoill Rollant;
Ço est merveille que Deus le soefret tant.
Ja prist il Noples seinz le vostre comant;   1775
Fors s'en eissirent li Sarrazins dedenz,
Sis cumbatirent al bon vassal Rollant;
Puis od les ewes (. . .) lavat les prez del sanc,
Pur cel le fist ne fust a[pa]rissant.
Pur un sul levre vat tute jur cornant,   1780
Devant ses pers vait il ore gabant.
Suz cel n'ad gent ki [l']osast (re)querre en champ.
Car chevalcez! Pur qu'alez arestant?
Tere Major mult est loinz ça devant.»   AOI.

135

Li quens Rollant ad la buche sanglente.   1785
De sun cervel rumput en est li temples.
L'olifan sunet a dulor e a peine.
Karles l'oït e ses Franceis l'entendent,
Ço dist li reis: «cCel corn ad lunge aleine!»
Respont dux Neimes: «Baron i fait la p[e]ine!   1790
Bataille i ad, par le men escientre.
Cil l'at traït ki vos en roevet feindre.
Adubez vos, si criez vostre enseigne,
Si sucurez vostre maisnee gente:
Asez oez que Rollant se dementet!»   1795

136

Li empereres ad fait suner ses corns.
Franceis descendent, si adubent lor cors
D'osbercs e de helmes e d'espees a or.
Escuz unt genz e espiez granz e forz,
E gunfanuns blancs e vermeilz e blois.   1800
Es destrers muntent tuit li barun de l'ost,
Brochent ad ait tant cum durent li port.

N'i ad celoi (a celoi) a l'altre ne parolt:
«Se veïssum Rollant einz qu'il fust mortz,
Ensembl'od lui i durriums granz colps.»   1805
De ço qui calt? car demuret i unt trop.

137

Esclargiz est li vespres e li jurz.
Cuntre le soleil reluisent cil adub,
Osbercs e helmes i getent grant flambur,
E cil escuz, ki ben sunt peinz a flurs,   1810
E cil espiez(z), cil oret gunfanun.
Li empereres cevalchet par irur
E li Franceis dolenz et cur[uçus](ius);
N'i ad celoi ki durement ne plurt,
E de Rollant sunt en grant poür.   1815
Li reis fait prendre le cunte Guenelun,
Sil cumandat as cous de sa maisun.
Tut li plus maistre en apelet, Besgun.
«Ben le me guarde, si cume tel felon!
De ma maisnee ad faite traïsun.»   1820
Cil le receit, si met .C. cumpaignons
De la quisine, des mielz e des pejurs.
Icil li peilent la barbe e les gernuns;
Cascun le fiert .IIII. colps de sun puign;
Ben le batirent a fuz e a bastuns;   1825
E si li metent el col un caeignun,
Si l'encaeinent altresi cum un urs;
Sur un sumer l'unt mis a deshonor.
Tant le guardent quel rendent a Charlun.

138

Halt sunt li pui e tenebrus e grant,   AOI.   1830
Li val parfunt e les ewes curant.
Sunent cil graisle e derere e devant,
E tuit rachatent encuntre l'olifant.
Li empereres chevalchet ireement,
E li Franceis cur(i[. . .]us)uçus e dolent;   1835
N'i ad celoi n'i plurt e se dement,
E p[ri]ent Deu qu'il guarisset Rollant
Josque il vengent el camp cumunement:
Ensembl'od lui i ferrunt veirement.
De ço qui calt? car ne lur valt nient.   1840
Demurent trop, n'i poedent estre a tens.   AOI.

139

Par grant irur chevalchet li reis Charles;
Desur (. . .) sa brunie li gist sa blanche barbe.
Puignent ad ait tuit li barun de France;
N'i ad icel ne demeint irance   1845
Que il ne sunt a Rollant le cataigne,
Ki se cumbat as Sarrazins d'Espaigne;
Si est blecet, ne quit que anme i remaigne.
Deus! quels seisante humes i ad en sa cumpaigne!
Unches meillurs n'en out reis ne c[at]aignes.   AOI.   1850

140

Rollant reguardet es munz e es lariz;
De cels de France i veit tanz morz gesir!
E il les pluret cum chevaler gentill:
«Seignors barons, de vos ait Deus mercit!
Tutes voz anmes otreit il pareïs!   1855
En seintes flurs il les facet gesir!
Meillors vassals de vos unkes ne vi.
Si lungement tuz tens m'avez servit,
A oes Carlon si granz païs cunquis!
Li empereres tant mare vos nurrit!   1860
Tere de France mult estes dulz païs
Oi desertet a tant rubostl exill.
Barons Franceis, pur mei vos vei murir:
Jo ne vos pois tenser ne guarantir.
Aït vos Deus, ki unkes ne mentit!   1865
Oliver, frere, vos ne dei jo faillir.
De doel murra, se altre ne m'i ocit.
Sire cumpainz, alum i referir!»

141

Li quens Rollant el champ est repairet:
Tient Durendal, cume vassal i fiert.   1870
Faldrun de Pui i ad par mi trenchet,
E .XXIIII. de tuz les melz preisez:
Jamais n'iert home plus se voeillet venger.
Si cum li cerfs s'en vait devant les chiens,
Devant Rollant si s'en fuient paiens.   1875
Dist l'arcevesque: «Asez le faites ben!
Itel valor deit aveir chevaler

Ki armes portet e en bon cheval set;
En bataille deit estre forz e fiers,
U altrement ne valt .IIII. deners;   1880
Einz deit monie estre en un de cez mustiers,
Si prierat tuz jurz por noz peccez.»
Respunt Rollant: «Ferez, nes esparignez!»
A icest mot l'unt Francs recumencet.
Mult grant damage i out de chrestiens.   1885

142

Home ki ço set, que ja n'avrat prisun
En tel bataill[e] fait grant defension:
Pur ço sunt Francs si fiers cume leuns.
As vus Marsilie en guise de barunt.
Siet el cheval qu'il apelet Gaignun,   1890
Brochet le ben, si vait ferir Bevon,
Icil ert sire de Belne e de Digun,
L'escut li freint e l'osberc li derumpt,
Que mort l'abat seinz altre descunfisun;
Puis ad ocis Yvoeries e Ivon   1895
Ensembl'od els Gerard de Russillun.
Li quens Rollant ne li est guaires loign;
Dist al paien: «Damnesdeus mal te duinst!
A si grant tort m'ociz mes cumpaignuns!
Colp en avras einz que nos departum,   1900
E de m'espee enquoi savras le nom.»
Vait le ferir en guise de baron:
Trenchet li ad li quens le destre poign.
Puis prent la teste de Jurfaleu le Blund,
Icil ert filz al rei Marsiliun.   1905
Paien escrient: «Aïe nos, Mahum!
Li nostre deu, vengez nos de Carlun.
En ceste tere nus ad mis tels feluns!
Ja pur murir le camp ne guerpirunt.»
Dist l'un a l'altre: «E! car nos en fuiums!»   1910
A icest mot tels .C. milie s'en vunt:
Ki ques rapelt, ja n'en returnerunt.   AOI.

143

De ço qui calt? Se fuit s'en est Marsilies,
Remes i est sis uncles, Marganices,
Ki tint Kartagene, Alfrere, Garmalie   1915

E Ethiope, une tere maldite.
La neire gent en ad en sa baillie;
Granz unt les nes e lees les oreilles,
E sunt ensemble plus de cinquante milie.
Icil chevalchent fierement e a íre,   1920
Puis escrient l'enseigne paenime.
Ço dist Rollant: «Ci recevrums ma[r]tyrie,
E or sai ben n'avons guaires a vivre;
Mais tut seit fel cher ne se vende primes!
Ferez, seignurs, des espees furbies,   1925
Si calengez e voz (e) mors e voz vies!
Que dulce France par nus ne seit hunie!
Quant en cest camp vendrat Carles, mi sire,
De Sarrazins verrat tel discipline,
Cuntre un des noz en truverat morz .XV.,   1930
Ne lesserat que nos ne beneïsse.»   AOI.

144
Quan Rollant veit la contredite gent
Ki plus sunt neirs que nen est arrement,
Ne n'unt de blanc ne mais que sul les denz,
Ço dist li quens: «Or sai jo veirement   1935
Que hoi murrum par le mien escient.
Ferez Franceis, car jol vos recumenz!»
Dist Oliver: «Dehet ait li plus lenz!»
A icest mot Franceis se fierent enz.

145
Quant paien virent que Franceis i out poi,   1940
Entr'els en unt e orgoil e cunfort.
Dist l'un a l'altre: «L'empereor ad tort.»
Li Marganices sist sur un ceval sor,
Brochet le ben des esperuns a or,
Fiert Oliver derere en mi le dos.   1945
Le blanc osberc li ad descust el cors,
Par mi le piz sun espiet li mist fors,
E dit apres: «Un col avez pris fort!
Carles li magnes mar vos laissat as porz!
Tort nos ad fait: nen est dreiz qu'il s'en lot,   1950
Kar de vos sul ai ben venget les noz.»

146

Oliver sent que a mort est ferut.
Tient Halteclere, dunt li acer fut bruns,
Fiert Marganices sur l'elme a or, agut,
E flurs e cristaus en acravenet jus;   1955
Trenchet la teste d'ici qu'as denz menuz,
Brandist sun colp, si l'ad mort abatut,
E dist apres: «Paien mal aies tu!
Iço ne di que Karles n'i ait perdut;
Ne a muiler ne a dame qu'aies veüd,   1960
N'en vanteras el regne dunt tu fus
Vaillant a un dener que m'i aies tolut,
Ne fait damage ne de mei ne d'altrui!»
Apres escriet Rollant qu'il li aiut.   AOI.

147

Oliver sent qu'il est a mort nasfret.   1965
De lui venger ja mais ne li ert lez.
En la grant presse or i fiert cume ber,
Trenchet cez hanstes e cez escuz buclers,
E piez e poinz e seles e costez.
Ki lui veïst Sarrazins desmembrer,   1970
Un mort sur altre geter,
De bon vassal li poüst remembrer.
L'enseigne Carle n'i volt mie ublier:
«Munjoie!» escriet e haltement e cler.
Rollant apelet, sun ami e sun per: 1975
«Sire cumpaign, a mei car vus justez!
A grant dulor ermes hoi desevrez.»   AOI.

148

Rollant reguardet Oliver al visage:
Teint fut e pers, desculuret e pale.
Li sancs tuz clers par mi le cors li raiet: 1980
Encuntre tere en cheent les esclaces.
«Deus!» dist li quens, «or ne sai jo que face.
Sire cumpainz, mar fut vostre barnage!
Jamais n'iert hume ki tun cors cuntrevaillet.
E! France dulce, cun hoi remendras guaste   1985
De bons vassals, cunfundue e chaiete!
Li emperere en avrat grant damage.»
A icest mot sur sun cheval se pasmet.   AOI.

149

As vus Rollant sur sun cheval pasmet,
E Oliver ki est a mort nasfret: 1990
Tant ad seinet (ki) li oil li sunt trublet;
Ne loinz ne pres (es) ne poet vedeir si cler
Que rec[on]oistre poisset nuls hom mortel.
Sun cumpaignun, cum il l'at encontret,
Sil fiert amunt sur l'elme a or gemet: 1995
Tut li detrenchet d'ici qu'al nasel;
Mais en la teste ne l'ad mie adeset.
A icel colp l'ad Rollant reguardet,
Si li demandet dulcement e suef:
«Sire cumpain, faites le vos de gred?   2000
Ja est ço Rollant, ki tant vos soelt amer!
Par nule guise ne m'aviez desfiet!»
Dist Oliver: «Or vos oi jo parler;
Jo ne vos vei, veied vus Damnedeu!
Ferut vos ai, car le me pardunez!»   2005
Rollant respunt: «Jo n'ai nient de mal.
Jol vos parduins ici e devant Deu.»
A icel mot l'un a l'altre ad clinet.
Par tel [. . .] amur as les vus desevred!

150

Oliver sent que la mort mult l'angoisset.   2010
Ansdous les oilz en la teste li turnent,
L'oíe pert e la veüe tute;
Descent a piet, a l[a] tere se culchet,
Durement en halt si recleimet sa culpe,
Cuntre le ciel ambesdous ses mains juintes,   2015
Si priet Deu que pareïs li dunget
E beneïst Karlun e France dulce,
Sun cumpaignun Rollant sur tuz humes.
Falt li le coer, le helme li embrunchet,
Trestut le cors a la tere li justet.   2020
Morz est li quens, que plus ne se demuret.
Rollant li ber le pluret, sil duluset;
Jamais en tere n'orrez plus dolent hume!

151

Or veit Rollant que mort est sun ami,
Gesir adenz, a la tere sun vis,   2025

Mult dulcement a regreter le prist:
«Sire cumpaign, tant mar fustes hardiz!
Ensemble avum estet e anz e dis;
Nem fesis mal ne jo nel te forsfis.
Quant tu es mor[t], dulur est que jo vif!»   2030
A icest mot se pasmet li marchis
Sur sun ceval que cleimet Veillantif.
Afermet est a ses estreus d'or fin:
Quel part qu'il alt, ne poet mie chaïr.

152

Ainz que Rollant se seit aperceüt,   2035
De pasmeisuns guariz ne revenuz,
Mult grant damage li est apareüt:
Morz sunt Franceis, tuz les i ad perdut,
Senz l'arcevesque e senz Gualter del Hum.
Repairez est des muntaignes jus;   2040
A cels d'Espaigne mult s'i est cumbatuz;
Mort sunt si hume, sis unt paiens (. . .) vencut;
Voeillet (illi) o nun, desuz cez vals s'en fuit,
Si reclaimet Rollant, qu'il li aiut:
«E! gentilz quens, vaillanz hom, ú ies tu?   2045
Unkes nen oi poür, la u tu fus.
Ço est Gualter, ki cunquist Maelgut,
Li nies Droün, al vieill e al canut!
Pur vasselage suleie estre tun drut.
Ma hanste est fraite e percet mun escut,   2050
E mis osbercs desmailet e rumput;
Par mi le cors hot une lances [. . .] ferut.
Sempres murrai, mais cher me sui vendut!»
A icel mot l'at Rollant entendut;
Le cheval brochet, si vient poignant vers lui.   AOI.   2055

153

Rollant ad doel, si fut maltalentifs;
En la grant presse cumencet a ferir.
De cels d'Espaigne en ad get[et] mort .XX.,
E Gualter .VI. e l'arcevesque .V.
Dient paien: «(Felun) Feluns humes ad ci!   2060
Guardez, seignurs, qu'il n'en algent vif!
Tut par seit fel ki nes vait envaïr,
E recreant ki les lerrat guar[ir]!»

Dunc recumencent e le hu e le cri;
De tutes parz le revunt envaïr.   AOI.   2065

154

Li quens Rollant fut noble guerrer,
Gualter de Hums est bien bon chevaler,
Li arcevesque prozdom e essaiet:
Li uns ne volt l'altre nient laisser.
En la grant presse i fierent as paiens.   2070
Mil Sarrazins i descendent a piet,
E a cheval sunt .XL. millers.
Men escientre nes osent aproismer.
Il lor lancent e lances e espiez,
E wigres e darz e museras e agiez e gieser.   2075
As premers colps i unt ocis Gualter,
Turpins de Reins tut sun escut percet,
Quasset sun elme, si l'unt nasfret el chef,
E sun osberc rumput e desmailet;
Par mi le cors nasfret de .IIII. espiez;   2080
Dedesuz lui ocient sun destrer.
Or est grant doel quant l'arcevesque chiet.   AOI.

155

Turpins de Reins, quant se sent abatut,
De .IIII. espiez par mi le cors ferut,
Isnelement li ber resailit sus;   2085
Rollant reguardet, puis si li est curut,
E dist un mot: «Ne sui mie vencut!
Ja bon vassal nen ert vif recreüt.»
Il trait Almace, s'espee de acer brun,
En la grant presse mil colps i fiert e plus,   2090
Puis le dist Carles qu'il n'en esparignat nul;
Tels .IIII. cenz i troevet entur lui:
Alquanz nafrez, alquanz par mi ferut,
Si out d'icels ki les chefs unt perdut.
Ço dit la Geste e cil ki el camp fut: 2095
Li ber Gilie, por qui Deus fait vertuz,
E fist la chartre el muster de Loüm.
Ki tant ne set ne l'ad prod entendut.

156

Li quens Rollant genteme[n]t se cumbat,
Mais le cors ad tressuet e mult chalt;   2100
En la teste ad e dulor e grant mal:
Rumput est li temples, por ço que il cornat.
Mais saveir volt se Charles i vendrat:
Trait l'olifan, fieblement le sunat.
Li emperere s'estut, si l'escultat: 2105
«Seignurs,» dist il, «mult malement nos vait!
Rollant mis nies hoi cest jur nus defalt.
Jo oi al corner que guaires ne vivrat.
Ki estre i voelt isnelement chevalzt!
Sunez voz graisles tant que en cest ost ad!»   2110
Seisante milie en i cornent si halt,
Sunent li munt e respondent li val:
Paien l'entendent, nel tindrent mie en gab;
Dit l'un a l'altre: «Karlun avrum nus ja!»

157

Dient paien: «L'emperere repairet!   AOI.   2115
De cels de France oe(n)z suner les graisles!
Se Carles vient, de nus i avrat perte.
Se R[ollant] vit, nostre guere renovelet,
Perdud avuns Espaigne, nostre tere.»
Tels .IIII. cenz s'en asemble[nt] a helmes,   2120
E des meillors ki el camp quient estre:
A Rollant rendent un estur fort e pesme.
Or ad li quens endreit sei asez que faire.   AOI.

158

Li quens Rollant, quant il les veit venir,
Tant se fait fort e fiers e maneviz!   2125
Ne lur lerat tant cum il serat vif.
Siet el cheval qu'om cleimet Veillantif,
Brochet le bien des esperuns d'or fin,
En la grant presse les vait tuz envaïr,
Ensem[b]l'od lui arcevesques Turpin.   2130
Dist l'un a l'altre: «Ça vus traiez ami!
De cels de France les corns avuns oït:
Carles repairet, li reis poesteïfs!»

159

Li quens Rollant unkes n'amat cuard
Ne orguillos, ne malvais (. . .) hume de male part,   2135
Ne chevaler, se il ne fust bon vassal.
Li arcevesques Turpin en apelat:
«Sire, a pied estes e jo sui a ceval;
Pur vostre amur ici prendrai estal;
Ensemble avruns e le ben e le mal;   2140
Ne vos lerrai pur nul hume de car.
Encui rendruns a paiens cest asalt.
Les colps des mielz, cels sunt de Durendal.»
Dist l'arcevesque: «Fel seit ki ben n'i ferrat.
Carles repairet, ki ben nus vengerat.»   2145

160

Paien dient: «Si mare fumes nez!
Cum pes[mes] jurz nus est hoi ajurnez!
Perdut avum noz seignurs e noz pers.
Carles repeiret od sa grant ost li ber;
De cels de France odum les graisles clers,   2150
Grant est la noise de «Munjoie!» escrier.
Li quens Rollant est de tant grant fiertet,
Ja n'ert vencut pur nul hume carnel.
Lancuns a lui, puis sil laissums ester.»
E il si firent darz e wigres asez,   2155
Espiez e lances e museraz enpennez;
(Le) L'escut Rollant unt frait e estroet,
E sun osberc rumput e desmailet;
Mais enz el cors ne l'unt mie adeset.
Mais Veillantif unt en .XXX. lius nafret,   2160
Desuz le cunte, si l'i unt mort laisset.
Paien s'en fuient, puis sil laisent ester.
Li quens Rollant i est remes a pied.   AOI.

161

Paien s'en fuient, curucus e irez;
Envers Espaigne tendent de l'espleiter.   2165
Li quens Rollant nes ad dunt encalcer:
Perdut i ad Veillantif sun destrer;
Voellet o nun, remes i est a piet.
A l'arcevesque Turpin alat aider:
Sun elme ad or li deslaçat del chef,   2170

Si li tolit le blanc osberc leger,
E sun blialt li ad tut detrenchet;
En ses granz plaies les pans li ad butet;
Cuntre sun piz puis si l'ad enbracet;
Sur l'erbe verte puis l'at suef culchet,   2175
Mult dulcement li ad Rollant preiet:
«E! gentilz hom, car me dunez cunget!
Noz cumpaignuns, que oümes tanz chers,
Or sunt il morz: nes i devuns laiser.
Joes voell aler querre e entercer,   2180
Dedevant vos juster e enrenger.»
Dist l'arcevesque: «Alez e repairez!
Cist camp est vostre, mercit Deu [. . .] mien.»

162

Rollant s'en turnet, par le camp vait tut suls,
Cercet les vals e si cercet les munz: 2185
Iloec truvat Gerin e Gerer sun cumpaignun.
E si truvat Berenger e Attun;
Iloec truvat Anseïs e Sansun,
Truvat Gerard le veill de Russillun.
Par uns e uns les ad pris le barun,   2190
A l'arcevesque en est venuz a tut,
Sis mist en reng dedevant ses genuilz.
Li arcevesque ne poet muer n'en plurt,
Lievet sa main, fait sa b[en]eïçun,
Apres ad dit: «Mare fustes, seignurs!   2195
Tutes voz anmes ait Deus li Glorius!
En pareïs les metet en se[i]ntes flurs!
La meie mort me rent si anguissus:
Ja ne verrai le riche empereuür!»

163

Rollant s'en turnet, le camp vait recercer,   2200
Sun cumpaignun ad truvet, Oliver:
Encuntre sun piz estreit l'ad enbracet;
Si cum il poet a l'arcevesques en vent,
Sur un escut l'ad as altres culchet,
E l'arcevesque (les) [l']ad asols e seignet.   2205
Idunc agreget le doel e la pitet.
Ço dit Rollant: «Bels cumpainz Oliver,
Vos fustes fils al duc Reiner

Ki tint la marche del val de Runers.
Pur hanste freindre e pur escuz peceier,   2210
Pur orgoillos veincre e esmaier,
E pur prozdomes tenir e cunseiller,
E pur glutun veincre e esmaier,
En nule tere n'ad meillor chevaler!»

164

Li quens Rollant, quant il veit mort ses pers,   2215
E Oliver, qu'il tant poeit amer,
Tendrur en out, cumencet a plurer.
En sun visage fut mult desculurez.
Si grant doel out que mais ne pout ester;
Voeillet o nun, a tere chet pasmet.   2220
Dist l'arcevesque: «Tant mare fustes ber!»

165

Li arcevesques quant vit pasmer Rollant,
Dunc out tel doel unkes mais n'out si grant.
Tendit sa main, si ad pris l'olifan:
En Rencesvals ad un ewe curant;   2225
Aler i volt, sin durrat a Rollant.
Sun petit pas s'en turnet cancelant.
Il est si fieble qu'il ne poet en avant;
N'en ad vertut, trop ad perdut del sanc.
Einz que om alast un sul arpent de camp,   2230
Falt li le coer, si est chaeit avant.
La sue mort l'i vait mult angoissant.

166

Li quens Rollant revient de pasmeisuns:
Sur piez se drecet, mais il ad grant dulur.
Guardet aval e si guardet amunt: 2235
Sur l'erbe verte, ultre ses cumpaignuns,
La veit gesir le nobilie barun,
Ço est l'arcevesque, que Deus mist en sun num.
Cleimet sa culpe, si reguardet amunt,
Cuntre le ciel amsdous ses mains ad juinz,   2240
Si priet Deu que pareïs li duinst.
[Morz est Turpin, le guerreier Charlun.]
Par granz batailles e par mult bels sermons,

Cuntre paiens fut tuz tens campiuns.
Deus li otreit (la sue) seinte beneïçun!   AOI.   2245

167

Li quens Rollant veit l'ar[ce]vesque a tere:
Defors sun cors veit gesir la buele;
Desuz le frunt li buillit la cervele.
Desur sun piz, entre les dous furceles,
Cruisiedes ad ses blanches [mains], les beles.   2250
Forment le pleignet a la lei de sa tere:
«E! gentilz hom, chevaler de bon aire,
Hoi te cumant al Glorius celeste!
Jamais n'ert hume plus volenters le serve.
Des les apostles ne fut hom tel prophete   2255
Pur lei tenir e pur humes atraire.
Ja la vostre anme nen ait sufraite!
De pareïs li seit la porte uverte!»

168

Ço sent Rollant que la mort li est pres
Par les oreilles fors se ist la cervel.   2260
De ses pers priet Deu ques apelt,
E pois de lui a l'angle Gabriel.
Prist l'olifan, que reproce n'en ait,
E Durendal s'espee en l'altre main.
D'un arcbaleste ne poet traire un quarrel,   2265
Devers Espaigne en vait en un guaret;
Muntet sur un tertre; desuz un arbre bel(e)
Quatre perruns i ad, de marbre fait(e).
Sur l'erbe verte si est caeit envers:
La s'est pasmet, kar la mort li est pres.   2270

169

Halt sunt li pui e mult halt les arbres.
Quatre perruns i ad luisant de marbre.
Sur l'erbe verte li quens Rollant se pasmet.
Uns Sarrazins tute veie l'esguardet:
Si se feinst mort, si gist entre les altres;   2275
Del sanc luat sun cors e sun visage.
Met sei en piez e de curre s'astet.
Bels fut e forz e de grant vasselage;

Par sun orgoill cumencet mortel rage;
Rollant saisit e sun cors e ses armes,   2280
E dist un mot: «Vencut est li nies Carles!
Iceste espee porterai en Arabe.»
En cel tirer(es) li quens s'aperçut alques.

170

Ço sent Rollant que s'espee li tolt.
Uvrit les oilz, si li ad dit un mot: 2285
«Men escientre, tu n'ies mie des noz!»
Tient l'olifan, que unkes perdre ne volt,
Sil fiert en l'elme, ki gemmet fut a or:
Fruisset l'acer e la teste e les ós,
Amsdous les oilz del chef li ad mis fors;   2290
Jus a ses piez si l'ad tresturnet mort.
Apres li dit: «Culvert paien, cum fus unkes si ós
Que me saisis, ne a dreit ne a tort?
Ne l'orrat hume, ne t'en tienget por fol.
Fenduz en est mis olifans el gros,   2295
Caiuz en est li cristals e li ors.»

171

Ço sent Rollant la veúe ad perdue;
Met sei sur piez, quanqu'il poet, s'esvertuet;
En sun visage sa culur ad perdue.
Dedevant lui ad une perre byse: 2300
.X. colps i fiert par doel e par rancune.
Cruist li acers, ne freint, [ne] n'esgruignet.
«E!» dist li quens, «sainte Marie, aiue!
E! Durendal, bone, si mare fustes!
Quant jo mei perd, de vos n'en ai mais cure.   2305
Tantes batailles en camp en ai vencues.
E tantes teres larges escumbatues,
Que Carles tient, ki la barbe ad canue!
Ne vos ait hume ki pur altre fuiet!
Mult bon vassal vos ad lung tens tenue: 2310
Jamais n'ert tel en France l'asolue.»

172

Rollant ferit el perrun de sardónie.
Cruist li acers, ne briset ne n'esgrunie.
Quant il ço vit que n'en pout mie freindre,

A sei meïsme la cumencet a pleindre: 2315
«E! Durendal, cum es bele, e clere, e blanche!
Cuntre soleill si luises e reflambes!
Carles esteit es vals de Moriane,
Quant Deus del cel li mandat par sun a[n]gle,
Qu'il te dunast a un cunte cataignie: 2320
Dunc la me ceinst li gentilz reis, li magnes.
Jo l'en cunquis Namon e Bretaigne,
Si l'en cunquis e Peitou e le Maine;
Jo l'en cunquis Normendie la franche,
Si l'en cunquis Provence e Equitaigne   2325
E Lumbardie e trestute (r)Romaine;
Jo l'en cunquis Baiver e tute Flandres,
E Burguigne e trestute Puillanie,
Costentinnoble, dunt il out la fiance,
E en Saisonie fait il ço, qu'il demandet;   2330
Jo l'en cunquis e Escoce e Vales Islonde,
E Engletere, que il teneit sa cambre;
Cunquis l'en ai païs e teres tantes,
Que Carles tient, ki ad la barbe blanche.
Pur ceste espee ai dulor e pesance: 2335
Mielz voeill murir qu'entre paiens remaigne.
Deus! Perre, n'en laise(i)t hunir France!»

                              173

Rollant ferit en une perre bise,
Plus en abat que jo ne vos sai dire.
L'espee cruist, ne fruisset, ne ne brise,   2340
Cuntre ciel amunt est resortie.
Quant veit li quens que ne la freindrat mie,
Mult dulcement la pleinst a sei meïsme:
«E! Durendal, cum es bele e seintisme!
En l'oriet punt asez i ad reliques: 2345
La dent seint Perre e del sanc seint Basilie,
E des chevels mun seignor seint Denise,
Del vestement i ad seinte Marie.
Il nen est dreiz que paiens te baillisent;
De chrestiens devrez estre servie.   2350
Ne vos ait hume ki facet cuardie!
Mult larges teres de vus avrai cunquises,
Que Carles les tent, ki la barbe ad flurie.
E li empereres en est ber e riches.»

174

Ço sent Rollant que la mort le tresprent,   2355
Devers la teste sur le quer li descent.
Desuz un pin i est alet curant,
Sur l'erbe verte s'i est culcet adenz,
Desuz lui met s'espee e l'olifan (en sumet);
Turnat sa teste vers la paiene gent;   2360
Pur ço l'at fait que il voelt veirement
Que Carles diet e trestute sa gent,
Li gentilz quens, qu'il fut mort cunquerant.
Cleimet sa culpe e menut e suvent;
Pur ses pecchez Deu (recleimet) en puroffrid lo guant.   AOI.   2365

175

Ço sent Rollant de sun tens n'i ad plus.
Devers Espaigne est en un pui agut;
A l'une main si ad sun piz batud:
«Deus, meie culpe vers les tues vertuz
De mes pecchez, des granz e des menuz   2370
Que jo ai fait des l'ure que nez fui
Tresqu'a cest jur que ci sui consoüt!»
Sun destre guant en ad vers Deu tendut:
Angles del ciel i descendent a lui.   AOI.

176

Li quens Rollant se jut desuz un pin;   2375
Envers Espaigne en ad turnet sun vis.
De plusurs choses a remembrer li prist:
De tantes teres cum li bers conquist,
De dulce France, des humes de sun lign,
De Carlemagne, sun seignor, kil nurrit.   2380
Ne poet muer n'en plurt e ne suspirt.
Mais lui meïsme ne volt mettre en ubli,
Cleimet sa culpe, si priet Deu mercit:
«Veire Patene, ki unkes ne mentis,
Seint Lazaron de mort resurrexis,   2385
E Daniel des leons guaresis,
Guaris de mei l'anme de tuz perilz
Pur les pecchez que en ma vie fis!»
Sun destre guant a Deu en puroffrit;
Seint Gabriel de sa main l'ad pris.   2390
Desur sun braz teneit le chef enclin;

Juntes ses mains est alet a sa fin.
Deus tramist sun angle Cherubin,
E seint Michel del Peril;
Ensembl'od els sent Gabriel i vint.   2395
L'anme del cunte portent en pareïs.

177

Morz est Rollant, Deus en ad l'anme es cels.
Li emperere en Rence[s]val[s] parvient.
Il nen i ad ne veie ne senter,
Ne voide tere, ne alne (illi) [ne] plein pied,   2400
Que il n'i ait o Franceis ó paien.
Carles escriet: «U estes vos, bels nies?
U est l'arcevesque e li quens Oliver?
U est Gerins e sis cumpainz Gerers?
U est Otes e li quens Berengers   2405
Ive e Ivorie, que jo aveie tant chers?
Que est devenuz li Guascuinz Engeler?
Sansun li dux e Anseïs li bers?
U est Gerard de Russillun li veilz?
Li .XII. per, que jo aveie laiset?»   2410
De ço qui chelt, quant nul n'en respundiet?
—«Deus!» dist li reis, «tant me pois esmaer
Que jo ne fui a l'estur cumencer!»
Tiret sa barbe cum hom ki est iret;
Plurent des oilz si baron chevaler;   2415
Encuntre tere se pasment .XX. millers.
Naimes li dux en ad mult grant pitet.

178

Il n'en i ad chevaler ne barun
Que de pitet mult durement ne plurt;
Plurent lur filz, lur freres, lur nevolz,   2420
E lur amis e lur lige seignurs;
Encuntre tere se pasment [. . .] li plusur.
Naimes li dux d'iço ad fait que proz,
Tuz premereins l'ad dit l empereür:
«Veez avant de dous liwes de nus,   2425
Ve[d]e[i]r puez les granz chemins puldrus,
(Que) Qu'ase(n)z i ad de la gent paienur.
Car chevalchez! Vengez ceste dulor!»
—«E! Deus!» dist Carles, «ja sunt il ja si luinz!

Cunse[i]l[l]ez mei e dreit[ure] e honur;   2430
De France dulce m'unt tolud la flur.»
Li reis cumandet Gebuin e Otun,
Tedbalt de Reins e le cunte Milun:
«Guardez le champ e les vals e les munz.
Lessez gesir les morz tut issi cun il sunt,   2435
Que n'i adeist ne beste ne lion,
Ne n'i adeist esquier ne garçun;
Jo vus defend que n'i adeist nuls hom,
Josque Deus voeil[l]e que en cest camp revengum.»
E cil respundent dulcement, par amur: 2440
«Dreiz emperere, cher sire, si ferum!»
Mil chevaler i retienent des lur.   AOI.

179

Li empereres fait ses graisles suner,
Puis si chevalchet od sa grant ost li ber.
De cels d'Espaigne unt lur les dos turnez,   2445
Tenent l'enchalz, tuit en sunt cumunel.
Quant veit li reis le vespres decliner,
Sur l'erbe verte descent li reis en un pred,
Culchet sei a tere, si priet Damnedeu
Que li soleilz facet pur lui arester,   2450
La nuit targer e le jur demurer.
Ais li un angle ki od lui soelt parler,
Isnelement si li ad comandet:
«Charle, chevalche, car tei ne faudrad clartet!
La flur de France as perdut, ço set Deus.   2455
Venger te poez de la gent criminel.»
A icel mot est l'emperere muntet.   AOI.

180

Pur Karlemagne fist Deus vertuz mult granz,
Car li soleilz est remes en estant.
Paien s'en fuient, ben les chalcent Franc.   2460
El Val Tenebrus la les vunt ateignant,
Vers Sarraguce les enchalcent [. . .] franc,
A colps pleners les en vunt ociant,
Tolent lur veies e les chemins plus granz.
L'ewe de Sebre, el lur est dedevant: 2465
Mult est parfunde, merveill[us]e e curant;
Il n'en i ad barge, ne drodmund ne caland.

Paiens recleiment un lur deu, Tervagant,
Puis saillent enz, mais il n'i unt guarant.
Li adubez en sunt li plus pesant,   2470
Env(er)ers les funz s'en turnerent alquanz;
Li altre en vunt cuntreval flotant.
Li miez guariz en unt boüd itant,
Tuz sunt neiez par merveillus ahan.
Franceis escrient: «Mare fustes, Rollant!»   AOI.   2475

181

Quant Carles veit que tuit sunt mort paiens,
Alquanz ocis e li plusur neiet,
Mult grant eschec en unt si chevaler,
Li gentilz reis descendut est a piet,
Culchet sei a tere, sin ad Deu graciet.   2480
Quant il se drecet, li soleilz est culchet.
Dist l'emperere: «Tens est del herberger;
En Rencesvals est tart del repairer:
Nos chevals sunt e las e ennuiez.
Tolez lur les seles, le freins qu'il unt es chefs,   2485
E par cez prez les laisez refreider.»
Respundent Franc: «Sire, vos dites bien.»   AOI.

182

Li emperere ad prise sa herberge.
Franceis descendent en la tere deserte,
A lur chevals unt toleites les seles,   2490
Les freins a or e metent jus des testes,
Livrent lur prez, asez i ad fresche herbe;
D'altre cunreid ne lur poent plus faire.
Ki mult est las, il se dort cuntre tere.
Icele noit n'unt unkes escalguaite.   2495

183

Li emperere s'est culcet en un pret:
Sun grant espiet met a sun chef li ber;
Icele noit ne se volt il desarmer,
Si ad vestut sun blanc osberc sasfret,
Laciet sun elme, ki est a or gemmet,   2500
Ceinte Joiuse, unches ne fut sa per,
Ki cascun jur muet .XXX. clartez.
Asez savum de la lance parler

Dunt Nostre Sire fut en la cruiz nasfret:
Carles en ad la mure, mercit Deu;   2505
En l'oret punt l'ad faite manuvrer.
Pur ceste honur e pur ceste bontet,
Li nums Joiuse l'espee fut dunet.
Baruns franceis nel deivent ublier:
Enseigne en unt de «Munjoie!» crier;   2510
Pur ço nes poet nule gent cuntrester.

184

Clere est la noit e la lune luisante.
Carles se gist, mais doel ad de Rollant
E d'Oliver li peiset mult forment,
Des .XII. pers e de la franceise gent.   2515
[Qu']en Rencesvals ad laiset morz sang[l]enz.
Ne poet muer n'en plurt e nes dement
E priet Deu qu'as anmes seit guarent.
Las est li reis, kar la peine est mult grant;
Endormiz est, ne pout mais en avant.   2520
Par tuz les prez or se dorment li Franc.
N'i ad cheval ki puisset ester en estant;
Ki herbe voelt, il la prent en gisant.
Mult ad apris ki bien conuist ahan.

185

Karles se dort cum hume traveillet.   2525
Seint Gabriel li ad Deus enveiet:
L'empereür li cumandet a guarder.
Li angles est tute noit a sun chef.
Par avisiun li ad anunciet
D'une bataille ki encuntre lui ert: 2530
Senefiance l'en demustrat mult gref.
Carles guardat amunt envers le ciel,
Veit les tuneires e les venz e les giels,
E les orez, les merveillus tempez,
E fous e flambes i est apareillez: 2535
Isnelement sur tute sa gent chet.
Ardent cez hanstes de fraisne e de pumer
E cez escuz jesqu'as bucles d'or mier,
Fruisent cez hanstes de cez trenchanz espiez,
Cruissent osbercs e cez helmes d'acer.   2540
En grant dulor i veit ses chevalers.

Urs e leuparz les voelent puis manger,
Serpenz e guivres, dragun e averser;
Grifuns i ad, plus de trente millers:
N'en i ad cel a Franceis ne s'agiet.   2545
E Franceis crient: «Carlemagne, aidez!»
Li reis en ad e dulur e pitet;
Aler i volt, mais il ad desturber.
Devers un gualt uns granz leons li vint,
Mult par ert pesmes e orguillus e fiers;   2550
Sun cors meïsmes i asalt e requert,
E prenent sei a braz ambesdous por loiter;
Mais ço ne set liquels abat ne quels chiet.
Li emperere n'est mie esveillet.

186

Apres icel li vien[t] un altre avisiun,   2555
Qu'il ert en France, ad Ais, a un perrun,
En dous chaeines si teneit un brohun.
Devers Ardene veeit venir .XXX. urs,
Cascun parolet altresi cume hum.
Diseient li: «Sire rendez le nus!   2560
Il nen est dreiz que il seit mais od vos;
Nostre parent devum estre a sucurs.»
De sun paleis uns veltres acurt;
Entre les altres asaillit le greignur
Sur l'erbe verte ultre ses cumpaignuns.   2565
La vit li reis si merveillus estur;
Mais ço ne set liquels veint ne quels nun.
Li angles Deu ço ad mustret al barun.
Carles se dort tresqu'al demain, al cler jur.

187

Li reis Marsilie s'en fuit en Sarraguce.   2570
Suz un olive est descendut en l'umbre,
S'espee rent e sun elme e sa bronie;
Sur la verte herbe mult laidement se culcet;
La destre main ad perdue trestute;
Del sanc qu'en ist se pasmet e angoiset.   2575
Dedevant lui sa muiller, Bramimunde,
Pluret e criet, mult forment se doluset;
Ensembl'od li plus de .XX. mil humes,
Si maldient Carlun e France dulce.

Ad Apolin (en) curent en une crute,   2580
Tencent a lui, laidement le despersunent:
«E! malvais deus, por quei nus fais tel hunte?
Cest nostre rei por quei lessas cunfundre?
Ki mult te sert, malvais luer l'en dunes!»
Puis si li tolent se sceptre e sa curune.   2585
Par les mains le pendent sur une culumbe,
Entre lur piez a tere le tresturnent,
A granz bastuns le batent e defruisent.
E Tervagan tolent sun escarbuncle,
E Mahumet enz en un fosset butent,   2590
E porc e chen le mordent e defulent.

188

De pa(i)smeisuns en est venuz Marsilies:
Fait sei porter en sa cambre voltice;
Plusurs culurs i ad peinz e escrites.
E Bramimunde le pluret, la reïne,   2595
Trait ses chevels, si se cleimet caitive,
A l'altre mot mult haltement s'escriet:
«E! Sarraguce, cum ies oi desguarnie
Del gentil rei ki t'aveit en baillie!
Li nostre deu i unt fait felonie,   2600
Ki en bataille oi matin le faillirent.
Li amiralz i ferat cuardie
S'il ne cumbat a cele gent hardie,
Ki si sunt fiers n'unt cure de lur vies.
Li emperere od la barbe flurie,   2605
Vasselage ad e mult grant estultie;
S'il ad bataill(i)e, il ne s'en fuirat mie.
Mult est grant doel que n'en est ki l'ociet!»

189

Li emperere par sa grant poestet,
.VII. anz tuz plens ad en Espaigne estet;   2610
Prent i chastels e alquantes citez.
Li reis Marsilie s'en purcacet asez:
Al premer an fist ses brefs seieler,
En Babilonie Baligant ad mandet,
Ço est l'amiraill, le viel d'antiquitet,   2615
Tut survesquiet e Virgilie e Omer,
En Sarraguce alt sucurre li ber;

E, s'il nel fait, il guerpirat ses deus
E tuz ses ydeles que il soelt adorer,
Si recevrat sainte chrestientet,   2620
A Charlemagne se vuldrat acorder.
E cil est loinz, si ad mult demuret;
Mandet sa gent de .XL. regnez,
Ses granz drodmunz en ad fait aprester,
Eschiez e barges e galies e nefs.   2625
Suz Alixandre ad un port juste mer:
Tut sun navilie i ad fait aprester.
Ço est en mai, al premer jur d'ested:
Tutes ses oz ad empeintes en mer.

190
Granz sunt les oz de cele gent averse: 2630
Siglent a fort e nagent e guvernent.
En sum cez maz e en cez (les) [h]altes vernes,
Asez i ad carbuncles e lanternes;
La sus amunt pargetent tel luiserne
Par la noit la mer en est plus bele.   2635
E cum il vienent en Espaigne la tere,
Tut li païs en reluist e esclairet.
Jesqu'a Marsilie en parvunt les noveles.   AOI.

191
Gent paienor ne voelent cesser unkes:
Issent de mer, venent as ewes dulces,   2640
Laisent Marbrose e si laisent Marbrise,
Par Sebre amunt tut lur naviries turnent.
Asez i ad lanternes e carbuncles:
Tute la noit mult grant clartet lur dunent.
A icel jur venent a Sarraguce.   AOI.   2645

192
Clers est li jurz et li soleilz luisant.
Li amiralz est issut del calan:
Espaneliz fors le vait adestrant,
.XVII. reis apres le vunt siwant;
Cuntes e dux i ad ben ne sai quanz.   2650
Suz un lorer, ki est en mi un camp,
Sur l'erbe verte getent un palie blanc:
U[n] faldestoed i unt mis d'olifan.

Desur s'asiet li paien Baligant;
Tuit li altre sunt remes en estant.   2655
Li sire d'els premer parlat avant:
«Oiez ore, franc chevaler vaillant!
Carles li reis, l'emperere des Francs,
Ne deit manger, se jo ne li cumant.
Par tute Espaigne m'at fait guere mult grant: 2660
En France dulce le voeil aler querant.
Ne finerai en trestut mun vivant
Josqu'il seit mort u tut vif recreant.»
Sur sun genoill en fiert sun destre guant.

193

Puis qu'il l'ad dit, mult s'en est afichet   2665
Que ne lairat pur tut l'or desuz ciel,
Que il ainz ad Ais, o Carles soelt plaider.
Si hume li lo[d]ent, si li unt cunseillet.
Puis apelat dous de ses chevalers,
L'un Clarifan e l'altre Clarïen: 2670
«Vos estes filz al rei Maltraïen,
Ki messages soleit faire volenters.
Jo vos cumant qu'en Sarraguce algez;
Marsiliun de meie part li nunciez,
Cuntre Franceis li sui venut aider.   2675
Se jo truis ó, mult grant bataille i ert;
Si l'en dunez cest guant ad or pleiet,
El destre poign si li faites chalcer.
Si li portez cest [bast]uncel d'or mer,
E a mei venget pur reconoistre sun feu.   2680
En France irai pur Carles guerreier;
S'en ma mercit ne se culzt a mes piez
E ne guerpisset la lei de chrestiens,
Jo li toldrai la co(r)rune del chef.»
Paien respundent «Sire, mult dites bien.»   2685

194

Dist Baligant: «Car chevalchez, barun!
L'un port le guant, li alt[r]e le bastun!»
E cil respundent «Cher sire, si ferum.»
Tant chevalcherent que en Sarraguce sunt.
Passent .X. portes, traversent .IIII. punz,   2690
Tutes les rues u li burgeis estunt.
Cum il aproisment en la citet amunt,

Vers le paleis oïrent grant fremur;
Asez i ad de cele gent paienur,
Plurent e crient, demeinent grant dolor,   2695
Pleignent lur deus Tervagan e Mahum
E Apollin, dunt il mie n'en unt.
Dist cascun a l'altre: «Caitifs, que devendrum?
Sur nus est venue male confusiun.
Perdut avum le rei Marsiliun: 2700
Li quens Rollant li trenchat ier le destre poign.
Nus n'avum mie de Jurfaleu le Blunt.
Trestute Espaigne iert hoi en lur bandun.»
Li dui message descendent al perrun.

195

Lur chevals laisent dedesuz un olive: 2705
Dui Sarrazin par les resnes les pristrent.
E li message par les mantels se tindrent,
Puis sunt muntez sus el paleis altisme.
Cum il entrent en la cambre voltice,
Par bel amur malvais saluz li firent: 2710
«Cil Mahumet ki nus ad en baillie,
E Tervagan e Apollin, nostre sire,
Sálvent le rei e guardent la reïne!»
Dist Bramimunde: «Or oi mult grant folie!
Cist nostre deu sunt en recreantise.   2715
En Rencesval m[al]vaises vertuz firent:
Noz chevalers i unt lesset ocire;
Cest mien seignur en bataille faillirent;
Le destre poign ad perdut, n'en ad mie,
Si li trenchat li quens Rollant, li riches.   2720
Trestute Espaigne avrat Carles en baillie.
Que devendrai, duluruse, caitive?
E! lasse, que n'en ai un hume ki m'ociet!»   AOI.

196

Dist Clarien «Dame, ne parlez mie itant!
Messages sumes al paien Baligant.   2725
Marsiliun, ço dit, serat guarant,
Si l'en enveiet sun bastun e sun guant.
En Sebre avum .IIII. milie calant,
Eschiez e barges e galees curant;
Drodmunz i ad ne vos sai dire quanz.   2730

Li amiralz est riches e puisant:
En France irat Carlemagne querant;
Rendre le quidet u mort ó recreant.»
Dist Bramimunde «Mar en irat itant!
Plus pres d'ici purrez truver les Francs.   2735
En ceste tere ad estet ja .VII. anz.
Li emperere est ber e cumbatant:
Meilz voel murir que ja fuiet de camp;
Suz ciel n'ad rei qu'il prist a un enfant.
Carles ne creint nuls hom ki seit vivant.»   2740

197

—«Laissez ço ester!« dist Marsilies li reis.
Dist as messages: «Seignurs, parlez a mei!
Ja veez vos que a mort sui destreit,
Jo si nen ai filz ne fille ne heir:
Un en aveie, cil fut ocis her seir.   2745
Mun seignur dites qu'il me vienge veeir.
Li amiraill ad en Espaigne dreit:
Quite li cleim, se il la voelt aveir,
Puis la defendet encuntre li Franceis!
Vers Carlemagne li durrai bon conseill: 2750
Cunquis l'avrat d'oi cest jur en un meis.
De Sarraguce les clefs li portereiz;
Pui li dites, il n'en irat, s'il me creit.»
Cil respundent: «Sire, vus dites veir.»   AOI.

198

Ço dist Marsilie: «Carles l'emperere   2755
Mort m'ad mes homes, ma tere deguastee,
E mes citez fraites e violees.
Il jut anuit sur cel ewe de Sebre:
Jo ai cunte n'i ad mais que .VII. liwes.
L'amirail dites que sun host i amein.   2760
Par vos li mand bataille i seit justee.»
De Sarraguce les clefs li ad livrees.
Li messager ambedui l'enclinerent,
Prenent cu(i)[n]get, a cel mot s'en turnerent.

199

Li dui message es chevals sunt muntet.   2765
Isnelement issent de la citet,

A l'amiraill en vunt esfreedement;
De Sarra[gu]ce li presentent les cles.
Dist Baligant: «Que avez vos truvet?
U est Marsilie, que jo aveie mandet?«   2770
Dist Clarïen: «Il est a mort nasfret.
Li emperere fut ier as porz passer,
Si s'en vuolt en dulce France aler.
Par grant honur se fist rereguarder:
Li quens Rollant i fut remes, sis nies,   2775
E Oliver e tuit li .XII. per,
De cels de France .XX. milie adubez.
Li reis Marsilie s'i cumbatit, li bers.
Il e Rollant el camp furent remes:
De Durendal li dunat un colp tel   2780
Le destre poign li ad del cors sevret;
Sun filz ad mort, qu'il tant suleit amer,
E li baron qu'il i out amenet.
Fuiant s'en vint, qu'il n'i pout mes ester.
Li emperere l'ad enchalcet asez.   2785
Li reis mandet que vos le sucurez.
Quite vus cleimet d'Espaigne le regnet.»
E Baligant cumencet a penser;
Si grant doel ad por poi qu'il n'est desvet.   AOI.

200

«Sire amiralz,» dist Clarïens,   2790
«En Rencesvals une bataille out ïer.
Morz est Rollant e li quens Oliver,
Li .XII. per, que Carles aveit tant cher;
De lur Franceis i ad mort .XX. millers.
Li reis Marsilie le destre poign i perdit,   2795
E l'emperere asez l'ad enchalcet,
En ceste tere n'est remes chevaler
Ne seit ocis o en Sebre neiet.
Desur la rive sunt Frances herbergiez:
En cest païs nus sunt tant aproeciez,   2800
Se vos volez, li repaires ert grefs.»
E Baligant le reguart en ad fiers,
En sun curage en est joüs e liet.
Del faldestod se redrecet en piez,
Puis escriet: «Baruns, ne vos targez!   2805
Eissez des nefs, muntez, si cevalciez!
S'or ne s'en fuit Karlemagne li veilz,

Li reis Marsilie enqui serat venget:
Pur sun poign destre l'en liverai le che(s)[f].»

201

Paien d'Arabe des nefs se sunt eissut,   2810
Puis sunt muntez es chevals e es muls;
Si chevalcherent, que fereient il plus?
Li amiralz, ki trestuz les esmut,
Sin apelet Gemalfin, un sun drut:
«Jo te cumant de tutes mes oz l'aunde.»   2815
Puis en un sun destrer brun est munte;
Ensembl'od lui emmeinet .IIII. dux.
Tant chevalchat qu'en Sarraguce fut.
A un perron de marbre est descenduz,
E quatre cuntes l'estreu li unt tenut.   2820
Par les degrez el paleis muntet sus,
E Bramidonie vient curant cuntre lui;
Si li ad dit: «Dolente, si mare fui!
A itel hunte, sire, mon seignor ai perdut!»
Chet li as piez, li amiralz la reçut;   2825
Sus en la chambre ad doel en sunt venut.   AOI.

202

Li reis Marsilie, cum il veit Baligant,
Dunc apelat dui Sarrazin espans:
«Pernez m'as braz, sim(e) drecez en seant.»
Al puign senestre ad pris un de ses guanz.   2830
Ço dist Marsilie: «Sire reis, amiralz,
Teres tutes ici [. . .] rengnes vos rendemas
E Sarraguce e l'onur qu'i apent.
Mei ai perdut e tute ma gent.»
E cil respunt: «Tant sy jo plus dolent.   2835
Ne pois a vos tenir lung parlement:
Jo sai asez que Carles ne m'atent,
E nepurquant de vos receif le guant.»
Al doel qu'il ad s'en est turnet plurant.   AOI.
Par les degrez jus del paleis descent,   2840
Muntet el ceval, vient a sa gent puignant.
Tant chevalchat, qu'il est premers devant,
De uns ad altres si se vait escriant:
«Venez paien, car ja s'en fuient Frant!»   AOI.

203

Al matin, quant primes pert li albe,   2845
Esveillez est li e[m]perere Carles.
Sein Gabriel, ki de part Deu le guarde,
Levet sa main, sur lui fait sun signacle.
Li reis descent, si ad rendut ses armes,
Si se desarment par tute l'ost li altre.   2850
Puis sunt muntet, par grant vertut chevalchent
Cez veiez lunges e cez chemins mult larges,
Si vunt ve[d]eir le merveillus damage
En Rencesvals, la ó fut la bataille.   AOI.

204

En Rencesvals en est Carles venuz.   2855
Des morz qu'il troevet cumencet a plurer.
Dist a Franceis: «Segnu[r]s, le pas tenez;
Kar mei meïsme estoet avant aler
Pur mun nev[ol]d que vuldreie truver.
A Eis esteie, a une féste anoel: 2860
Si se vant(t)[er]ent mi vaillant chevaler
De granz batailles, de forz esturs pleners.
D'une raisun oï Rollant parler:
Ja ne (ne) murreit en estrange regnet
Ne trespassast ses hume[s] e ses pers;   2865
Vers lur païs avreit sun chef turnet;
Cunquerrantment si finereit li bers.»
Plus qu'en ne poet un bastuncel jeter,
Devant les altres est en un pui muntet.

205

Quant l'empereres vait querre sun nevold,   2870
De tantes herbes el pre truvat les flors,
Ki sunt vermeilz del sanc de noz barons!
Pitet en ad, ne poet muer n'en plurt.
Desuz dous arbres parvenuz est [. . .] li reis.
Les colps Rollant conut en treis per(r)uns,   2875
Sur l'erbe verte veit gesir sun nevuld;
Nen est merveille se Karles ad irur.
Descent a pied, aled i est pleins curs,
Entre ses mains ansdous prent le priest suus;
Sur lui se pasmet, tant par est anguissus.   2880

206

Li empereres de pasmeisuns revint.
Naimes li dux e li quens Acelin,
Gefrei d'Anjou e sun frere Henri
Prenent le rei, sil drecent suz un pin.
Guardet a la tere, veit sun nevold gesir.   2885
Tant dulcement a regreter le prist:
«Amis Rollant, de tei ait Deus mercit!
Unques nuls hom tel chevaler ne vit
Por granz batailles juster e defenir.
La meie honor est turnet en declin.»   2890
Carles se pasmet, ne s'en pout astenir.   AOI.

207

Carles li reis se vint de pasmeisuns;
Par mains le tienent .III. de ses barons.
Guardet a tere, veit gesir sun nev[u]ld:
Cors ad gaillard, perdue ad sa culur,   2895
Turnez ses oilz, mult li sunt tenebros.
Carles le pleint par feid e par amur:
«Ami Rollant, Deus metet t'anme en flors,
En pareïs, entre les glorius!
Cum en Espaigne venis [a] mal seignur!   2900
Jamais n'ert jurn que de tei n'aie dulur.
Cum decarrat ma force e ma baldur!
N'en avrai ja ki sustienget m'onur;
Suz ciel ne quid aveir ami un sul!
Se jo ai parenz, n'en i ad nul si proz.»   2905
Trait ses crignels, pleines ses mains amsdous,
Cent milie Franc en unt si grant dulur
N'en i ad cel ki durement ne plurt.   AOI.

208

«Ami Rollant, jo m'en irai en France.
Cum jo serai a Loün, en ma chambre,   2910
De plusurs regnes vendrunt li hume estrange;
Demanderunt: «U est quens cataignes?»
Jo lur dirrai qu'il est morz en Espaigne.
A grant dulur tendrai puis mun reialme:
Jamais n'ert jur que ne plur ne n'en pleigne.»   2915

209

—«Ami Rollant, prozdoem, juvente bele,
Cum jo serai a Eis, em ma chapele,
Vendrunt li hume, demanderunt noveles;
Jes lur dirrai, merveilluses e pesmes:
«Morz est mis nies, ki tant me fist cunquere.»   2920
Encuntre mei revelerunt li Seisne,
E Hungre e Bugre e tante gent averse,
Romain, Puillain e tuit icil de Palerne
E cil d'Affrike e cil de Califerne;
Puis entrerunt mes peines e mes suffraites.   2925
Ki guierat mes oz a tel poeste,   .
Quant cil est [morz] ki tuz jurz nos cadelet?
E! France, cum remeines deserte!
Si grant doel ai que jo ne vuldreie estre!»
Sa barbe blanche cumencet a detraire,   2930
Ad ambes mains les chevels de sa teste.
Cent milie Francs s'en pasment cuntre tere.

210

«Ami Rollant, de tei ait Deus mercit!
L'anme de tei seit mise en pareïs!
Ki tei ad mort France ad mis en exill.   2935
Si grant dol ai que ne voldreie vivre,
De ma maisnee, ki por mei est ocise!
Ço duinset Deus, le filz sainte Marie,
Einz que jo vienge as maistres porz de Sirie,
L'anme del cors me seit oi departie,   2940
Entre les lur aluee e mise,
E ma car fust delez els enfuïe!»
Ploret des oilz, sa blanche bar[b]e tiret.
E dist dux Naimes: «Or ad Carles grant ire.»   AOI.

211

—«Sire emperere,» ço dist Gefrei d'Anjou,   2945
«Ceste dolor ne demenez tant fort!
Par tut le camp faites querre les noz,
Que cil d'Espaigne en la bataille unt mort;
En un carne(l)[r] cumandez que hom les port.»
Ço dist li reis: «Sunez en vostre corn!»   AOI.   2950

212

Gefreid d'Anjou ad sun greisle sunet.
Franceis descendent, Carles l'ad comandet.
Tuz lur amis qu'il i unt morz truvet,
Ad un carne(l)[r] sempres les unt portet.
Asez i ad evesques e abez,   2955
Munies, canonies, proveires coronez:
Si sunt asols e seignez de part Deu.
Mirre e timoine i firent alumer,
Gaillardement tuz les unt encensez;
A grant honor pois les unt enterrez.   2960
Sis unt laisez: qu'en fereient il el?   AOI.

213

Li emperere fait Rollant costeïr
E Oliver e (e) l'arcevesque Turpin,
Devant sei les ad fait tuz uvrir
E tuz les quers en paile recuillir: 2965
Un blanc sarcou de marbre sunt enz mis;
E puis les cors des barons si unt pris,
En quirs de cerf les seignurs unt mis:
Ben sunt lavez de piment e de vin.
Li reis cumandet Tedbalt e Gebuin,   2970
Milun le cunte e Otes le marchis:
«En .III. carettes les guiez [. . .] tres ben.»
Bien sunt cuverz d'un palie galazin.   AOI.

214

Venir s'en volt li emperere Carles,
Quant de paiens li surdent les enguardes.   2975
De cels devant i vindrent dui messages,
De l'amirail li nuncent la bataille:
«Reis orguillos, nen est fins que t'en alges!
Veiz Baligant, ki apres tei chevalchet:
Granz sunt les oz qu'il ameinet d'Arabe.   2980
Encoi verrum se tu as vasselage.»   AOI.
Carles li reis en ad prise sa barbe;
Si li remembret del doel e [del] damage,
Mult fierement tute sa gent reguardez;
Puis si s'escriet a sa voiz grand e halte: 2985
«Barons franceis, as chevals e as armes!»   AOI.

215

Li empereres tuz premereins s'adubet:
Isnelement ad vestue sa brunie,
Lacet sun helme, si ad ceinte Joiuse,
Ki pur soleill sa clartet n'en muet;   2990
Pent a sun col un escut de Biterne,
Tient sun espiet, sin fait brandir la hanste,
En Tencendur, sun bon cheval, puis muntet:
Il le cunquist es guez desuz Marsune,
Sin getat mort Malpalin de Nerbone;   2995
Laschet la resne, mult suvent l'esperonet,
Fait sun eslais, veant cent mil humes,   AOI.
Recleimet Deu e l'apostle de Rome.

216

Par tut le champ cil de France descendent,
Plus de cent milie s'en adubent ensemble;   3000
Guarnemenz unt ki ben lor atalente[n]t,
Cevals curanz e lur armes mult gentes;
Puis sunt muntez e unt grant science.
S'il troevent oí, bataille quident rendre.
Cil gunfanun sur les helmes lur pendent.   3005
Quant Carles veit si beles cuntenances,
Sin apelat Jozeran de Provence,
Naimon li duc, Antelme de Maience:
«En tels vassals deit hom aveir fiance!
Asez est fols ki entr'els se dem[ent]et.   3010
Si Arrabiz de venir ne se repentent,
La mort Rollant lur quid cherement rendre.»
Respunt dux Neimes: «E Deus le nos cunsente!»   AOI.

217

Carles apelet Rabe[l] e Guinemán.
Ço dist li reis: «Seignurs, jo vos cumant,   3015
Seiez es lius Oliver e Rollant:
L'un port l'espee e l'altre l'olifant,
Si chevalcez el premer chef devant,
Ensembl'od vos .XV. milie de Franc(ei)s,
De bachelers, de noz (. . .) meillors vaillanz.   3020
Apres icels en avrat altretant,
Sis guierat Gibuins e Guinemans.»
Naimes li dux e li quens Jozerans

Icez eschieles ben les vunt ajustant.
S'il troevent oí, bataille i ert mult grant.   AOI.   3025

218

De Franceis sunt les premeres escheles.
Apres les dous establisent la terce;
En cele sunt li vassal de Baivere,
A .XX. [milie] chevalers la preiserent;
Ja devers els bataille n'ert lessee.   3030
Suz cel n'ad gent que Carles ait plus chere,
Fors cels de France, ki les regnes cunquerent.
Li quens Oger li Daneis, li puinneres,
Les guierat, kar la cumpaigne est fiere.   AOI.

219

Treis escheles ad l'emperere Carles.   3035
Naimes li dux puis establist la quarte
De tels barons qu'asez unt vasselage:
Alemans sunt e si sunt d'Alemaigne;
Vint milie sunt, ço dient tuit li altre.
Ben sunt guarniz e de chevals e d'armes;   3040
Ja por murir ne guerpirunt bataille.
Sis guierat Hermans li dux de Trace.
Einz i murat que cuardise i facet.   AOI.

220

Naimes li dux e li quens Jozerans
La quinte eschele unt faite de Normans: 3045
.XX. milie sunt, ço dient tuit li Franc.
Armes unt beles e bons cevals curanz;
Ja pur murir cil n'erent recreanz.
Suz ciel n'ad gent ki plus poissent en camp.
Richard li velz les guierat el camp: 3050
Cil i ferrat de sun espiet trenchant.   AOI.

221

La siste eschele unt faite de Bretuns:
.XXX. milie chevalers od els unt.
Icil chevalchent en guise de baron,
Peintes lur hanstes, fermez lur gunfanun.   3055
Le seignur d'els est apelet Oedun:

Icil cumandet le cunte Nevelun,
Tedbald de Reins e le marchis Otun:
«Guiez ma gent, jo vos en faz le dun!»   AOI.

222

Li emperere ad .VI. escheles faites.   3060
Naimes li dux puis establist la sedme
De Peitevins e des barons d'Alverne:
.XL. milie chevalers poeent estre.
Chevals unt bons e les armes mult beles.
Cil sunt par els en un val suz un tertre;   3065
Sis beneïst Carles de sa main destre.
Els guierat Jozerans e Godselmes.   AOI.

223

E l'oidme eschele ad Naimes establie:
De Flamengs est [e] des barons de Frise.
Chevalers unt plus de .XL. milie;   3070
Ja devers els n'ert bataille guerpie.
Ço dist li reis «Cist ferunt mun servise.»
Entre Rembalt e Hamon de Galice
Les guierunt tut par chevalerie.   AOI.

224

Entre Naimon e Jozeran le cunte   3075
La noefme eschele unt faite de prozdomes
De Loherengs e de cels de Borgoigne.
.L. milie chevalers unt par cunte,
Helmes laciez e vestues lor bronies;
Espiez unt forz e les hanstes sunt curtes.   3080
Si Arrabiz de venir ne demurent,
Cil les ferrunt, s'il a els s'abandunent.
Sis guierat Tierris, li dux d'Argone.   AOI.

225

La disme eschele est des baruns de France:
Cent milie sunt de noz meillors cataignes.   3085
Cors unt gaillarz e fieres cuntenances,
Les chefs fluriz e les barbes unt blanches,
Osbercs vestuz e lur brunies dubleines,
Ceintes espees franceises e d'Espaigne;

Escuz unt genz, de multes cunoisances.   3090
Puis sunt muntez, la bataille demandent;
«Munjoie!» escrient: Od els est Carlemagne.
Gefreid d'Anjou portet l'orieflambe:
Seint Piere fut (. . .), si aveit num Romaine;
Mais de Munjoie iloec out pris eschange.   AOI.   3095

226

Li emperere de sun cheval descent;
Sur l'erbe verte se est culchet adenz,
Turnet su[n] vis vers le soleill levant,
Recleimet Deu mult escordusement:
«Veire Paterne, hoi cest jor me defend,   3100
Ki guaresis Jonas tut veirement
De la baleine ki en sun cors l'aveit
E espar(i)gnas le rei de Niniven
E Daniel del merveillus turment
Enz en la fosse des leons o fut enz,   3105
Les .III. enfanz tut en un fou ardant:
La tue amurs me seit hoi en present!
Par ta mercit, se tei plaist, me cunsent
Que mun nevold pois[se] venger Rollant!»
Cum ad oret, si se drecet en estant,   3110
Seignat sun chef de la vertut poisant.
Muntet li reis en sun cheval curant;
L'estreu li tindrent Neimes e Jocerans;
Prent sun escut e sun espiet trenchant.
Gent ad le cors, gaillart e ben seant,   3115
Cler le visage e de bon cuntenant.
Puis si chevalchet mult aficheement.
Sunent cil greisle e derere e devant;
Sur tuz les altres bundist li olifant.
Plurent Franceis pur pitet de Rollant.   3120

227

Mult gentement li emperere chevalchet:
Desur sa bronie fors ad mise sa barbe.
Pur sue amor altretel funt li altre:
Cent milie Francs en sunt reconoisable.
Passent cez puis e cez roches plus haltes,   3125
E cez parfunz val(ee)s, ces destreit anguisables,
Issent des porz e de la tere guaste,

Devers Espaigne sunt alez en la marche;
En un emplein unt prise lur estage.
A Baligant repairent ses enguardes.   3130
Uns Sulians ki ad dit sun message:
«Veüd avum li orguillus reis Carles.
Fiers sunt si hume, n'unt talent qu'il li faillent.
Adubez vus, sempres avrez bataille!»
Dist Baligant: «Or oi grant vasselage.   3135
Sunez voz graisles, que mi paien le sace[n]t!»

228

Par tute l'ost funt lur taburs suner,
E cez buisines e cez greisles mult cler:
Paien descendent pur lur cors aduber.
Li amiralz ne se voelt demurer: 3140
Vest une bronie dunt li pan sunt sasfret,
Lacet sun elme, ki ad or est gemmet,
Puis ceint s'espee al senestre costet.
Par sun orgoill li ad un num truvet:
Par la spee Carlun dunt il oït parler   3145
. . . .
Ço ert s'enseigne en bataille campel:
Ses chevalers en ad fait escrier.
Pent a sun col un soen grant escut let:
D'or est la bucle e de cristal listet,   3150
La guige en est d'un bon palie roet;
Tient sun espiet, si l'apelet Maltet:
La hanste grosse cume uns tinels;
De sul le fer fust uns mulez trusset.
En sun destrer Baligant est muntet;   3155
L'estreu li tint Marcules d'Ultremer.
La forcheüre ad asez grant li ber,
Graisles les flancs e larges les costez;
Gros ad le piz, belement est mollet,
Lees les espalles e le vis ad mult cler,   3160
Fier le visage, le chef recercelet,
Tant par ert blancs cume flur en estet;
De vasselage est suvent esprovet.
Deus! quel baron, s'oüst chrestientet!
Le cheval brochet, li sancs en ist tuz clers,   3165
Fait sun eslais, si tressalt un fosset,
Cinquante pez i poet hom mesurer.
Paien escrient: «Cist deit marches tenser!

N'i ad Franceis, si a lui vient juster,
Voeillet o nun, n'i perdet sun edet.   3170
Carles est fols que ne s'en est alet.»   AOI.

229

Li amiralz ben resemblet barun.
Blanche ad la barbe ensement cume flur,
E de sa lei mult par est saives hom,
E en bataille est fiers e orgoillus.   3175
Ses filz Malpramis mult est chevalerus:
Granz est e forz e trait as anceisurs.
Dist a sun perre: «Sire, car cevalchum!
Mult me merveill se ja verrum Carlun.»
Dist Baligant: «Oïl, car mult est proz.   3180
En plusurs gestes de lui sunt granz honurs.
Il n'en at mie de Rollant sun nevold:
N'avrat vertut ques tienget cuntre nus.»   AOI.

230

—«Bels filz Malpramis,» ço li dist Baligant,
«Li altrer fut ocis le bon vassal Rollant   3185
E Oliver, li proz e li vaillanz,
Li .XII. per qui Carles amat tant,
De cels de France .XX. milie cumbatanz.
Trestuz les altres ne pris jo mie un guant.
Li empereres repairet veirement,   3190
S'il m'at nunciet mes mes, li Sulians,
.X. escheles en unt faites mult granz.
Cil est mult proz ki sunet l'olifant,
D'un graisle cler racatet ses cumpaignz;
E si cevalcent el premer chef devant,   3195
Ensembl'od els .XV. milie de Francs,
De bachelers que Carles cleimet enfanz.
Apres icels en i ad ben altretanz:
Cil i ferrunt mult orgoillusement.»
Dist Malpramis: «Le colp vos en demant.»   AOI.   3200

231

—«Filz Malpramis,» Baligant li ad dit,
«Jo vos otri quanque m'avez ci quis.
Cuntre Franceis sempres irez ferir;

Si i merrez Torleu, le rei persis,
E Dapamort, un altre rei leutiz.   3205
Le grant orgoill se ja puez matir,
Jo vos durrai un pan de mun païs
Des Cheriant entresqu'en Val Marchis.»
Cil respunt: «Sire, vostre mercit!»
Passet avant, le dun en requeillit,   3210
Ço est de la tere ki fut al rei Flurit,
A itel ore unches puis ne la vit,
Ne il n'en fut ne vestut ne saisit.

232

Li amiraill chevalchet par cez oz.
Sis filz le siut, ki mult ad grant le cors.   3215
Li reis Torleus e li reis Dapamort
.XXX. escheles establissent mult tost:
Chevalers unt a merveillus esforz;
En la menur .L. milie en out.
La premere est de cels de Butentrot,   3220
E l'altre apres de Micenes as chefs gros;
Sur les eschines qu'il unt en mi les dos
Cil sunt seiet ensement cume porc.   AOI.
E la t(er)erce est de Nubles e de Blos,
E la quarte est de Bruns e d'Esclavoz,   3225
E la quinte est de Sorbres e de Sorz,
E la siste est d'Ermines e de Mors,
E la sedme est de cels de Jericho,
E l'oitme est de Nigres e la noefme de Gros,
E la disme est de Balide la fort: 3230
Ço est une gent ki unches ben ne volt.   AOI.
Li amiralz en juret quanqu'il poet
De Mahumet les vertuz e le cors:
«Karles de France chevalchet cume fols.
Bataille i ert, se il ne s'en destolt;   3235
Jamais n'avrat el chef corone d'or.»

233

Dis escheles establisent apres.
La premere est des Canelius les laiz,
De Val Fuit sun venuz en traver.
L'altre est de Turcs e la terce de Pers,   3240
E la quarte est de Pinceneis e de Pers,

E la quinte est de Solteras e d'Avers,
E la siste est d'Ormaleus e d'Eugiez,
E la sedme est de la gent Samuel,
L'oidme est de Bruise e la noefme de Clavers,   3245
E la disme est d'Occian le desert:
Ço est une gent ki Damnedeu ne sert;
De plus feluns n'orrez parler jamais.
Durs unt les quirs ensement cume fer:
Pur ço n'unt soign de elme ne d'osberc;   3250
En la bataille sunt felun e engres.   AOI.

234

Li amiralz .X. escheles ad justedes:
La premere est des jaianz de Malprese,
L'altre est de Hums e la terce de Hungres,
E la quarte est de Baldise la lunge   3255
E la quinte est de cels de Val Penuse
E la siste est de [. . .] Maruse,
E la sedme est de Leus e d'Astrimónies;
L'oidme est d'Argoilles e la noefme de Clarbone,
E la disme est des barbez de Fronde: 3260
Ço est une gent ki Deu nen amat unkes.
Geste Francor .XXX. escheles i numbrent.
Granz sunt les oz u cez buisines sunent.
Paien chevalchent en guise de produme.   AOI.

235

Li amiralz mult par est riches hoem.   3265
Dedavant sei fait porter sun dragon
E l'estandart Tervagan e Mahum
E un ymagene Apolin le felun.
Des Canelius chevalchent envirun.
Mult haltement escrient un sermun: 3270
«Ki par noz Deus voelt aveir guarison,
Sis prit e servet par grant afflictiun!»
Paien i baissent lur chefs e lur mentun;
Lor helmes clers i suzclinent enbrunc.
Dient F[r]anceis: «Sempres murrez, glutun!   3275
De vos seit hoi male confusiun!
Li nostre Deu, guarantisez Carlun!
Ceste bataille seit ju(ic)get en sun num!»   AOI.

236

Li amiralz est mult de grant saveir;
A sei apelet sis filz e les dous reis: 3280
«Seignurs barons, devant chevalchereiz,
Mes escheles tutes les guiereiz;
Mais des meillors voeill jo retenir treis:
L'un ert de Turcs e l'altre d'Ormaleis,
E la terce est des jaianz de Malpreis.   3285
Cil d'Ociant ierent e[n]sembl'ot mei,
Si justerunt a Charles e a Franceis.
Li emperere, s'il se cumbat od mei,
Desur le buc la teste perdre en deit.
Trestut seit fiz, n'i avrat altre dreit.»   AOI.   3290

237

Granz sunt les oz e les escheles beles;
Entr'els nen at ne pui ne val ne tertre,
Selve ne bois; asconse n'i poet estre;
Ben s'entreveient en mi la pleine tere.
Dist Baligant: «La meie gent averse,   3295
Car chevalchez pur la bataille quere!»
L'enseigne portet Amborres d'Oluferne.
Paien escrient, «Precieuse» l'apelent.
Dient Franceis: «De vos seit hoi grant perte!»
Mult haltement: «Munjoie!» renuvelent.   3300
Li emperere i fait suner ses greisles,
E l'olifan, ki tres(tu)tuz les esclairet.
Dient paien: «La gent Ca[r]lun est bele.
Bataille avrum e aduree e pesme.»   AOI.

238

Grant est la plaigne e large la cuntree.   3305
Luisent cil elme as perres d'or gemmees,
E cez escuz e cez bronies safrees,
E cez espiez, cez enseignes fermees.
Sunent cez greisles, les voiz en sunt mult cleres;
De l'olifan haltes sunt les menees.   3310
Li amiralz en apelet sun frere,
Ço est Canabeus, li reis de Floredee:
Cil tint la terre entresqu'en Val Sevree.
Les escheles Charlun li ad mustrees:
«Veez l'orgoil de France la loee!   3315

Mult fierement chevalchet li emperere;
Il est darere od cele gent barbee.
Desur lur bronies lur barbes unt getees,
Altresi blanches cume neif sur gelee.
Cil i ferrunt de lances e d'espees,   3320
Bataille avrum e forte e aduree:
Unkes nuls hom ne vit tel ajustee.»
Plus qu'om ne lancet une verge pelee,
Baligant ad ses cumpaignes trespassees.
Une raisun lur ad dit e mustree: 3325
«Venez, paien, kar jo(n) irai en l'estree.»
De sun espiet la hanste en ad branlee;
Envers Karlun la mure en ad turnee.   AOI.

239

Carles li magnes, cum il vit l'amiraill,
E le dragon, l'enseigne e l'estandart,   3330
De cels d'Arabe si grant force i par (ar)ad,
De la cuntree unt purprises les parz,
Ne mes que tant (scue)[cume] l'empereres en ad,
Li reis de France s'en escriet mult halt:
«Barons franceis, vos estes bons vassals.   3335
Tantes batailles avez faites en camps!
Veez paien: felun sunt e cuart,
Tutes lor leis un dener ne lur valt.
S'il unt grant gent, d'iço, seignurs, qui calt?
Ki errer voelt, a mei venir s'en alt!»   3340
Des esperons puis brochet le cheval,
E Tencendor li (a)ad fait .IIII. salz.
Dient Franceis: «Icist reis est vassals!
Chevalchez, bers! Nul de nus ne vus falt.»

240

Clers fut li jurz e li soleilz luisanz.   3345
Les oz sunt beles e les cumpaignes granz.
Justees sunt les escheles devant.
Li quens Rabels e li quens Guinemans
Lascent les resnes a lor cevals curanz,
Brochent a eit; dunc laisent curre Francs: 3350
Si vunt ferir de lur espiez trenchanz.   AOI.

241

Li quens Rabels est chevaler hardiz,
Le cheval brochet des esperuns d'or fin,
Si vait ferir Torleu, le rei persis,
N'escut ne bronie ne pout sun colp tenir: 3355
L'espiet a or li ad enz el cors mis,
Que mort l'abat sur un boissun petit.
Dient F[r]anceis: «Damnedeus nos aït!»
Carles ad dreit, ne li devom faillir.»   AOI.

242

E Guineman justet a un rei leutice.   3360
Tute li freint la targe, ki est flurie;
Apres li ad la bronie descunfite;
Tute l'enseigne li ad enz el cors mise,
Que mort l'abat, ki qu'en plurt u kin riet.
A icest colp cil de France s'esc(ri)rient: 3365
«Ferez, baron, ne vos targez mie!
Carles ad dreit vers la gent [pa]iesnie;
Deus nus ad mis al plus verai juïse.»   AOI.

243

Malpramis siet sur un cheval tut blanc;
Cunduit sun cors en la presse des Francs.   3370
De (u) uns es altres granz colps i vait ferant,
L'un mort sur l'altre suvent vait trescevant.
Tut premereins s'escriet Baligant:
«Li mien baron, nurrit vos ai lung tens.
Veez mun fils, Carlun le vait querant,   3375
A ses armes tanz barons calunjant:
Meillor vassal de lui ja ne demant.
Succurez le a voz espiez trenchant!»
A icest mot paien venent avant,
Durs colps i fierent, mult est li caples granz.   3380
La bataille est merveilluse e pesant:
Ne fut si fort enceis ne puis cel tens.   AOI.

244

Granz sunt les oz e les cumpaignes fieres,
Justees sunt trestutes les escheles,
E li paien merveillusement fierent.   3385
Deus! tantes hanstes i ad par mi brisees,

Escuz fruisez e bronies desmaillees!
La veïsez la tere si junchee:
L'erbe del camp, ki est verte e delgee
. . . .   3390
Li amiralz recleime sa maisnee:
«Ferez, baron, sur la gent chrestiene!»
La bataille est mult dure e afichee;
Unc einz ne puis ne fut si fort ajustee;
Josqu'a la [nuit] nen ert fins otriee.   AOI.   3395

245

Li amiralz la sue gent apelet:
«Ferez, paien: por el venud n'i estes!
Jo vos durrai muillers gentes e beles,
Si vos durai feus e honors e teres.»
Paien respundent: «Nus le devuns ben fere.»   3400
A colps pleners de lor espiez i perdent:
Plus de cent milie espees i unt traites.
Ais vos le caple e dulurus e pesmes;
Bataille veit cil ki entr'els volt estre.   AOI.

246

Li emperere recleimet ses Franceis: 3405
«Seignors barons, jo vos aim, si vos crei.
Tantes batailles avez faites pur mei,
Regnes cunquis e desordenet reis!
Ben le conuis que gueredun vos en dei
E de mun cors, de terres e d'aveir.   3410
Vengez voz fi[l]z, voz freres e voz heirs,
Qu'en Rencesvals furent morz l'altre seir!
Ja savez vos cuntre paiens ai dreit.»
Respondent Franc: «Sire, vos dites veir.»
Itels .XX. miliers en ad od sei,   3415
Cumunement l'en prametent lor feiz,
Ne li faldrunt pur mort ne pur destreit.
N'en i ad cel sa lance n'i empleit;
De lur espees i fierent demaneis.
La bataille est de merveillus destreit.   AOI.   3420

247

E Malpramis parmi le camp chevalchet;
De cels de France i fait mult grant damage.

Naimes li dux fierement le reguardet,
Vait le ferir cum hume vertudable.
De sun escut li freint la pene halte,   3425
De sun osberc les dous pans li desaffret;
El cors li met tute l'enseigne jalne,
Que mort [l'abat] entre .VII.C. des altres.

248

Reis Canabeus, le frere a l'amiraill,
Des esporuns ben brochot sun cheval;   3430
Trait ad l'espee, le punt est de cristal,
Si fiert Naimun en l'elme principal:
L'une meitiet l'en fruissed d'une part,
Al brant d'acer l'en trenchet .V. des laz,
Li capelers un dener ne li valt;   3435
Trenchet la coife entresque a la char,
Jus a la tere une piece en abat.
Granz fut li colps, li dux en estonat,
Sempres caïst, se Deus ne li aidast.
De sun destrer le col en enbraçat.   3440
Se li paiens une feiz recuvrast,
Sempres fust mort li nobilies vassal.
Carles de France i vint, kil succurat.   AOI.

249

Naimes li dux tant par est anguissables,
E li paiens de ferir mult le hastet.   3445
Carles li dist: «Culvert, mar le baillastes!»
Vait le ferir par sun grant vasselage:
L'escut li freint, cuntre le coer li quasset,
De sun osberc li desrumpt la ventaille,
Que mort l'abat: la sele en remeint guaste.   3450

250

Mult ad grant doel Carlemagnes li reis,
Quant Naimun veit nafret devant sei,
Sur l'erbe verte le sanc tut cler caeir.
Li empereres li ad dit a cunseill:
«Bel sire Naimes, kar chevalcez od mei!   3455
Morz est li gluz ki en destreit vus teneit;
El cors li mis mun espiet une feiz.»
Respunt li dux: «Sire, jo vos en crei.

Se jo vif alques, mult grant prod i avreiz.»
Puis sunt justez par amur e par feid,   3460
Ensembl'od els tels .XX. milie Franceis.
N'i ad celoi que n'i fierge o n'i capleit.   AOI.

251

Li amiralz chevalchet par le camp,
Si vait ferir le cunte Guneman,
Cuntre le coer li fruisset l'escut blanc,   3465
De sun osberc li derumpit les pans,
Les dous costez li deseivret des flancs,
Que mort l'abat de sun cheval curant.
Puis ad ocis Gebuin e Lorain,
Richard le Veill, li sire des Normans.   3470
Paien escrient: «Preciuse est vaillant!
Ferez, baron, nus i avom guarant!»   AOI.

252

Ki puis veist li chevaler d'Arabe,
Cels d'Occiant e d'Argoillie e de Bascle!
De lur espiez ben i fierent e caplent;   3475
E li Franceis n'unt talent que s'en algent;
Asez i moerent e des uns e des altres.
Entresqu'al vespre est mult fort la bataille,
Des francs barons i ad mult gran damage.
Doel i avrat, enceis qu'ele departed.   AOI.   3480

253

Mult ben i fierent Franceis e Arrabit;
Fruissent cil hanste se cil espiez furbit.
Ki dunc veïst cez escuz si malmis,
Cez blancs osbercs ki dunc oïst fremir,
E cez escuz sur cez helmes cruisir,   3485
Cez chevalers ki dunc veïst caïr
E humes braire, contre tere murir,
De grant dulor li poüst suvenir!
Ceste bataille est mult fort a suffrir.
Li amiralz recleimet Apolin   3490
E Tervagan e Mahumet altresi:
«Mi Damnedeu, jo vos ai mult servit!
Tutes tes ymagenes ferai d'or fin.»   AOI.
. . . .

As li devant un soen drut, Gemalfin.   3495
Males nuveles li aportet e dit:
«Baligant, sire, mal este oi baillit.
Perdut avez Malpramis vostre fils,
E Canabeus, vostre frere, est ocis.
A dous Franceis belement en avint.   3500
Li empereres en est l'uns, ço m'est vis:
Granz ad le cors, ben resenblet marchis;
Blanc[he] ad la barbe cume flur en avrill.»
Li amiralz en ad le helme enclin,
E en apres sin enbrunket sun vis: 3505
Si grant doel ad sempres quiad murir.
Sin apelat Jangleu l'Ultremarin.

254

Dist l'amiraill: «Jangleu, venez avant!
Vos estes proz e vostre saveir est grant;
Vostre conseill ai oc evud tuz tens.   3510
Que vos en semblet d'Arrabiz e de Francs?
Avrum nos la victorie del champ?»
E cil respunt: «Morz estes, Baligant!
Ja vostre deu ne vos erent guarant.
Carles est fiers e si hume vaillant;   3515
Unc ne vi gent ki si fust cumbatant.
Mais reclamez les barons d'Occiant,
Turcs e Enfruns, Arabiz e Jaianz.
Ço que estre en deit, ne l'alez demurant.»

255

Li amiraill ad sa barbe fors mise,   3520
Altresi blanche cume flur en espine:
Cument qu'il seit, ne s'i voelt celer mie.
Met a sa buche une clere buisine,
Sunet la cler, que si paien l'oïrent;
Par tut le camp ses cumpaignes ralient.   3525
Cil d'Ociant i braient e henissent,
Arguille si cume chen i glatissent;
Requerent Franc par si grant estultie,
El plus espes ses rumpent e partissent:
A icest colp en jetent mort .VII. milie.   3530

256

Li quens Oger cuardise n'out unkes;
Meillor vassal de lui ne vestit bronie.
Quant de Franceis les escheles vit rumpre,
Si apelat Tierri, le duc d'Argone,
Gefrei d'Anjou e Jozeran le cunte,   3535
Mult fierement Carles en araisunet:
«Veez paien cum ocient voz humes!
Ja Deu ne placet qu'el chef portez corone,
S'or n'i ferez pur venger vostre hunte.»
N'i ad icel ki un sul mot respundet: 3540
Brochent ad eit, lor cevals laissent cure,
Vunt les ferir la o il les encuntrent.

257

Mult ben i fiert Carlemagnes li reis,   AOI.
Naimes li dux e Oger li Daneis,
Geifreid d'Anjou ki l'enseigne teneit.   3545
Mult par est proz danz Ogers li Daneis!
Puint le ceval, laisset curre ad espleit,
Si vait ferir celui ki le dragun teneit,
Qu'Ambure cravente en la place devant sei
E le dragon e l'enseigne le rei.   3550
Baligant veit sun gunfanun cadeir
E l'estandart Mahumet remaneir.
Li amiralz alques s'en aperceit
Que il ad tort e Carlemagnes dreit.
Paien d'Arabe s'en turnent plus .C.   3555
Li emperere recleimet ses parenz:
«Dites, baron, por Deu, si m'aidereiz.»
Respundent Francs: «Mar le demandereiz.
Trestut seit fel ki n'i fierget a espleit!»   AOI.

258

Passet li jurz, si turnet a la vespree.   3560
Franc e paien i fierent des espees.
Cil sunt vassal ki les oz ajusterent.
Lor enseignes n'i unt mie ubliees:
Li amira[l]z «Preciuse!» ad criee,
Carles «Munjoie!», l'enseigne renumee.   3565
L'un conuist l'altre as haltes voiz e as cleres;
En mi le camp amdui s'entr'encuntrerent:

Si se vunt ferir, granz colps s'entredunerent
De lor espiez en lor targes roees.
Fraites les unt desuz cez bucles lees.   3570
De lor osbercs les pans en deseverent:
Dedenz cez cors mie ne s'adeserent:
Rumpent cez cengles e cez seles verserent,
Cheent li rei, a tere se turbecherent,
Isnelement sur lor piez releverent.   3575
Mult vassalment unt traites les espees.
Ceste bataille n'en ert mais destornee:
Seinz hume mort ne poet estre achevee.   AOI.

259

Mult est vassal Carles de France dulce;
Li amiralt, il nel crent ne ne dutet.   3580
Cez lor espees tutes nues i mustrent,
Sur cez escuz mult granz colps s'entredunent,
Trenchent les quirs e cez fuz ki sunt dubles;
Cheent li clou, si pecerent les bucles;
Puis fierent il nud a nud sur les bronies;   3585
Des helmes clers li fous en escarbunet.
Ceste bataille ne poet remaneir unkes,
Josque li uns sun tort i reconuisset.   AOI.

260

Dist l'amiraill: «Carles, kar te purpenses,
Si pren cunseill que vers mei te repentes!   3590
Mort as (. . .) mun filz, par le men esciente;
A mult grant tort mun païs me calenges;
Deven mes hom, en fedeltet voeill rendre;
Ven mei servir d'ici qu'en Oriente!»
Carles respunt: «Mult grant viltet me sembl[e];   3595
Pais ne amor ne dei a paien rendre.
Receif la lei que Deus nos apresentet,
Christientet, e pui te amerai sempres;
Puis serf e crei le rei omnipotente!»
Dist Baligant: «Malvais sermun cumences!»   3600
Puis vunt ferir des espees qu'unt ceintes.   AOI.

261

Li amiralz est mult de grant vertut.
Fier Carlemagne sur l'elme d'acer brun,

Desur la teste li ad frait e fendut;
Met li l'espee sur les chevels menuz,   3605
Prent de la carn grant pleine palme e plus:
Iloec endreit remeint li os tut nut.
Carles cancelet, por poi qu'il n'est caüt;
Mais Deus ne volt qu'il seit mort ne vencut.
Seint Gabriel est repairet a lui,   3610
Si li demande: «Reis magnes, que fais tu?»

262

Quant Carles oït la seinte voiz de l'angle,
N'en ad poür ne de murir dutance;
Repairet loi vigur e remembrance.
Fiert l'amiraill de l'espee de France,   3615
L'elme li freint o li gemme reflambent,
[T]renchet la teste pur la cervele espandre
[E] tut le vis tresqu'en la barbe blanche,
Que mort l'abat senz nule recuvrance.
«Munjoie!» escriet pur la reconuisance.   3620
A icest mot venuz i est dux Neimes:
Prent Tencendur, muntet i est li reis magnes.
Paien s'en turnent, ne volt Deus qu'il i remainent.
Or sunt Franceis a icels qu'il demandent.

263

Paien s'en fuient, cum Damnesdeus le volt.   3625
Encalcent Francs e l'emperere avoec.
Ço dist li reis: «Seignurs, vengez voz doels,
Si esclargiez voz talenz e voz coers,
Kar hoi matin vos vi plurer des oilz.»
Respondent Franc: «Sire, çó nus estoet.»   3630
Cascuns i fiert tanz granz colps cum il poet.
Poi s'en estoerstrent d'icels ki sunt iloec.

264

Granz est li calz, si se levet la puldre.
Paien s'en fuient e Franceis les anguissent;
Li enchalz duret d'ici qu'en Sarraguce.   3635
En sum sa tur muntee est Bramidonie,
Ensembl'od li si clerc e si canonie
De false lei, que Deus nen amat unkes:

Ordres nen unt ne en lor chefs corones.
Quant ele vit Arrabiz si cunfundre,   3640
A halte voiz s'escrie: «Aiez nos, Mahum!
E! gentilz reis, ja sunt vencuz noz humes,
Li amiralz ocis a si grant hunte!»
Quant l'ot Marsilie, vers sa pareit se turnet,
Pluret des oilz, tute sa chere enbrunchet: 3645
Morz est de doel. Si cum pecchet l'encumbret,
L'anme de lui as vifs diables dunet.   AOI.

265

Paien sunt morz, alquant cunfundue,
E Carles ad sa bataille vencue.
De Sarraguce ad la porte abatue: 3650
Or set il ben que n'est mais defendue.
Prent la citet, od sa gent i est venue;
Par poestet icele noit i jurent.
Fiers est li reis a la barbe canue,
E Bramidonie les turs li ad rendues: 3655
Les dis sunt grandes, les cinquante menues.
Mult ben espleitet qui Damnesdeus aiuet.

266

Passet li jurz, la noit est aserie;
Clers est la lune e les esteiles flambient.
Li emperere ad Sarraguce prise.   3660
A mil Franceis funt ben cercer la vile,
Les sinagoges e les mahumeries;
A mailz de fer e a cuignees qu'ils tindrent,
Fruissent les ymagenes e trestutes les ydeles:
N'i remeindrat ne sorz ne falserie.   3665
Li reis creit en Deu, faire voelt sun servise;
E si evesque les eves beneïssent,
Meinent paien ent[r]esqu'al baptisterie:
S'or i ad cel qui Carles cuntredie voillet,
Il le fait pendre o ardeir ou ocire.   3670
Baptizet sunt asez plus de .C. milie
Veir chrestien, ne mais sul la reïne.
En France dulce iert menee caitive:
Ço voelt li reis par amur cunvertisset.

267

Passet la noit, si apert le cler jor.   3675
De Sarraguce Carles guarnist les turs;
Mil chevalers i laissat puigneürs;
Guardent la vile a oes l'empereor.
Mandet li reis e si hume trestuz
E Bramidonie, qu'il meinet en sa prisun;   3680
Mais n'ad talent que li facet se bien nun.
Repairez sunt a joie e a baldur.
Passent Nerbone par force e par vigur;
Vint a Burdeles la citet de . . .
Desur l'alter seint Severin le baron   3685
Met l'oliphan plein d'or e de manguns:
Li pelerin le veient ki la vunt.
Passet Girunde a mult granz nefs qu'i sunt;
Entresque a Blaive ad cunduit sun nevold
E Oliver, sun nobilie cumpaignun,   3690
E l'arcevesque, ki fut sages e proz.
En blancs sarcous fait metre les seignurs
A Seint Romain; la gisent li baron.
Francs les cumandent a Deu e a ses nuns.
Carles cevalchet e les vals e les munz;   3695
Entresqu'a Ais ne volt prendre sujurn.
Tant chevalchat qu'il descent al perrun.
Cume il est en sun paleis halçur,
Par ses messages mandet ses jugeors:
Baivers e Saisnes, Loherencs e Frisuns;   3700
Alemans mandet, si mandet Borguignuns,
E Peitevins e Normans e Bretuns,
De cels de France des plus saives qui sunt.
Des ore cumencet le plait de Guenelun.

268

Li empereres est repairet d'Espaigne,   3705
E vient a Ais, al meillor sied de France;
Muntet el palais, est venut en la sale.
As li Alde venue, une bele damisele.
Ço dist al rei: «O est Rollant le catanie,
Ki me jurat cume sa per a prendre?»   3710
Carles en ad e dulor e pesance,
Pluret des oilz, tiret sa barbe blance:
«Soer, cher'amie, de hume mort me demandes.
Jo t'en durai mult esforcet eschange:

Ço est Loewis, mielz ne sai a parler;   3715
Il est mes filz e si tendrat mes marches.»
Alde respunt: «Cest mot mei est estrange.
Ne place Deu ne ses seinz ne ses angles
Apres Rollant que jo vive remaigne!»
Pert la culor, chet as piez Carlemagne,   3720
Sempres est morte, Deus ait mercit de l'anme!
Franceis barons en plurent e si la pleignent.

269

Alde la bel[e] est a sa fin alee.
Quidet li reis que el[le] se seit pasmee;
Pited en ad, sin pluret l'emperere;   3725
Prent la as mains, si l'en ad relevee.
Desur l(es)['] espalles ad la teste clinee.
Quant Carles veit que morte l'ad truvee,
Quatre cuntesses sempres i ad mandees.
A un muster de nuneins est portee;   3730
La noit la guaitent entresqu'a l 'ajurnee.
Lunc un alter belement l'enterrerent.
Mult grant honor i ad li reis dunee,   AOI.

270

Li emperere est repairet ad Ais.
Guenes li fels, en caeines de fer,   3735
En la citet est devant le paleis.
A un estache l'unt atachet cil serf,
Les mains li lient a curreies de cerf;
Tres ben le batent a fuz e a jamelz:
N'ad deservit que altre ben i ait;   3740
A grant dulur iloec atent sun plait.

271

Il est escrit en l'anciene geste
Que Carles mandet humes de plusurs teres.
Asemblez sunt ad Ais, a la capele.
Halz est li jurz, mult par est grande la feste,   3745
Dient alquanz del baron seint Silvestre.
Des ore cumencet le plait e les noveles
De Guenelun, ki traïsun ad faite.
Li emperere devant sei l'ad fait traire.   AOI.

272

«Seignors barons» dist Carlemagnes li reis,   3750
«De Guenelun car me jugez le dreit!
Il fut en l'ost tresque en Espaigne od mei,
Si me tolit .XX. milie de mes Franceis
E mun nevold, que ja mais ne verreiz,
E Oliver, li proz e li curteis;   3755
Les .XII. pers ad traït por aveir.»
Dist Guenelon: «Fel seie se jol ceil!
Rollant me forfist en or et en aveir,
Pur que jo quis sa mort e sun destreit;
Mais traïsun nule n'en i otrei.»   3760
Respundent Franc: «Ore en tendrum cunseill.»

273

Devant le rei la s'estut Guenelun:
Cors ad gaillard, el vis gente color;
S'il fust leials, ben resemblast barun.
Veit cels de France e tuz les jugeürs,   3765
De ses parenz .XXX. ki od lui sunt;
Puis s'escriat haltement, a grant voeiz:
«Por amor Deu, car m'entendez, barons!
Seignors, jo fui en l'ost avoec l'empereür,
Serveie le par feid e par amur.   3770
Rollant sis nies me coillit en haür,
Si me jugat a mort e a dulur.
Message fui al rei Marsiliun;
Par mun saveir vinc jo a guarisun.
Jo desfiai Rollant le poigneor   3775
E Oliver e tuiz lur cumpaignun;
Carles l'oïd e si nobilie baron.
Venget m'en sui, mais n'i ad traïsun.»
Respundent Francs: «A conseill en irums.»

274

Quant Guenes veit que ses granz plaiz cumencet,   3780
De ses parenz ensemble [od li] i out trente.
Un en i ad a qui li altre entendent:
Ço est Pinabel del castel de Sorence;
Ben set parler e dreite raisun rendre;
Vassals est bons por ses armes defendre,   AOI.   3785
Ço li dist Guenes: «En vos [. . .] ami . . .

Getez mei hoi de mort e de calunje!»
Dist Pinabel: «Vos serez guarit sempres.
N'i ad Frances ki vos juget a pendre,
U l'emper[er]e les noz dous cors en asemblet,   3790
Al b(a)rant d'acer que jo ne l'en desmente.»
Guenes li quens a ses piez se presente.

275

Bavier e Saisnes sunt alet a conseill,
E Peitevin e Norman e Franceis;
Asez i ad Alemans e Tiedeis.   3795
Icels d'Alverne(ne) i sunt li plus curteis;
Pur Pinabel se cuntienent plus quei.
Dist l'un a l'altre: «Bien fait a remaneir!
Laisum le plait e si preium le rei
Que Guenelun cleimt quite ceste feiz,   3800
Puis si li servet par amur e par feid.
Morz est Rollant, ja mais nel revereiz;
N'ert recuvret por ór ne por aveir:
Mult sereit fols ki [l]a(a) se cumbatreit.»
N'en i ad celoi nel graant e otreit,   3805
Fors sul Tierri, le frere(re) dam Geifreit.   AOI.

276

A Charlemagne repairent si barun;
Dient al rei: «Sire, nus vos prium
Que clamez quite le cunte Guenelun,
Puis si vos servet par feid e par amor.   3810
Vivre le laisez, car mult est gentilz hoem.
Ja por murir n'en ert veüd gerun,
Ne por aveir ja nel recuverum.»
Ço dist li reis: «Vos estes mi felun!»   AOI.

277

Quant Carles veit que tuz li sunt faillid,   3815
Mult l'enbrunchit e la chere e le vis;
Al doel qu'il ad si se cleimet caitifs.
Ais li devant uns chevalers, [Tierris],
Frere Gefrei a un duc angevin.
Heingre out le cors e graisle e eschewid,   3820
Neirs les chevels e alques bruns [le vis];

N'est gueres granz ne trop nen est petiz.
Curteisement a l'emperere ad dit:
«Bels sire reis, ne vos dementez si.
Ja savez vos, que mult vos ai servit;   3825
Par anceisurs dei jo tel plait tenir.
Que que Rollant a Guenelun forsfesist,
Vostre servise l'en doüst bien guarir!
Guenes est fels d'iço qu'il le traït;
Vers vos s'en est parjurez e malmis.   3830
Pur ço le juz jo a prendre e a murir
E sun cors metre . . .
Si cume fel ki felonie fist.
Se or ad parent ki m'en voeille desmentir,
A ceste cspee, que jo ai ceinte ici,   3835
Mun jugement voel sempres guarantir.»
Respundent Franc: «Or avez vos ben dit.»

278

Devant lu rei est venuz Pinabel,
Granz est e forz e vassals e isnel:
Qu'il fiert a colp, de sun tens n'i ad mais.   3840
E dist al rei: «Sire, vostre est li plaiz:
Car cumandez, que tel noise n'i ait!
Ci vei Tierri, ki jugement ad fait.
Jo si li fals, od lui m'en cumbatrai.»
Met li el poign de cerf le destre guant.   3845
Dist li emper[er]es: «Bons pleges en demant.»
.XXX. parenz l'i plevissent leial.
Ço dist li reis: «E jol vos recr[e]rai.»
Fait cels guarder tresque li dreiz en serat.   AOI.

279

Quant veit Tierri qu'or en ert la bataille,   3850
Sun destre guant en ad presentet Carle.
Li emperere l'i recreit par hostage,
Puis fait porter .IIII. bancs en la place;
La vunt sedeir cil kis deivent cumbatre.
Ben sunt malez, par jugement des altres,   3855
Sil purparlat Oger de Denemarche;
E puis demandent lur chevals e lur armes.

280

Puis que il sunt a bataille jugez,   AOI.
Ben sunt cunfes e asols e seignez:
Oent lur messes e sunt acuminiez;   3860
Mult granz offrendes metent par cez musters.
Devant Carlun andui sunt repairez:
Lur esperuns unt en lor piez calcez,
Vestent osberc blancs e forz e legers,
Lur helmes clers unt fermez en lor chefs,   3865
Ceinent espees enheldees d'or mier,
En lur cols pendent lur escuz de quarters,
En lur puinz destres unt lur trenchanz espiez;
Puis sunt muntez en lur curanz destrers.
Idunc plurerent .C. milie chevalers,   3870
Qui pur Rollant de Tierri unt pitiet.
Deus set asez cument la fins en ert.

281

Dedesuz Ais est la pree mult large:
Des dous baruns justee est la bataille.
Cil sunt produme e de grant vasselage   3875
E lur chevals sunt curanz e aates.
Brochent les bien, tutes les resnes lasquent;
Par grant vertut vait ferir l'uns li altre;
Tuz lur escuz i fruissent e esquassent,
Lur osbercs rumpent e lur cengles depiecent,   3880
Les alves turnent, les seles cheent a tere.
.C. mil humes i plurent, kis esguardent.

282

A tere sunt ambdui li chevaler,   AOI.
Isnelement se drecent sur lur piez.
Pinabels est forz e isnels e legers.   3885
Li uns requiert l'altre, n'unt mie des destrers.
De cez espees enheldees d'or mer,
Fierent e caplent sur cez helmes d'acer;
Granz sunt les colps, as helmes detrencher.
Mult se dementent cil Franceis chevaler.   3890
«E! Deus,» dist Carles, «le dreit en esclargiez!»

283

Dist Pinabel: «Tierri, car te recreiz!
Tes hom serai par amur e par feid,
A tun plaisir te durrai mun aveir,
Mais Guenelun fai acorder al rei!»   3895
Respont Tierri: «Ja n'en tendrai cunseill.
Tut seie fel se jo mie l'otrei!
Deus facet hoi entre nus dous le dreit!»   AOI.

284

Ço dist Tierri: «Pinabel mult ies ber,
Granz ies e forz e tis cors ben mollez;   3900
De vasselage te conoissent ti per;
Ceste bataille, car la laisses ester!
A Carlemagne te ferai acorder;
De Guenelun justise ert faite tel,
Jamais n'ert jur que il n'en seit parlet.»   3905
Dist Pinabel: «Ne placet Damnedeu!
Sustenir voeill trestut mun parentet;
N'en recrerrai pur nul hume mortel;
Mielz voeill murir que il me seit reprovet.»
De lur espees cumencent a capler   3910
Desur cez helmes, ki sunt a or gemez;
Cuntre le ciel en volet li fous tuz clers.
Il ne poet estre qu'il seient desevrez:
Seinz hume mort ne poet estre afinet.   AOI.

285

Mult par est proz Pinabel de Sorence;   3915
Si fiert Tierri sur l'elme de Provence:
Salt en li fous, que l'erbe en fait esprendre;
Del brant d'acer la mure li presentet,
Desur le frunt li ad faite descendre.
Parmi le vis (li ad faite descendre):   3920
La destre joe en ad tute sanglente;
L'osberc del dos josque par sum le ventre.
Deus le guarit, que mort ne l'acraventet.   AOI.

286

Ço veit Tierris, que el vis est ferut:
Li sancs tuz clers en chiet el pred herbus   3925

Fiert Pinabel sur l'elme d'acer brun,
Jusqu'al nasel li ad frait e fendut,
Del chef li ad le cervel espandut,
Brandit sun colp, si l'ad mort abatut.
A icest colp est li esturs vencut.   3930
Escrient Franc: «Deus i ad fait vertut!
Asez est dreiz que Guenes seit pendut
E si parent, ki plaidet unt pur lui.»   AOI.

287

Quant Tierris ad vencue sa bataille,
Venuz i est li emperere Carles,   3935
Ensembl'od lui de ses baruns quarante,
Naimes li dux, Oger de Danemarche,
Geifrei d'Anjou e Willalme de Blaive.
Li reis ad pris Tierri entre sa brace,
Tert lui le vis od ses granz pels de martre,   3940
Celes met jus, puis li afublent altres;
Mult suavet le chevaler desarment.
[Munter l'unt] fait en une mule d'Arabe;
Repairet s'en a joie e a barnage;
Vienent ad Ais, descendent en la place.   3945
Des ore cumencet l'ocisiun des altres.

288

Carles apelet ses cuntes e ses dux:
«Que me loez de cels qu'ai retenuz?
Pur Guenelun erent a plait venuz,
Pur Pinabel en ostage renduz.»   3950
Respundent Franc: «Ja mar en vivrat uns!»
Li reis cumandet un soen veier, Basbrun:
«Va, sis pent tuz a l'arbre de mal fust!
Par ceste barbe dunt li peil sunt canuz,
Se uns escapet, morz ies e cunfunduz.»   3955
Cil li respunt: «Qu'en fereie jo e el?»
Od .C. serjanz par force les cunduit.
.XXX. en i ad d'icels ki sunt pendut.
Ki hume traïst, sei ocit e altroi.   AOI.

289

Puis sunt turnet Bavier e Aleman   3960
E Peitevin e Bretun e Norman.

Sor tuit li altre l'unt otriet li Franc
Que Guenes moerget par merveillus ahan.
Quatre destrers funt amener avant,
Puis si li lient e les piez e les mains.   3965
Li cheval sunt orgoillus e curant;
Quatre serjanz les acoeillent devant,
Devers un'ewe ki est en mi un camp.
Guenes est turnet a perdiciun grant;
Trestuit si nerf mult li sunt estendant   3970
E tuit li membre de sun cors derumpant:
Sur l'erbe verte en espant li cler sanc.
Guenes est mort cume fel recreant.
Hom ki traïst altre, nen est dreiz qu'il s'en vant.

290

Quant li empereres ad faite sa venjance,   3975
Sin apelat ses evesques de France,
Cels de Baviere e icels d'Alemaigne:
«En ma maisun ad une caitive franche.
Tant ad oït e sermuns e essamples,
Creire voelt Deu, chrestientet demandet.   3980
Baptizez la, pur quei Deus en ait l'anme.»
Cil li respundent: «Or seit faite par marrenes:
Asez cruiz e linees dames . . . »
As bainz ad Aís mult sunt granz les ci . . .
La baptizent la reïne d'Espaigne: 3985
Truvee li unt le num de Juliane.
Chrestiene est par veire conoisance.

291

Quant l'emperere ad faite sa justise
E esclargiez est la sue grant ire,
En Bramidonie ad chrestientet mise,   3990
Passet li jurz, la nuit est aserie.
Culcez s'est li reis en sa cambre voltice.
Seint Gabriel de part Deu li vint dire:
«Carles, sumun les oz de tun emperie!
Par force iras en la tere de Bire,   3995
Reis Vivien si succuras en Imphe,
A la citet que paien unt asise:
Li chrestien te recleiment e crient.»
Li emperere n'i volsist aler mie:

«Deus,» dist li reis, «si penuse est ma vie!»   4000
Pluret des oilz, sa barbe blanche tiret.
Ci falt la geste que Turoldus declinet.